"For anyone considering joining a board, this book offers invaluable practical insight. The chapter on Environment, Social and Governance (ESG) is particularly relevant at a time when stakeholder capitalism is on the rise. This is something I think about frequently and it is the talk of boardrooms around the world."

Ann Cairns, *Executive Vice Chair – Mastercard, Global Chair 30% Club, Lead Director – Government Department for Business, Energy and Industrial Strategy (BEIS), Chair Intercontinental Exchange and Chair – Financial Alliance for Women*

"It offers a practical guide for non-executive and executive board directors in the private, public and charity sectors of the UK. Its unusual but compelling combination of factual information and personal insights provided by practicing board members, offering insights that are just not available anywhere else."

Peter Allanson, *Good Governance Institute*

"This topic is of extreme importance to all Boards. Every director should understand the implications and ramifications for their business. The editors and contributing authors add to the growing body of scholarly and other works that provide a grounding and underpinning to the understanding of good governance."

Jonathan Geldart, *Director General, Institute of Directors*

T0293128

A DIRECTOR'S GUIDE TO GOVERNANCE IN THE BOARDROOM

This book is a practical guide for executive and non-executive directors and aspiring directors to lead, govern, and steer UK-based organisations to long-term sustainable success.

In today's turbulent environment, corporate governance is increasingly scrutinised, and this book will consider how directors can 'bring the future forward' with respect to responsible and ethical governance and leadership against the challenging political, environmental, and economic backdrop. While other books discuss UK corporate governance, this one uniquely demonstrates how the work of directors can build an organisation's antifragility, and offers a view of stewardship approaches to every sector and type of UK organisation, from large premium listed companies to start-ups, the public sector, not-for-profits, partnerships, and family-owned and private-equity-backed organisations.

Aspiring and experienced directors will each benefit from this book as well as those who provide board evaluation services, professional advisers, auditors, and those who provide training and other support for board members.

ARTURO LANGA is an experienced Non-executive Director. His executive career has spanned in excess of 30 years in the NHS and includes senior management roles and chairing leadership committees relating to clinical governance and oversight. This has led to a passion for board governance, which he brings to his non-executive Board roles. His current roles include being a non-executive director of NHS National Services Scotland (NSS) and serving on the Court of Queen Margaret University and he is still a practicing senior clinician (Consultant) in the NHS. Previous board roles have included large charities where he chaired board committees. He has also been a board adviser to a number of MedTech companies. He provides strategic input, business knowledge, and seeks to adhere to strong governance principles in every boardroom setting. Arturo is an active investor in early-stage companies. He has been an editor and an editorial board member of a number of professional journals and a published author in academic publications as well as a Visiting Professor at the University of the Highlands and Islands.

MONICA LANGA is the Chair and Non-executive Director of a number of private-equity-backed companies and of an Angel Investment Syndicate. She is a former Fund Manager/Investment Director and also worked at the Institute of Directors. She has over 20 years' Non-executive Board experience in the charity/voluntary and the venture capital sectors. As a Director of an executive search practice, Monica specialises in Non-executive Board appointments and independent Board evaluations for the listed investment company and financial mutual sectors, so she spends the majority of her time both advocating for and experiencing best practice in governance in some of the most highly regulated boards in the UK. She holds the Institute of Director's Certificate in Company Direction, holds an MSc in Investment Analysis, is a qualified banker (Chartered Institute of Bankers in Scotland), and a qualified HR professional (CIPD).

A DIRECTOR'S GUIDE TO GOVERNANCE IN THE BOARDROOM

ACROSS THE PRIVATE, PUBLIC, AND VOLUNTARY SECTORS

Edited by Arturo Langa and Monica Langa

Routledge
Taylor & Francis Group

NEW YORK AND LONDON

Cover image: Getty Images – Rawpixel

First published 2022
by Routledge
605 Third Avenue, New York, NY 10158

and by Routledge
4 Park Square, Milton Park, Abingdon, Oxon, OX14 4RN

Routledge is an imprint of the Taylor & Francis Group, an informa business

Library of Congress Cataloging-in-Publication Data
Names: Langa, Arturo, editor. | Langa, Monica, editor.
Title: A director's guide to governance in the boardroom :
across the private, public and charity sectors / [edited by]
Arturo Langa and Monica Langa.
Description: New York, NY : Routledge, 2022. |
Includes bibliographical references and index.
Subjects: LCSH: Boards of directors—Great Britain. |
Corporate governance—Great Britain. | Charities—Great
Britain—Management. | Public administration—Great Britain.
Classification: LCC HD2745 .D572 2022 |
DDC 658.4/220941—dc23/eng/20220202
LC record available at https://lccn.loc.gov/2021052039

ISBN: 978-0-367-69682-5 (hbk)
ISBN: 978-0-367-69680-1 (pbk)
ISBN: 978-1-003-14285-0 (ebk)

DOI: 10.4324/9781003142850

Typeset in Minion Pro
by codeMantra

CONTENTS

List of Figures   xiii
List of Tables   xiv
Notes on Contributors   xv
Foreword   xxii
ANN CAIRNS

Foreword   xxiv
PETER ALLANSON

Foreword   xxv
JONATHAN GELDART

Preface   xxvi
ARTURO LANGA AND MONICA LANGA

CHAPTER 1   GOVERNANCE AND THE ROLE OF THE
             BOARD   **1**

             DAVID WATT, ARTURO LANGA, AND
             EILEEN MACLEAN

             Introduction   2
             Governance   2
             Understanding the Role of the Board   7
             Strategic View   15
             Board Make-Up   16
             Board Structure   22
             Subsidiary Boards   26
             Role of the Chair of the Board   28
             Board Committees   30
             Appointment to Board Committees   31
             Comparisons between Sectors (private, public, and
                 charity/voluntary)   33

What the Board Should Do	34
What the Board Should Not Do	37
What Makes a Board of Value to the Organisation?	37
Role of External Advisors to the Board	42
Insolvency – What the Board Should Know	43
When to Resign	47
Directors and Officers Liability Insurance (D&O)	51
Key Messages	51
Further Reading	52
References	52

CHAPTER 2   GOVERNANCE CODES   **55**

CARUM BASRA AND MONICA LANGA

Introduction	56
Emergence of Governance Codes	56
Understanding the Role of Governance Codes	57
Why Apply a Code?	59
Reporting against a Code	60
Governance Codes in the Private Sector	60
Governance Codes in the Public Sector	69
Governance Codes in the Charity/Voluntary Sector	74
Support on Governance Code Compliance	88
Key Messages	89
Further Reading	89
References	90

CHAPTER 3   RISK MANAGEMENT IN THE BOARDROOM   **93**

VICKY KUBITSCHECK

Introduction	94
Under the Spotlight	94
The Concept of Risk Management	96
The Key Principles of Risk Management	100
Defining the Board's Risk Appetite	101
Identifying Risks	106
Assessing Risks	108
Monitoring and Reporting of Risks	110
Pitfalls and Lessons: Why Organisations Fail …	113
Future Proofing: Forewarned Is Forearmed	124
Key Messages	129
Further Reading	130
Notes	130
References	132

CHAPTER 4   ENVIRONMENT, SOCIAL, AND
            GOVERNANCE (ESG) AND
            SUSTAINABILITY   **135**

SITAL CHEEMA AND MONICA LANGA

Introduction   136
Defining ESG and Why It Has Increased in Importance   136
ESG and Sustainability   143
ESG in the Boardroom   151
Approaches to ESG in the 3 Sectors (private, public, and
    charity/voluntary)   159
Taking the Lead – Post-COVID-19   166
Key Messages   169
Further Reading   169
References   170

CHAPTER 5   EXECUTIVE DIRECTORS ON THE BOARD   **173**

CHRIS PEARSE, MONICA LANGA, AND
LORRAINE CLINTON

Introduction   174
Executive Director versus Non-executive Director   174
Functions of the Most Common Executive Directors on
    the Board   178
Employee Directors   184
Challenges Faced by Executive Board Directors   186
Executive Board Directors in Different Sectors (private,
    public, and charity/voluntary) – Some Practicalities   191
Newly Appointed Executive Board Directors   199
The Board and Executive Director Team Dynamics   200
Key Messages   203
Further Reading   204
References   204

CHAPTER 6   ROLE OF THE COMPANY SECRETARY   **207**

SHEELAGH DUFFIELD AND GAYLE WATSON

Introduction   208
Company Secretary – Main Duties   208
The Need for Qualifications for the Company Secretary   211
The Governance Framework   213
The Governance Facilitator   217
Board Induction   221

Board Meetings	223
The Respected "Governance Adviser"	228
Important Aspects of the Role in the Private Sector	229
Important Aspects of the Role in the Public Sector	231
Important Aspects of the Role in the Charity/Voluntary Sector	232
Key Messages	234
Further Reading	234
References	235

CHAPTER 7 **RECRUITING AND MAINTAINING AN EFFECTIVE BOARD** **237**

MONICA LANGA AND ARTURO LANGA

Introduction	238
What Is a Board Made Up Of?	239
Executive and Non-executive Board Members	242
Structuring a Board	244
Deciding the Board Composition	247
Common Mistakes in Board Recruitment	248
Board Diversity	252
Approaches to Board Recruitment	257
Private Sector	257
Public Sector	262
Charity/Voluntary Sector	264
How to Recruit the Right Board Members	265
Director Selection	268
Board Matrices	270
Board Behaviours	273
Recruiting for the Optimal Behaviour Mix	277
Maintaining an Effective Board	278
Independent Board Evaluations	280
Board Chemistry	282
Key Messages	284
Further Reading	284
References	285

CHAPTER 8 **GAINING YOUR FIRST NON-EXECUTIVE BOARD APPOINTMENT** **287**

FRANCESCA ECSERY

Introduction	288
Top Tips	288
NED CV – Your Personal Brand	292

Networking 297
Creating a Digital Brand 298
Why Do Boards Hire NEDs? 300
To NED or Not to NED? 301
No NED Experience? Leverage Your Executive Skills! 305
Securing a NED While Still in Full-Time Employment 306
Private Sector Appointments 307
Public Sector (Ministerial) Appointments 310
Charity/Voluntary Sector Appointments 314
The Importance of a Good Chair 317
Key Messages 318
Further Reading 319
References 319

CHAPTER 9   GOVERNANCE IN THE PRIVATE SECTOR   **321**

CHARLOTTE VALEUR, CLAIRE FARGEOT,
AND PATRICIA BARCLAY

Introduction 322
Defining the Sector 323
Scale of the Sector 324
Role of the Private Sector 325
How Is the Sector Governed? 326
Legal Structures 332
Why Be a Non-executive Director in the Private Sector 348
COVID-19 and Company Governance 349
Key Messages 350
Further Reading 350
References 351

CHAPTER 10   GOVERNANCE IN THE PUBLIC SECTOR   **355**

RACHEL GWYON AND ARTURO LANGA

Introduction 356
Defining the Public Sector across the UK 357
History 361
The Nature of Public Bodies 362
Common Legal Structures of Public Bodies 363
The Role of Public Body Boards 368
Working Effectively with Ministers and the Civil Service 376
Important Aspects of Public Body Governance 379
Why Join a Public Sector Board? 386
COVID-19 and Public Body Governance 387

Key Messages	390
Further Reading	390
References	391

CHAPTER 11 GOVERNANCE IN THE CHARITY/
VOLUNTARY SECTOR **393**

PATRICIA ARMSTRONG AND MARGARET WRIGHT

Introduction	394
Defining the Sector	396
The Scale of the Sector	398
How Is the Sector Governed?	399
Legal Structures	400
The Governing Document	409
Why Be a Charity Trustee?	414
COVID-19 and Charity/Voluntary Organisation Governance	417
Key Messages	417
Further Reading	418
References	418

Index	419

FIGURES

3.1 A dynamic framework 102

3.2 The assurance food chain 112

4.1 Calculating the ecological footprint (The Economics of Biodiversity: The Dasgupta Review, Feb 2021.) 145

4.2 The UN SDGs (Neshovski, 2018) 150

6.1 Typical example of the structure and main powers of a board 214

6.2 Suggested induction documents/activities for new board members 222

7.1 Example structure of a board 240

7.2 IoD Director Competency Framework – Institute of Directors (2016) 267

7.3 Pillars underpinning the creation of a board matrix 271

10.1 The governance model – NHS Scotland Blueprint for Governance (Jan. 2019) 370

11.1 Examples of a single-, two-, and three-tier structure with committees 408

TABLES

1.1   A checklist for board participation   41

2.1   Governance codes by sector and nation   85

4.1   Environmental, social, and governance issues and potential solutions   139

4.2   Mandatory Task Force on Climate-Related Financial Disclosures (TCFD) (2020)   154

4.3   Guidance for boards to build back better   167

5.1   Advantages and disadvantages of multiple executive directors on a board   182

5.2   Summary of challenges faced by executive board members and possible solutions   190

7.1   Example board matrix   272

8.1   Comparison of public body board appointments within the UK   312

9.1   Private sector definitions and terminology (GOV.UK, n.d.)   325

10.1   The three sub-classifications of public bodies in the UK   359

11.1   Number of organisations by size and UK country, 2017/18   397

11.2   Income sources, 2017/18 (£m)   397

CONTRIBUTORS

Patricia Armstrong OBE is a highly experienced board member. Currently, chief executive of ACOSVO, the Association of Chief Officers of Scottish Voluntary Organisations, she is vice chair of the Office of the Scottish Charities Regulator and a Board Member of EUCLID, the European Network of Third Sector Leaders. She has worked in the charity/voluntary sector for over 30 years and has gained experience of both local and national voluntary organisations from a range of thematic areas. Patricia has a particular interest in leadership development in the third sector. This interest led her to establish the Leadership Exchange Programme which brings together leaders from across the charity/voluntary and public sectors for peer support, good practice sharing, and personal development. She holds an MBA and is currently a doctoral research student at Edinburgh Napier University Business School exploring resilience in third sector leadership.

Patricia Barclay is an internationally recognised and multi-award-winning lawyer working primarily with science-based companies and those who invest in them. Now based in the UK she has been involved both as in-house and external counsel in the governance of public and private companies in various countries around the world and in the organisation and management of their boards, and is an experienced board member. Patricia holds an LLB law degree from the University of Edinburgh and a bachelor of civil law degree from Oxford University.

Carum Basra is an associate director at Purpose Union, a specialist social purpose strategy firm. He joined Purpose Union from the Institute of Directors (IoD) where he was senior policy advisor. In this role he worked closely with business leaders to represent their views on sustainability and corporate governance issues to government. Carum also worked to establish the IoD Centre for Corporate Governance, and worked extensively on the development of governance codes as part of the European Corporate Governance Codes Network (ECGCN). Having undertaken a Master of Laws degree (LLM) in International Corporate Governance, Carum has a detailed knowledge and critical understanding of the fundamental doctrines, principles, and features of corporate governance. Carum also holds a BA degree in politics.

Sital Cheema is the Sustainability Director at Habitability, working within the Futureproof model, maintaining zero carbon eco-thriving and self-governed housing communities. Habitability will have a significant positive societal and environmental impact. As an investment consultant, her purpose is to help people retire with dignity in a sustainable manner supporting a society and environment that is worth retiring into. Sital was a member of the BSI Steering Group, where she was the sustainability investment technical expert on the BSI Sustainability Investment Management Standards Project responsible for developing the new Environmental, Social, and Governance Standard published by the British Standards Institution in November 2020. In July 2021 she was asked to join the review board for the asset class specific standards currently in the development phase. She is also the Sustainability Ambassador for the Transparency Task Force a certified Social Enterprise. She has over 21 years of investment experience across a broad range of disciplines including ESG and climate change. Sital has a BSc (Hons) in Economics and a MPhil in Management, Economics and Politics from St Andrews University. She is an Associate of the Chartered Institute of Bankers (ACIB) and holds a master's in wealth management awarded by the Chartered Institute for Securities and Investments.

Lorraine Clinton is an experienced, executive director, with multi-industry positions and extensive commercial, operational, and global manufacturing capability. She is well-recognised for both her private and public sector experience and has won several awards. She has a strong track record of delivering strategic change, alongside commercial and operational accountability, embedded via the mentoring of the senior executive team. She is an experienced practitioner in all aspects of governance and risk. She is an enthusiastic and innovative ex-FTSE 100 global executive with key skills in strategy definition, major change management, operational excellence, and stakeholder engagement. She was named in the 2017 "Northern Power Women list" and the 2016 Cranfield "100 Women to Watch" report. She holds a master's degree in maths, French, and economics from the University of Glasgow.

Sheelagh Duffield is a senior executive and qualified lawyer with over 20 years of board level experience and a successful track record of leading complex projects and transactions in FTSE 100 and 250 companies; private equity owned businesses and public sector organisations. Over many years as general counsel and company secretary, Sheelagh has developed a thorough and practical understanding of corporate governance and the effective operation of boards. Sheelagh has held senior executive roles within the corporate departments of Scottish Power plc, Scottish Television plc, and The Miller Group Limited and has a wide range of experience in corporate strategy, business planning, risk management, in-house legal management, and company secretarial and governance practices. Sheelagh is chair of IndiNature, a non-executive director with the National Theatre of Scotland and Cricket Scotland, and a course leader for the Institute of Directors delivering the role of the director and the board (part of the chartered director qualification). She is a corporate governance consultant with Burness Paull.

Francesca Ecsery is a portfolio non-executive director and chair. She is currently on the boards of the F&C Investment Trust PLC, Marshall

Motor Holdings plc, Air France, and the Association of Investment Companies. With 30+ years' board director experience Francesca previously worked for McKinsey & Company, PepsiCo, Thorn EMI, Thomas Cook, STA Travel, and many other consumer brands. An Angel investor in the hospitality sector, Francesca also assesses business on behalf of private equity houses and is working with a new internet start-up company. She holds an MBA from Harvard University and an MSc in international political sciences. Francesca is a business mentor and executive coach as well as a keynote speaker on topics related to diversity in the boardroom, corporate governance, and remuneration committees.

Claire Fargeot has board experience in entrepreneurial, youth and health charity, local authority, and education sectors. As chief operating officer of the Global Governance Group, she works strategically with listed companies as well as other types of organisations to improve governance and sustainability practices. With more than 25 years of capital market, finance, and management consulting experience, Claire is a board reviewer, London Stock Exchange trainer, as well as a business leader mentor. Claire is a doctoral candidate and an associate lecturer, undertaking research in behaviours and actions of directors.

Rachel Gwyon is a senior Government and board leader. She has qualified as a chartered director and been awarded fellowship of the Institute of Directors. She is a former non-executive director of the Scottish Prison Service and of Disclosure Scotland, both public agencies. Her board experience also extends to trustee roles with two charities: Scottish Ballet and Scottish Ensemble. Rachel has worked as a senior civil servant for both the Scottish and UK Governments, and has also sponsored a range of public bodies. She is currently the Director for Nations and Agriculture, Food and Drink in the UK Department for International Trade, based in Edinburgh. Rachel holds a Master's degree in physics from Oxford University.

Vicky Kubitscheck is a non-executive director and board advisor
following a long career leading specialist teams and establishing
systems of risk management, assurance and governance. She has
broad cross sector experience in listed and private companies as
well as public organisations and start-ups. Vicky's non-executive
directorships span the banking, insurance and asset management
industries with responsibilities including chair of the risk and audit
committees and member of the remuneration and nomination
committees. Vicky also advises boards on the effectiveness of their
governance, risk and assurance arrangements. As a member of the
FRC advisory group consulting on the risk management and internal
control guidance and the integrated Corporate Governance Code
(2014), she was responsible for shifting the focus onto the 'principal
risks' of firms. She was the sector technical advisor to the Chartered
Institute of Internal Auditors for evaluating the effectiveness
of internal audit functions in financial services. She authored
'Integrated Assurance: Risk governance beyond boundaries' (Gower,
2014) and has written for the FTAdviser and a number of other
publications. She was described as 'One of the most original and
thorough thinkers in the risk management world' by governance
commentator and FT columnist Robert Bruce.

Eileen Maclean is a licensed insolvency practitioner with over 30
years' experience of all aspects of personal and corporate insolvency.
She is the founding director of Insolvency Support Services, an
award-winning provider of training, outsourcing, compliance, and
practice support services to the UK insolvency market. A member
of the Association of Business Recovery Professionals (R3) and
licensed by the Insolvency Practitioners Association (IPA), Eileen
has represented Scotland on R3's National Council, is a member of
R3's Scottish Technical Committee, and sits on the IPA's Standards,
Ethics and Regulatory Liaison Committee; the AiB's PTD Standing
Committee; Bankruptcy Stakeholder Group and Policy and Cases
Committee; and the Scottish Statutory Debt Solutions Forum.

Chris Pearse is the director of Clarity Space – providing leadership development programmes for CEOs, directors, and senior managers, with clients including Exertis, LAMDA, Mars, BT, Rolls-Royce, Wellcome Trust, BAE Systems, Pernod Ricard, Saudi Aramco, and many others. His career includes being an executive director of a number of international PLCs and he is also the author of the book *THE BROKEN CEO: How To Be The Leader You Always Wanted To Be.* Chris has many years of executive and non-executive board experience with an early executive career in engineering and electronics industries; he is a chartered engineer with a BSc in electrical and electronic engineering.

Charlotte Valeur has extensive experience in financial markets as an investment banker and is an experienced FTSE non-executive director and chair. She is a regular public speaker and delivers training in corporate governance globally. In addition, she conducts board reviews and advices boards on corporate governance through her company Global Governance Group and is a visiting professor of governance at University of Strathclyde. Charlotte has substantial board experience as chair of FTSE250 Kennedy Wilson Europe Real Estate Plc, chair of DW Catalyst Fund Ltd, NED of Renewable Energy Generation Ltd, NED of Phoenix Spree Deutschland Ltd, NED of JPMorgan Convertibles Income Fund, NED of FTSE250 3i Infrastructure Plc, chair of the U.K. Institute of Directors, chair of Blackstone Loan Financing Ltd, NED of NTR Plc, NED of Digital 9 Infrastructure Plc, and NED of Laing O'Rourke Ltd and FSN Capital. She is also chair and founder of Board Apprentice. She is a member of the London Stock Exchange Primary Markets Group and serves on the Advisory Board of the Moller Institute, Churchill College, University of Cambridge.

Gayle Watson is a member of the Institute of Chartered Accountants for England and Wales (ICAEW) who has worked as a director of finance and corporate services/company secretary in the public and charitable sectors for 18 years. An experienced and highly regarded company secretary, Gayle has also had roles on the other side of the fence as both a board member and chair of an audit committee. Gayle currently chairs the Scottish Credit and Qualifications Framework Partnership (SCQF) and is a non-executive director of the Rural and Urban Training Scheme. She has also been responsible for running the finance directors and board secretaries networks in the Scottish college sector and was involved with the production of the Code of Good Governance for Scotland's colleges. She holds a BSc in applied biochemistry.

David Watt is chair of Fife College and of the Scottish Forum on Natural Capital and a non-executive director of Colleges Scotland and Goodison Group. He is a former executive director of the Institute of Directors in Scotland, with considerable board experience in private, public, and charity/voluntary sectors. David is the author of several international texts on management and administration as well as events in the leisure and tourism sectors. He continues to be a sought-out contributor of media articles on governance and civic policy matters and has over many years contributed to live programmes on television and radio. David holds a doctorate in business management and administration, a BSc in Social sciences, and an advanced diploma in education.

Margaret Wright has over 20 years' experience working in the charity/voluntary sector, having led local and national voluntary organisations across the UK. She is currently working as an independent consultant and interim executive specialising in voluntary sector business leadership. Margaret also has experience working in the health care field in the private and public sectors. Having gained an MBA from the University of Glasgow, Margaret has embarked on doctorate level studies, researching governance in the voluntary sector. Margaret supports the work of the Chairs Network in Scotland and has been a trustee in several organisations, including being chair of ACOSVO (Association of Chief Officers of Scottish Voluntary Organisations).

FOREWORD

ANN CAIRNS

Serving on a board is a position of both responsibility and privilege. There are many different types of boards and roles within them, but whatever the structure or role, the main job of members is the same. It is your duty to oversee the running of the organisation and hold the leadership to account. This requires deep understanding of its objectives, strategy, obligations, and challenges. Effective board members are able to draw on their expertise and experience to offer guidance and stewardship, ensuring that the company is doing the best it can for its customers, people, investors, and community. The ability to listen and read between the lines is essential.

There have been many books written on the topic of governance, often focussing on large multinational corporations or a specific sector. However, it is rare to see a publication that brings together the private, public, and third sectors and considers organisations large and small while delving into the practical issues faced by board directors across them all. Written by experienced board members from across the UK, the book explores the nuances of being a board member, covering a wide range of topics that many serving and aspiring directors would wish to know about. It is clear from the straightforward language that the authors have gained considerable insight into what serving in the boardroom really means.

For anyone considering joining a board, this book offers an invaluable practical insight. The chapter on environment, social, and governance (ESG) is particularly relevant at a time when stakeholder capitalism is on the rise. This is something I think about frequently and it is the talk of boardrooms around the world.

Ann Cairns (EXECUTIVE VICE CHAIR – Mastercard; global chair – 30% Club, lead director – Government Department for Business, Energy and Industrial Strategy (BEIS); chair – Intercontinental Exchange; and chair – Financial Alliance for Women)

FOREWORD

This is the book I would very much like to have had at my disposal over the last 20 years to be able to give to new directors and aspirant directors. It offers a practical guide for non-executive and executive board directors in the private, public, and charity sectors of the UK. Its unusual but compelling combination of factual information and personal insights provided by practicing board members offers insights that are just not available anywhere else. Good governance is essential for the health, wealth, and prosperity of the country and we are reliant on its being discharged professionally and with the utmost integrity.

This is a useful guide for directors, aspiring directors, trustees, board secretaries, professional board advisers, and anyone with an interest in best practice governance in large and small organisations, in any UK sector. As it shines a light onto the challenges faced by UK board directors while highlighting easy-to-follow learning points, this book compares the similarities of good governance between different types of organisations as well as contrasts some of the important differences that exist. It demystifies some of the complexities of risk management as well as the important topic of environmental, social, and governance (ESG) alongside that other essential subject – equality, diversity, and inclusion.

Written by highly experienced chairs, non-executive and executive directors, I highly recommend the book for its wisdom, advice, and guidance.

PETER ALLANSON, GOOD GOVERNANCE INSTITUTE

FOREWORD

Jonathan Geldart

The topic of this book is of extreme importance to all Boards. Every director should understand the implications and ramifications for their business. The editors and contributing authors add to the growing body of scholarly and other works that provide a grounding and underpinning to the understanding of good governance.

Jonathan Geldart, Director General, Institute of Directors.

PREFACE

ARTURO LANGA AND MONICA LANGA

It is said that good board governance is much easier to write about than to achieve in practice; the aim of *A Director's Guide to Governance in the Boardroom* is to present a UK-wide practical perspective of governance in the private, public, and charity/voluntary sectors – it is written by board directors/practitioners for experienced and aspiring directors alike and those who provide board evaluation services, as well as professional advisers, auditors, and those who provide training and any other support for board members. The idea for the book was born from a shared passion for good governance and a strong interest in boardroom dynamics – you might even describe the editors as "boardroom geeks". The combination of the differing sectoral board experience of all contributing authors has led to a rich variety of views and perspectives being reflected in the book's content. We believe the end result is all the better for it in much the same way as the sharing of diverse views and perspectives leads to better board decisions.

With the input of highly experienced, practicing board members, readers are offered unique insights not only into best practice governance but also into what it is actually like to serve on a board within a complex regulatory, social, and economic landscape. As governance is increasingly scrutinised, this book considers how directors can be at the forefront of responsible and ethical governance and leadership.

Uniquely bringing together facts and anecdotes/learning points and, like many serving board directors who take up board roles in different sectors, topics explored include board dynamics, succession, board committees, stakeholders, risk management, strategy, governance codes, and sustainability, through the lens of the private, public, and charity sectors, readers can "dip in and out" of chapters and sections as appropriate to the sector or topic they are interested at the time.

A valuable and insightful resource to support directors in the vital role they play in the effective governance of business, civil society, and public services as well as offer an international audience a deep perspective on UK organisational governance.

The editors wish to thank all the contributing authors for their continued passion for excellence in boardroom governance and we hope all readers of this book enjoy it and find it of practical help.

CHAPTER ONE

Governance and the Role of the Board

David Watt, Arturo Langa, and Eileen Maclean

DOI: 10.4324/9781003142850-1

INTRODUCTION

For any organisation, how it is governed is crucial and the board it appoints and empowers to ensure that the process is well done can be absolutely vital.

Other chapters in this book consider the nature of the individuals on a board and the way to recruit the best people, as well as the context in which they operate. However, there is a need to understand in some depth what a board is, what is does or, indeed, does not do – or more accurately, in many cases, what it should do and what it should not do.

There are legal obligations on the board and the directors who make it up, but there is more to being effective as a board than just knowing how to comply with legislation. A board needs to add value to the organisation and in the 21st-century world that can be quite complex and very onerous for the individuals concerned.

There will be some differences highlighted between the private, public, and voluntary/charity sectors, but what always amazes people is the similarities in good governance and potential problems far outweigh any differences which are often of tone and accountability rather than board operation.

GOVERNANCE

This is an oft-used and little understood term which stretches back to the early days of the private sector and company construction in the UK. When companies began to have shareholders and not just patriarchal ownership it was realised that a wider group must be involved in the oversight of how a company operated and what direction it would take.

The topic is a vast subject that enjoys a long and rich history. The issue of governance began with the beginning of corporations, dating back to the East India Company, the Hudson's Bay Company, the Levant Company, and other major chartered companies during the 16th and 17th centuries.

While the concept of corporate governance – the term gained popularity initially in the United States, during the post-Second World War boom, it has existed for centuries, albeit the name did not come into vogue until the 1970s. The balance of power and decision-making between board directors, executives and shareholders has evolved over centuries. The issue has continued to be a "hot topic" among academic experts, regulators, executives, investors, and other stakeholders. It should also be noted, as pointed out by the Institut Européen d'Administration des Affaires (INSEAD) that the UK has one of the oldest systems of corporate governance in the world (Commonalities, Differences, and Future Trends Board Chairs' Practices across Countries Contents, n.d.). While the term "corporate" is often seen as applying to companies in the private sector, in this case it applies to any incorporated body or body established under statute and therefore, this chapter uses the term corporate governance as applying equally to organisations in the public sector and the charity/voluntary sector as well.

Since the 1970s corporate governance had become the subject of debate worldwide by academics, regulators, executives, and investors. By the end of the 1990s, the term "corporate governance" was well-entrenched as academic and regulatory shorthand.

Recent developments and the need to maintain the inter-relationship between directors, executives and shareholders of publicly traded companies and other entities mean that the concept of corporate governance is likely to be with us for the foreseeable future. More recently structures have been established in all sectors of civic society to ensure that wider stakeholder views are represented in how organisations are run, the actions they take, and the values they portray.

It is amusing, for example, to witness sports journalist deliberate on terms such as corporate governance every time a football club gets into financial trouble or a rugby club is struggling to survive, when clearly, they have little or no idea what it is. Equally politicians can use the term quite loosely in criticising others when, it could be argued, they are not quite so good at keeping their own house in order.

To be fair there are many definitions and to some degree the reader can take their pick or look to a whole variety of texts and find different definitions or emphasis.

Investopedia (Chen, n.d.) defines it as,

> Corporate governance is the structure of rules, practices, and processes used to direct and manage a company.

The OECD Principles of Corporate Governance (Oecd.org, 2015) states,

> Corporate governance involves a set of relationships between a company's management, its board, its shareholders and other stakeholders. Corporate governance also provides the structure through which the objectives of the company are set, and the means of attaining those objectives and monitoring performance are determined.

The Chartered Governance Institute (ICSA) (www.icsa.org.uk, n.d.) has a much more comprehensive definition:

> Corporate Governance refers to the way in which companies are governed and to what purpose. It identifies who has power and accountability, and who makes decisions. It is, in essence, a toolkit that enables management and the board to deal more effectively with the challenges of running a company. Corporate governance ensures that businesses have appropriate decision-making processes and controls in place so that the interests of all stakeholders (shareholders, employees, suppliers, customers, and the community) are balanced.

All such definitions are fine and in their own way correct – people, processes, policies, and procedure must all be in place, but experience shows that this is not enough. The governance piece is certainly about what is in place to ensure things are done but we also need to remember that the corporate word added means that we are usually applying that to an organisation and sharing the responsibility.

If you consider the many organisational failures we have seen over many years – such as Carillion, or the highly concerning cases of abuse in USA Gymnastics – do we really think that the board did not believe that all these mechanics were in place? It is very likely that all the directors – right up until the crisis blew up in their face, were totally confident of their governance and they had all the necessary checks and balance in place.

Certainly, governance is about the proper monitoring and control as well as ensuring compliance with legal and regulatory requirements, as well as financial probity.

It is always about ensuring that governance delivers long term relationships which deal with checks and balances, incentives for manager and communications between management and investors/ stakeholders; in addition to transactional relationships which involve dealing with disclosure and authority.

Governance is also about a culture based on a foundation of sound leadership ethics which fulfils the long-term strategic goal of the owners/members/beneficiaries while considering the expectations of all the key stakeholders, and in particular considering and caring for the interests of employees, past, present, and future. It works to maintain excellent relations with both customers and suppliers and takes account of the needs of the environment and the local community, while maintaining proper compliance with all the applicable legal and regulatory requirements under which the organisation is carrying out its activities.

For the board in the 21st century the real question in governance is,

Is what we believe going on and what we agreed, actually happening?

Sounds an easy question but in truth so many boards get caught out with what they believe to be happening is not true in practice – they might have agreed something, but they always have real challenges to know if that is being implemented day to day.

It is doubtful that the board of Boeing knew that the 737Max Airplanes were not fit to fly in their early days, but they were still responsible, or the boards of the banks when they banned the use of credit derivatives squared – only to find they were still being operated by lower-level staff.

For many voluntary organisations, the health and safety and wellbeing of clients and staff is paramount and is a great example of how boards must "walk the walk" to find out what is going on. For example, as a board member is a sports and leisure trust board members should visit sites and ask what exactly is going on and not just sit round a table asking questions. That way you will get genuine feeling for the staff commitment and involvement in the process as well as their faith in the senior management and indeed the board in backing the culture of health and safety.

So, despite all your best efforts as a board, there may be things going on which you do not desire or did not agree – the real challenge of corporate governance is not just that all the policies and procedures are in place but the delivery of the business controls and action on the ground.

The key activity then of the board is to be the agent who delivers this proper organisational governance and ensures that the organisation keeps on track to deliver its purpose. Ensuring that mechanisms are in place to deliver your policies and an audit – internal and external – is carried out to check that they are being effective, is the crucial action a board must take.

Governance is about:

- Accountability.
- Probity.
- Transparency.
- Integrity.

UNDERSTANDING THE ROLE OF THE BOARD

A s far back as 1995 the business guru John Harvey-Jones said,

> The job of the board is all to do with creating momentum, movement, improvement, and direction. If the board is not taking the company purposefully into the future, who is?

While not all organisations are incorporated as companies, for example, some public bodies and some charities, the majority of organisations in the private, public, and charity/voluntary sectors are incorporated so it is helpful to consider the key legal duties and potential liabilities of Directors as outlined by Companies House are as follows.

GENERAL DUTIES

As a director, you must perform a set of seven duties under the Companies Act 2006 (Legislation.gov.uk, 2010).

These still apply if:

- You are not active in your role as director.
- Someone else tells you what to do.
- You act as a director but have not been formally appointed.
- You control a board of directors without being on it.

CONSTITUTION

You must follow the organisation's constitution and its articles of association (governing documents). These are written rules about running the company, agreed by the members, directors, and the company secretary.

The constitution sets out what powers you are granted as a director, and the purpose of those powers.

PROMOTE THE SUCCESS OF THE ORGANISATION

You must act in the company's best interests to promote its success. You must consider the:

- Consequences of decisions, including the long term.
- Interests of its employees.
- Need to support business relationships with suppliers, customers, and others.
- Impact of its operations on the community and environment.
- Company's reputation for high standards of business conduct.
- Need to act fairly to all members of the company.

If the company becomes insolvent, your responsibilities as director will apply towards the creditors, as well as the company. A creditor is anyone owed money by the company.

INDEPENDENT JUDGEMENT

You must not allow other people to control your powers as a director. You can accept advice, but you must use your own independent judgement to make final decisions.

EXERCISE REASONABLE CARE, SKILL, AND DILIGENCE

You must perform to the best of your ability. The more qualified or experienced you are, the greater the standard expected of you.

You must use any relevant knowledge, skill, or experience you have (e.g. if you are a qualified accountant).

AVOID CONFLICTS OF INTEREST

You must avoid situations where your loyalties might be divided. You should consider the positions and interests of your family, to avoid possible conflicts.

You should tell other directors and members about any possible conflict of interest, and follow any process set out in the company's articles of association.

This duty continues to apply if you are no longer a director. You must not take advantage of any property, information, or opportunity you became aware of as a director.

THIRD-PARTY BENEFITS

You must not accept benefits from a third party that are offered to you because you are a director. This could cause a conflict of interest.

The company may allow you to accept benefits like reasonable corporate hospitality if it is clear there is no conflict of interest.

INTERESTS IN A TRANSACTION

You must tell the other directors and members if you might personally benefit from a transaction the organisation makes. For example, if the organisation plans to enter a contract with a business owned by a member of your family.

OTHER DUTIES

There are other duties you must perform as a company director. For example, you must:

- Not misuse the company's property.
- Apply confidentiality about the company's affairs.

In addition, there are a number of broad roles and responsibilities to be followed.

- Ensure annual accounts and returns are produced and received by Companies House.
- Keep accurate and up to date company records.
- Be responsible for the health and safety of employees.
- Be answerable to the owners of the limited company.
- Be responsible for entering into credit agreements on behalf of the company.
- Register to pay business tax and file tax returns and annual accounts to HMRC.
- Use or disclose the company's confidential information only for the benefit of the company.
- Report company changes to Companies House.

The Institute of Directors defines a good board as,

> A well-balanced board of well-chosen executive and non-executive directors, with the chairman's leadership and co-ordination, should provide a totally integrated team to shape the destiny of the company, ensure its profitable performance and safeguard its interests.

As a board, we take on these responsibilities – jointly and severally – on the basis of cabinet responsibility, meaning that we together have accountability for our actions on behalf of the organisation. It is worth mentioning that liability is "joint and several"; this means that should legal action be taken against a board, or in the case of insolvency/ administration, it is possible to pursue the personal assets of only the wealthiest board member, and it is not necessary to pursue all board members equally. At the same time, while there is no distinction in the Companies Act between executive and non-executive directors, in practice the courts recognise that it is not possible for non-executive board members to have the same detailed knowledge of the organisation as executive directors do and some allowances have been known to be made in light of this. Equally, the level of professional knowledge a director has would also be taken into account, for example a board member with little knowledge of background in finance would be treated less severely on matters on accountancy irregularities than a board member who is a chartered accountant.

In the UK there has often been a debate about the duties, responsibilities and accountabilities of directors and boards, especially when things go wrong – for example, when companies who wind up have inadequate funds to cover pension liabilities or their organisation fails to properly protect its employees in health and safety terms.

It has always proved quite difficult, although far from impossible to prosecute directors on the basis of their individual culpability – more often the charge has been made corporately.

The Institute of Directors (IoD) factsheet on the Role of the Board (2018) highlights four key areas of focus for directors which include:

- Establishing vision, mission, and values.
- Setting strategy and structure.
- Delegating to management.
- Exercising accountability to shareholders/stakeholders.

The Financial Reporting Council (FRC) (the FRC was replaced by the Audit Reporting and Governance Authority – ARGA) report Guidance on Board Effectiveness (July 2018) recommends,

> The boardroom should be a place for robust debate where challenge, support, diversity of thought and teamwork are essential features. Diversity of skills, background and personal strengths is an important driver of a board's effectiveness, creating different perspectives among directors, and breaking down a tendency towards 'group think'.

DAVID WATT ET AL.

All of this is true, but what should the board be debating and deliberating on – and just as important what should it not be considering.

Investopedia again suggests,

> A company's board of directors is the primary force influencing corporate governance.

In a similar vein to the above, the charity/voluntary sector highlights the board's key responsibilities as including:

STRATEGY

- Setting the direction and strategic aims.
- Monitoring of performance against strategic priorities.

FINANCE

- Setting annual budget.
- Approval of changes to budget out with delegated authority.
- Maintenance of financial regulations.
- Scrutiny and approval of management accounts and of statutory accounts.
- Setting and reviewing reserves policy.

HUMAN RESOURCES

- Approval of policies and terms and conditions of employment.
- Recruitment, induction, supervision, and appraisal of the CEO.

RISK

- Maintaining and regularly reviewing a risk register.

- Monitoring and reviewing delegated authorities.
- Maintaining a business continuity plan.

Trustees must work together to ensure that the organisation's staff are protected and supported. The National Occupation Standards for Volunteer Management committee members outlines five key areas of responsibility that are essential principles for committee/board members to follow to ensure good governance, described as the 5 S's of governance (support, stretch, stewardship, scrutiny, and strategy).

Trustees have a responsibility to act reasonably and prudently in all matters relating to the organisation and have a responsibility to act in the best interest of the organisation.

In order to avoid the most common difficulties that can arise trustees should:

- Appreciate their responsibilities for the organisation and its resources.
- Make themselves familiar with the governing document to ensure clarity of their powers to act.
- Spot any circumstances in which they need to get specialist advice, for example on legal or financial issues.
- Ensure measures are in place to ensure no individual trustee or staff member can make decisions without accountability or control.
- Recognise and manage conflicts of interest and not allow personal matters and resources to become entangled with those of the organisation.
- Manage the organisation in the interest of the organisation.

SUPPORT

There are times when the function of the Board is to support the management team and enable them to manage by ensuring that the infrastructure of the organisation works – that systems work, and that staff are encouraged and enabled to do their work. Boards in support mode may say:

- "Have you got what you need?"
- "We really ought to celebrate that".
- "We really can't allow you to be treated like that".

STRETCH

Equally there are times when the Board needs to stretch the organisation and to challenge and improve. Boards that are stretching may say:

- "Can we do any better than that?"
- "Have you thought of doing it differently?"
- "Couldn't we develop a process to do this?"

SCRUTINY

Boards scrutinise and question the information and proposals put to them, challenge them and hold them to account. Scrutinising Boards may say:

- "Does this make sense?"
- "Have you thought of the implications of doing this?"
- "I don't think you have made the case that …"

STEWARDSHIP

Boards are the stewards who guard the assets of the organisation. They protect the funds, the reputation and the long-term functioning of the organisation. As good stewards they need to protect and conserve, and preserve assets for current and future beneficiaries. In the stewardship role the Boards may say:

- "But will the money be here in five years' time?"
- "Are we giving away our intellectual property too easily?"
- "Is reputational risk too great if we do this?"

STRATEGY

Boards also determine strategy by listening to others, consult experts and all the stakeholders. The board makes the decisions that affect the future direction of the organisation. Boards in strategy mode may say:

- "The external environment means that we have to re-think …".
- "This is a golden opportunity to open our doors to people from …".
- "We can come out of this a stronger organisation".

Another way to access peer support is to connect to other trustees or chair of a different board. This can be done independently, but there are also organisations and events which can enable connections. Examples such as The Association of Chairs and Scotland's Chairs network would all be conduits to a wider network for peer support and good practice sharing.

LEADERSHIP

- Chair and board
- Chief and chair

STRATEGIC VIEW

In 2015 Larry Fink, founder and CEO of BlackRock, issued a public letter pressing fellow CEOs to forego making business decisions based on short-term considerations (Fink, 2015).

> It is critical however to understand that corporate leaders' duty of care and loyalty is not to every investor or trader who owns their company's shares at any moment in time, but to the company and its long-term owners.

This warning clearly highlights the board's duty to take a longer view and to guide executives who often drive for short term benefit – to the longer aim of sustainability and continuity. New CEOs in particular often wish to make their mark and make changes instead of "making haste slowly" and reflecting on what is working and what is not and what will endure successfully over time.

If one duty of the board stands out it is perhaps this – being longer term and strategic – considering the durability of the organisation and how it will sustain and thrive into the future – five and ten years away – not just next month or next year. The individuals – executive or non-executive may be gone by then, but the body should survive and grow successfully without them. The private sector, in particular, has been all too good at rewarding short-term success and finding that after CEOs have left with their package they have not built for the long term. Interestingly this trend has begun to change and now with executive remuneration often linked to share price and value in five years' time. Again, a board duty is to set the future focus in its remuneration schemes.

BOARD MAKE-UP

Fulfilled by the board of directors, which may also be called trustees or governors and in some organisations, it is called a board of management, is this vital commitment to the success and long-term sustainability of their organisation.

Boards may vary from organisation to organisation, but it is quite normal to find a mixture of participants in attendance and contributing at board meetings. A private limited company which might be limited by shares or by guarantee (the latter is often the legal form of a charity or public sector organisation) is required, by law, to have at least one director, while publicly listed companies must have at least two, although the various members of the board may have different roles within the board and within the organisation.

The composition varies, but most boards across the private, public, and charity/voluntary sectors, are made up from a combination of executive and non-executive directors. There may be others with the courtesy title of director or functional director/head of division or department that may attend all or parts of board meetings but have no standing in law.

Non-executive directors (NEDs) may be given different names in different types of organisations and are sometimes called lay members, trustees, governors, independent directors, and some organisations appoint a senior independent director (SID). One of the NEDs fulfils the role of chair of the board; sometimes the title used is convenor.

It is worth noting that in some organisations in both the private and charity/voluntary sectors, the entire board comprises only non-executive directors. It is interesting that the charity/voluntary sector commonly does not have the CEO or any executive staff member as a fully signed up board director or trustee. There is no specific reason for this position which occurs in many charities of all sizes. It may simply be historic where the view was that the Trustees would decide what was to be done and then tell the staff to carry out their orders. It probably comes from the platonic and authoritarian start of the sector and its links to an older military management style.

Whatever the history, by tradition many charity/voluntary organisation CEOs do not sit on the board. This CEO "not a board member" position is considered somewhat outdated – for effectiveness, and probably from a legal perspective. The clear legal position is that anyone who is "a moving force in decision making" is liable for board decisions, whether or not they are a signed-up Trustee. Additionally, not involving people fully in the decisions which dictate their work can be seen as not motivating or stimulating. Clearly chief officers must be fully engaged with and involved in the board if we want to get them fully engaged and ensure we get best out of them.

Most would agree that the definition includes "not for profit" and that the "voluntary board of management", board members do not get paid. Over recent years in some charities (mostly larger), board members are remunerated – and charity regulations do allow for this (as long as it is allowed in their governing documents and by the regulator.). It is the norm that expenses are paid to board members. The general position is that the board agree the strategic direction and the paid staff carry out the work from an operational perspective. Often a "scheme of delegation" will be in place to clarify what powers are delegated and to whom.

In some smaller community organisations, there can be the case when the board look to the CEO for advice and guidance on operational matters and it can be a fine line as to "who is in charge". In England and Wales, under the Charities Act 2011, it specifies that "It's not the name that matters, it's what they do [...] the persons having the general control and management of the administration of a charity", regardless of their title. The Office of the Scottish Charities Regulator (OSCR) explains that "A charity must be managed and controlled by charity trustees who are acting in the interests of the charity".

Members of the board hold the legal role of registered directors of the company/organisation, once they have officially registered with Companies House in the UK – where all the records of registered companies, annual accounts and named directors are held; with the authority to act as specified in the governing documents of the organisation, they can vote on board matters.

Those in attendance may attend for part or for the entirety of board meetings but are not legal directors as defined by the Companies Act (2006) and have no voting powers on board matters, this may include the Board/Company Secretary who advises on matters of board process and governance but has sometimes has no part in board decision-making. Bear in mind, though, that those who have a significant influence on board decisions can be held responsible and liable in law even if they are not officially signed up as directors. This view of the CEO of a charity being a potential "de facto" director was tested in the courts in 2021 in the case of the former CEO of the charity the Kids Company which went into insolvency in 2015.

The Official Receiver had applied to the High Court to disqualify the CEO as a company director for six years for her alleged part in the collapse of the charity together with six trustees of the charity. Although the CEO was not formally a member of the board, the receiver argued her importance as the charity's founder and chief executive made her a "de facto" trustee.

LEARNING POINT

Kids Company was established by Camila Batmanghelidjh in south London in 1996; it became one of the most high-profile charities of the early 21st century. With political and celebrity backing from UK Prime Ministers Gordon Brown and David Cameron, and support from artists such as Coldplay and JK Rowling.

Not only did the case fail, the judge also praised the trustees for their role in the final months of Kids Company. The judge Mrs Justice Falk commented,

> Most charities would, I think, be delighted to have available to them individuals with the abilities and experience that the trustees in this case possess. It is vital that the actions of public bodies do not have the effect of dissuading able and experienced individuals from becoming or remaining charity trustees.

In fact, the Official Receiver was criticised for attempting to hold the board and management team of a charity to commercial company standards.

According to UK law (Companies Act, 2006) there is no distinction between the executive and non-executive directors (NEDs) on a board, the entire board is collectively responsible for the long-term success of the organisation and is required to fulfil its legal responsibilities by ensuring effective stewardship and governance oversight.

In the most general sense, the role of the Board is to set the strategy and direction of travel, set the risk appetite and to make the important, collective decisions acting in the best interests of the organisation, protecting the interests of shareholders/stakeholders.

While the Companies Acts do not differentiate between executive and non-executive directors, the UK Corporate Governance Code 2018 (the Code) does (Financial Reporting Council, 2018).

The Code is only mandatory for UK public listed companies (with a premier listing) also known as (Public Limited Companies shortened to PLCs) and although there is no requirement for other types of organisation, to adhere to the Code, it is considered a "gold standard" in governance terms and therefore worthwhile for board members of any organisation to be aware of. Chapter 2 on Governance Codes provides much more detail on this Code and also many of the variety of other governance codes in existence in the UK. Many such codes are to some extent, based on the UK Governance Code so there are familiar threads and common themes are noticeable.

The Financial Reporting Council (FRC), the body responsible for the UK Corporate Governance Code, at present has very few "teeth" to enforce the Code or such good practice. At present there is reliance on shareholder and peer pressure to encourage compliance – except in extreme cases. This "voluntary" approach is constantly under review and many feel that it needs to be strengthened.

In the public sector the body will be established by statute or government departmental edict and will have a lengthy a detailed form of oversight. This will be done on an on-going basis by the responsible government department and will normally require a detailed, wide ranging annual report and may even involve a member of the civil service sitting on the board regularly.

In the voluntary sector this role is taken by the appropriate oversight body, for example, in Scotland by the Office of the Scottish Charity Regulator or in England and Wales by the Charity Commission and in Northern Ireland by the Charity Commission for Northern Ireland. These bodies will check regularly on the behaviour of the individual organisations, as well as checking their articles of association and constitution when they first apply for registration.

In the UK, there are many forms of oversight for organisations and their proper behaviour in the sight of the law and the regulators, so boards and individual directors/trustees must be aware of the legal and regulatory requirements and ensure they are met, as the number one priority of their work.

It is also absolutely vital that we consider the individuals that compose the board and that a proper skills matrix is developed containing all the skills we want on our board, then we can set off to recruit them and so produce a balanced board. It is equally vital that any board understands the business it is in and in some way reflects the customer or client or shareholder interest in its deliberations.

For example, many will remember when Marks & Spencer PLC refused to accept credit cards when other retailers did or how it lost its way in the clothing business – quite possibly because the board was out of touch with the people who were buying their range. The board does not need to be made up of users, but it does have to understand the world in which they exist.

This is often evidenced too in board room diversity – which often focusses solely on gender, when the issue is much bigger than this. All the evidence, over many years, has demonstrated that a diverse board delivers business success in terms of numbers but also in terms of positive perception. That diversity is crucially of thought but that derives from difference – of background, experience, age, gender, disability, education, ethnicity, technical knowledge, etc.

Any review of board effectiveness must assess the achievement of diversity and the impact if it is not achieved.

BOARD STRUCTURE

The first step to establishing and maintaining an effective board is to consider the best structure and size for the board which is most appropriate to the age, stage, size, and nature of the organisation.

The detail of board composition and recruitment will be considered in further in Chapter 7 (Recruiting and Maintaining an Effective Board), but recognising that all directors with board-level roles retain a fiduciary duty the Code suggests that at least 50% of board members are non-executive or independent.

The balance of non-executive directors to executive directors will vary depending on the type of organisation and its governing documents. In some charities, for example, the entire board is made up or non-executive directors – or trustees, while members of executive management may attend board meetings but sometimes have no official board decision-making role.

The chief executive officer (CEO), the managing director (MD), and the chief financial officer (CFO) or finance director are executives who are typically members of the board. This may extend to other executive roles, for example in a banking institution, the chief compliance officer or chief risk officer may be board members, in a healthcare organisation, the chief medical officer and so on.

It is always worth remembering that when deciding on or reviewing the size and structure of a board of directors is that "one size does not fit all". The way in which directors are appointed and the number will be prescribed by a company's articles of association, but if they are out of date, they can be changed.

Turning to what the Code mentions on this subject, it does not specify a number of directors, instead suggesting,

> The board should be of sufficient size that the requirements of the business can be met and that changes to the board's composition and that of its committees can be managed without undue disruption and should not be so large as to be unwieldy.

The Chartered Governance Institute, states in its 2019 report – The Future Board – Getting in Shape for Tomorrow's Challenges (www.cgi. org.uk, 2019):

> When contemplating possible future models for the structure and role of the board, there are perhaps four overlapping considerations to be borne in mind:
>
> - Capacity – how much time does the board need to carry out its responsibilities, and how can use it most effectively? If the board does not have sufficient time to do all the work that is expected of it, is the answer to increase the time commitment or reduce the workload?
> - Capability – what skills and information does the board need, and where does it get them from? Do you need all the relevant expertise and all the different perspectives around the board table, or can they be obtained more efficiently in a different way?
> - Control – what visibility does the board have over the organisation it leads, and what levers can it pull to influence behaviour and performance? Are they sufficient?
> - Closeness to the issue concerned – is the view from the top necessarily the best view? Is the boardroom the best place in the organisation to deal with all the issues currently on the board's agenda?

The vital characteristic of a successful and productive board is a balance of skills and experience – ideally with a diversity of backgrounds as we must drive for diversity of thought and input. The code also recommends that the chair should not be a former chief executive of the same organisation and that the roles of chair and chief executive should not be held by the same individual.

The number on the board is another issue which should be determined in the same way – by appropriateness to the age, stage, size, and nature of the organisation.

It has been said that "the best board is three – two at home in bed and me – making the decisions".

This type of thinking which often weakens family businesses and almost certainly caused the downfall of some of the big banks during the financial crash. It is a type of elitist or cliquish behaviour which tends to only listen to people who think in the same way and so damages the long-term future of any organisation.

While that sort of autocracy does not work, there is some sense in thinking that larger boards take longer to get to a decision. A smaller board size may improve the quality of communication, with more focussed discussions, although it can create problems if one board member is suddenly indisposed and can easily be overpowered by "savvy" executives.

Often in the start-up or early stages of a business there might be only one non-executive chair or director to act as a guiding hand, partly because the business cannot afford or does not need any more input, which would probably overwhelm the often-small executive team anyway.

An important concept too, for early-stage businesses, is "sweat equity" – where a non-exec will come in to help in growing the business in return for a small stake in the business. This stake, of course, is only producing any return for the non-exec effort should the company develop well and produce value. One cautionary note here is to be aware of predatory non-execs who look for massive stakes – for example, 20% plus. The norm should be 5–10% and even that should be tied up clearly in a contract dictating what level of input will be given.

On the other hand, start-ups can also struggle with governance and support from a board if they leave it too late to bring the external view and experience, they lack – it genuinely can be transforming to have a good board and the timing of its formation can be life improving or damaging if done badly.

Having touched on the UK Corporate Governance Code, it is worth highlighting that the Corporate Governance Guidance and Principles that exist for other types of organisations such as unlisted organisations including privately owned companies and those in the public and third sectors are covered in more detail in Chapter 2. While the Wates Principles were introduced as a voluntary code for large privately owned companies in 2018, the IoD in association with ecoDa and sponsored by Deloitte, produced a guidance in 2010 with all sizes of organisation in mind, it is not a recognised governance code as such albeit it contains useful guidance and states that

> Once a company reaches a certain size and level of complexity, an independent board, i.e., a board containing independent non-executive directors and not entirely composed of company or family insiders, becomes essential to the long-term success and survival of the company.

That said it is worth again remembering that Drucker – the renowned US management guru was often quoted as saying that

> the only thing that was common to all boards is that they are dysfunctional!

Getting the appropriate size and structure will help avoid this – as will recruiting the best people – as identified in subsequent chapters.

SUBSIDIARY BOARDS

A UK subsidiary is an officially incorporated body formed in the UK in accordance with local rules on company formation and registration. The subsidiary's capital is normally fully or partially owned by its parent company. There are many reasons that a UK-based subsidiary board might exist, for example it may be the trading arm of a charity/voluntary sector organisation, or the UK trading entity of an international company. Subsidiaries are required to have their own board structure and a board, which has non-executive directors and executive directors, some of whom may be common to the parent as well as the subsidiary board and some who are independent of the parent company.

Certain regulators, such as the Financial Conduct Authority require international asset management firms to establish UK subsidiary boards to ensure that the interests of the UK clients are protected – this is a good example of the tricky balancing act that subsidiary board directors face. A "Balancing Act" is how Susan Fadil, director – Funds and Corporate Services at JTC plc (provider of fund management services), described subsidiary board governance (JTC, Apr. 2018). She commented,

> It's a fact that often corporate governance failings occur at the subsidiary level, largely due to a lack of attention or an ineffective oversight mechanism. It is not good enough to just take a group-wide corporate governance code and ask the subsidiary board to apply it.

The risk and challenge faced in particular by members of a subsidiary board is that the parent company may not have a good understanding of the culture, climate, and environment that any subsidiary boards operate in. Equally, establishing and maintaining an effective and respectful relationship between board members of the parent and the subsidiary organisation is vital, the parent company may decide on a strategy that has a negative impact on the stakeholders of the subsidiary organisation. Ongoing dialogue between subsidiary and parent boards is absolutely vital to make sure that all parties clearly understand each other's objectives. If they can do this, they will be a good way along the road to achieving an effective balance between the level of independence of the subsidiary while allowing the overall group to achieve its strategic objectives.

The Institute of Chartered Accountants England and Wales (ICAEW Helpsheet, 2016.) Highlights a number of areas that can make subsidiary board governance effective, with the starting points of "a precise statement (terms of reference) on the role of the subsidiary board, with guidance on the level of autonomy and the flexibility granted to the subsidiary body".

Another tool which can facilitate the alignment of governance processes while still allowing for some local flexibility is putting in place a subsidiary governance framework template.

ICSA the Chartered Governance Institute has developed a helpful "at a glance" subsidiary governance framework template checklist as presented by Diligent Corporation, the governance, risk and compliance (GRC) SaaS provider (Diligent Insights, 2019):

- Get buy-in and establish processes – this assists in "setting the tone from the top" and can be followed by an audit and due diligence on all subsidiaries.
- Build in some flexibility for local needs – the governance framework template should be built on best practice corporate governance throughout the group, while taking into account any local legal or regulatory and customs that may require subsidiaries to tweak to suit the jurisdiction.
- Audits and reviews are key – auditing the composition and effectiveness of subsidiary boards and consider remuneration policies and practices that are appropriate for each subsidiary.
- Documents, policies, and procedures – all group-wide policies, such as anti-bribery policies, codes of ethics, health and safety needs, and whistle-blowing procedures, should be easily accessible to all staff and there may be a need to refresh the policies to fit the subsidiary governance framework template needs.

- Communications and training – clear reporting lines to keep the flow of communication open between the parent and the subsidiaries are vital. Encouraging communication and engagement between members of subsidiary boards and the parent board as well as keeping staff and stakeholders informed of relevant changes is important. Regular training especially for subsidiary directors as well as consideration to how new directors are inducted and onboarded is also helpful.

ROLE OF THE CHAIR OF THE BOARD

Arguably the most important post in any organisation – certainly, any board is the chair. Their behaviour, attitude, knowledge, and expertise set the tone for the board and relationships at all levels. Most likely this will work its way through the whole set up and can have a major impact on the organisation's psyche and so its performance.

Clearly, they have certain duties and roles to perform, as below but this setting of values and behaviours is very important too.

We may want a chair with situation specific skills – for example, knowledge of the financial sector or a large company background as well as a number of other needs such as a knowledge of raising funds or working in certain aspect of the public sector. On searching for the best person for the role, it is vital to be very specific about any such requirements and to be clear about which are essential, and which are desirable.

So, for a good chair we also need some very specific chairing skills which relate to the board and the practical duties they have. The list is long and again will vary in terms of importance depending on the precise situation. It is critical to understand that these specific chairing skills are not optional though nor should it be assumed that people with industry experience or reputation necessarily have the required aptitudes.

Chair skills/abilities/characteristics

Diplomacy Tact Engaging Others Empathy Technical Knowledge
Leadership

Intellect Charisma Good Timekeeper Well Organised Hard-
working Caring Involved

Understanding Listener Reflective Thinker Keeps Focus
Visionary Prepared Fair Emotional Intelligence

Decisive Mentor Guide Independent Enhances
Organisation Humour.

Deep knowledge of board procedures and mechanics Board
member appraisal

Board recruitment and development Reviewing board performance.

The best tip ever, and the critical one if you are asked to join a board
is – *check out the chair* – if you can work them and if you are going to
learn from them, then this may be a great board to join.

LEARNING POINT

If you have reached a point in your executive career, which makes
you believe that you have some time and expertise to take into the
non-executive space. It might also help you expand your range of
experience and help build your CV in the future.

To make this move you will have to consider what you would
add to the board you might join, but also what sector you would
want to work in, as well as the nature of the board you might
want to join.

Assessing your skills and abilities and examining the fit of the
host organisation and its board – will ensure a sound and lasting
relationship, which will see you both maximise benefit.

BOARD COMMITTEES

The existence and number of board committees depends on the size and needs of each specific board; however, typically committees include audit committee, risk committee, nomination committee, and remuneration committee. Sometimes these are combined, for example, audit and risk assurance committee or remuneration and nominations committee. Nominations Committees take on responsibility for board recruitment, although it is not uncommon for this process to be led by the chair of the board. A remuneration committee, if one exists, would be responsible for proposing the remuneration levels for executive directors as well as any remuneration paid to the chair, for approval by the board. It would be inappropriate for NEDs to propose their own remuneration levels so this is often determined by the governance documents of the organisation and/or the chair of the board.

Modern boards will also consider other committees or short-term working groups which report to the board and these might include – stakeholder/shareholder engagement; innovation driving; environmental responses and actions; or constitutional review. For example, a finance, risk, and audit committee will:

- Review the management accounts and provide a narrative for the board.
- Conduct the annual organisation risk assessment and provide a report and action plan for the board.

Board committees are expected to have a formal Terms of Reference (TOR), which outlines how each committee will operate, how often it will meet, what the membership will comprise of and the process followed to decide how board members will be appointed to it. It is worth noting that board committees also often have staff members attend meetings, which gives all committee members a better understanding of the operations and governance of the organisation.

There is also scope for working groups to be convened for a specific task. For example, an organisation may need to find new premises.

A working group may be convened to consider the needs or the organisation, conduct a search and advise the board accordingly. Once the work has concluded, the working group is disbanded.

APPOINTMENT TO BOARD COMMITTEES

In practice, it is unlikely that the full board will be able to consider all the issues that it should in the necessary detail to stop potential problems arising, and this is increasingly true in the increasingly complex environment that boards operate in. For this reason, the role and significance of the board committees becomes more important as they will have more responsibility for challenging the executive team and for a more detailed interrogation of key issues.

This being true it is important that the correct people with the requisite skills and experience are on the correct committee. It is crucial that the selection process gets the best person in and does not allow a clique to rule any aspect or the board to get false feedback due to lack of non-executive expertise in committees.

While there is considerable guidance, via many of the codes of governance and even regulatory guidance on appropriate methods of recruiting directors to a board, there is not so much guidance on appropriate frameworks for the appointment of existing board members to a board committee or to the position of chairing such a committee. While some governance codes describe the fact that board committee chairs should have relevant skills to perform the function, for example a chair of the audit committee, where the UK Corporate Code suggests that the individual taking up this role has recent and relevant financial experience, it is silent on the topic of what process the board should undertake to make the appointment – there might be two suitably experienced and qualified board members who both want to chair the audit committee. Publicly listed companies often take the approach of appointing a qualified accountant to the role as do other organisations, such as privately owned companies, public bodies and charity/voluntary bodies. Equally, a number of governance codes specify that the chair of the board should not chair of be a member of the audit committee and that chairs of all board sub-committees should be non-executive directors; however, there is no guidance on a best practice approach to going about fairly and impartially choosing which board member should sit on or chair which committee.

The selection process should be in line with the organisation's governing documents, such as articles of association, terms of reference of standing committee. The appointments process should be conducted on the same impartial skills assessed basis as when recruiting board members – the key difference is the committee work will demand some genuine expertise in the specific area of the committee (e.g. HR or finance or remuneration). The mechanics must be fair and impartial, and all board members, who are eligible, should go through the same process of skills matching to committee requirements.

Considerations which should be taken into account include:

- Relevant skills and experience;
- The need to provide sufficient continuity of membership to maintain committee performance levels;
- The need for cross committee membership to provide appropriate governance links;
- Robust succession planning in terms of both the chairs and membership;
- A fair and transparent approach (this should include written guidelines outlining the procedure that will be followed highlighting an open process and understood by all board members);
- The remaining terms of office of members;
- Timings of any appointment – does this give an opportunity for a handover period; and
- The length of service of members on each of the committees.

It is also possible for committees to bring other non-executive input from out with the board itself should the necessary skills not be available from within. This is particularly effective in the charity/voluntary sector where someone could assist greatly just by sitting on a committee.

This process would normally be led by the chair of the board, or the nominations committee, if one exists. As mentioned above, the process of appointment to board committees may also be laid out in the organisation's governing documents and/or the committee Terms of Reference and may require whole board approval. It is important that any board committee appointments process is seen as fair and transparent. Therefore, when a board committee vacancy arises, the appointments process should be clear for all eligible board members.

Should this process become problematic at any time then – an approach that could be considered is to seek out external guidance, perhaps in the form of an external non-executive director or from a recruitment professional, may be useful.

COMPARISONS BETWEEN SECTORS (PRIVATE, PUBLIC, AND CHARITY/VOLUNTARY)

People often fixate about being in one sector or other when talking about boards and their operation – believing that there are major differences which must always be in the forefront of directors' minds.

This really is not true! While there are some issues which vary, the most interesting fact is that the similarities far outweigh any differences in how the board should operate and what its concerns and duties are. How the board should behave in terms of focussing on strategy and oversight and not being caught up in day-to-day detail, is the same.

Yes, practical purpose will usually be quite different:

Private Sector = making profit

Public Sector = delivering defined task or service

Charity/Voluntary Sector = pursuing the charity mission to provide a service for users/beneficiaries.

And there may be some variation in other areas, such as in levels of public profile; the influence of shareholders/stakeholders; image; volunteer engagement; and the empathy for purpose.

However, there will still be more commonalities like complying with Health and Safety and employment legislation, as well as a large range of other common agenda items like marketing, social media, and cybersecurity.

The other very significant variance will be the nature of the regulator. For the private sector in the UK, it is the Financial Reporting Council; while the Charity Commission for England and Wales, the Charity Commission for Northern Ireland, and the Office of the Scottish Charity regulator will oversee mainland Great Britain; and for the public sector they will be governed by their sponsoring government department. Again, the sensible organisation will ensure it complies with all the regulator's requirements and keeps a positive, co-operative relationship going with them – regardless of sector.

Crucially the one feature that certainly has grown over recent years, is the focus in all sectors on improving governance and assuring all key stakeholders that we are delivering proper control and oversight to keep the body healthy, sustainable, and successful.

WHAT THE BOARD SHOULD DO

It is really important for there to be 100% agreement on what our organisation's board is going to do and, on the other hand, what it is not going to do. Crucially it has overall responsibility for the everything that goes on in our name, but it does not have any operational role. A position that many non-executive directors find challenging.

For some it is quite simple – the board should simply be about:

- Strategy.
- Evaluation.
- CEO succession.
- Risk management.
- Board education.
- Audit.
- Regulatory compliance.
- Onboarding/outboarding.

But, as we will see, this is a bit simplistic.

Many believe "the board shouldn't do anything but ensure that others do!" and, while that is clearly flippant, it has a grain of truth, that is, boards get into the most trouble when they start doing things, which often equates to interfering with the executive team and their actions – a recipe for trouble and discord.

The INSEAD research into Board Chair practices conducted in 2016 (Commonalities, Differences, and Future Trends Board Chairs' Practices across Countries Contents, 2016), mentions a phrase to describe to role of non-executive directors as "sticking my nose in the pie but keeping my fingers out".

The board, in fact, does a lot but not in the hands-on sense; rather, it should oversee, check, monitor, and challenge on key issues such as:

- Finance and accounting.
- Compliance with regulations and legislation.
- Risk assessment and management.
- Strategic planning.
- Showing leadership.

- Growth and prosperity.
- Preparation of the annual report.
- Relationships with shareholders/stakeholders.
- Monitoring policies and procedures.
- Challenge, question, and scrutinise.
- Hold accountable.
- Delegation of powers.
- Remuneration policies.
- Appointment of the CEO.
- Being independent.
- Being visible.
- Establish values, culture, and behaviours.

LEARNING POINT

As our world and the environment that organisations operate in become more complex, so too do the areas of concern for board members, and crucially they must keep a close watch on potential new developments.

Key issues include:

- The growth and impact of social media.
- The impact of a pandemic.
- Climate change.
- Cybersecurity – the link to The National Cyber Security Centre Board Toolkit can be found in the Further Reading section at the end of the chapter.

Board members are responsible for asking the questions to assure themselves that there is good governance in all the areas above, in addition to "business as usual" and should develop their knowledge to "know the questions to ask" or ensure individuals with skills in these areas are added to the board.

WHAT THE BOARD SHOULD NOT DO

Almost as important (some would say more important) as agreeing what the board will do is not going to do and definitely keeping it out of the day-to-day running of the business. It is often said "Eyes on fingers out!" and that is a great motto for a board – observe and oversee, but do not try to do!

The board should not be:

- Managing.
- Interfering.
- Dictating.
- Implementing.
- Squabbling or in-fighting.
- All thinking the same way.
- Recruiting staff (unless there are exceptional circumstances or when appointing a CEO).
- Accept things at face value or fail to follow up.

Just as a good board can add great deal to any organisation, so too one can detract from the organisation and prove a diversion from the really important work to be done.

Time spent on board room politics is time wasted and interference with staff in their day-to-day running of the business is de-motivating and demoralising.

WHAT MAKES A BOARD OF VALUE TO THE ORGANISATION?

Boards and their members – directors or trustees – need to know their place and their role and that starts form recruitment, through induction and practice to annual appraisal. This is the first and vital step to an effective board – stop any bad practice through clarity from day on as to what is expected from the individuals and the board as a collective.

It absolutely has to be a value add and not a burden on the organisation.

It is necessary for every entity to be very specific about its board composition and role, the expectations, and the detail of what it will be doing for the business in addition to any statutory duties it has. It also vital that the Articles of Association are clear about the appointment and powers of the board and they are constructed to allow the board to function legally, but also helpfully.

The board must be focussed on the business strategy and what it can add to the prosperity of the organisation. For example, how much outside influence or context the combined group weight of the board can bring. The board and its members must be a bonus – an addition to the skills knowledge, experience, and expertise of the executive team.

Crucially this value-added and clear role must be – and not often enough is – noted and closely measured to check that the board is actually performing its identified duties. The board as well as compliance should have its own agenda and objectives for the year, and this should be measured and assessed. Only then will we know whether the board is effective in our setting.

This measurement should be annual and internal and then at least every three years an external reviewer should be brought in to assess board performance against relevant codes and good practice.

In early 2020, the audit watchdog the Financial Reporting Council (FRC) conducted an examination of corporate governance practices of FTSE companies (Annual Review of the UK Corporate Governance Code, 2020). Most worryingly, the FRC concluded that many companies appeared to struggle with both defining *purpose* and in defining what effective *culture* means. The report went further and states,

> too many [boards are] substituting slogans or marketing lines for a clear purpose.

On the basis that one of the most important functions of directors on a board is to set the strategy, purpose, and the culture of the organisation, the recent FRC findings are concerning, indeed.

The purpose of an organisation defines it reason for being and so it must be the overarching focus and commitment for any board because it defines what the organisation exists to do.

This is critical for many different reasons:

- First clear purpose needs to be enshrined in the Articles of Association and/or construction of the body.
- Once this is done the board must pursue this as described and may well break the law and fall foul of the regulator if they try to wander to far from the purpose in setting strategy
- Shareholders/stakeholders need to know what they are investing in.
- Potential customers and employees will consider the body's purpose in deciding where to buy or work with the company.
- Without clear purpose there is nothing which the board can use as a measure of progress.

Increasingly businesses are almost defined by their purpose in the public eye and it has become a significant influence on commercial success for many in the private sector.

For example, Microsoft's corporate mission is "to empower every person and every organization on the planet to achieve more".

Clearly like other private sector businesses its ultimate raison d'être is to make money for its shareholders, but Microsoft, like so many others, now realises that you have to bring others with you for the greater good to achieve that and have a greater purpose about wider impact.

That "buy in" to the organisation's purpose is a basic responsibility of the board as the body which sets the vision and direction of the entity and its strategy.

Interestingly in the charity/voluntary sector, purpose is even more core to the central conviction about what we are there to do. Most people in almost every role will be there because they believe in the purpose, for example, to provide for disadvantaged young children or to give all under 15 girls the chance to play soccer or whatever it may be – it tends to be very clear and to be the focus for all involved. The whole organisation is about that mission.

In the public sector purpose tends to be set or self-explanatory, since the body will be established to deliver that one focus – for example, to oversee the running of college or to deliver economic development in a locality (a local enterprise partnership in England). Again, though it can be necessary to constantly refocus on that purpose to avoid being side-tracked or not delivering efficiently.

It can be argued that the top team in any organisation, which the board of directors leads, sets the tone for every other team throughout the organisation, thereby effectively setting the culture and the values by which the rest of the teams act. Yet in his book, Lencioni (2002) comments that "It is not finance, not strategy, not technology, it is teamwork that remains the ultimate competitive advantage both because it is so powerful and so rare".

Research conducted by Thomas, Kidd, and Fernandez-Araoz (2007) points to organisations failing to obtain full value from their boards of directors through a combination of,

> inadequate competencies (especially around difficult and high-risk matters), lack of diversity of thought, underutilisation of the skills of directors, dereliction of duties (debate focussed on relatively minor issues and a lack of debate around big strategic issues), lack of robust selection and assessment methods.

Board effectiveness is often measured on the basis of profit or profile or impact on organisational process and practice. All of this is true, and these outcomes are, of course, important, but so too, and increasingly more so, are the commitment to, and operating by, positive values and behaviours. By building their governance *culture* of positivity and focussing on proactive factors like respect, integrity, honesty and transparency, the trustees/directors together as the board can set the whole tone of the business and what it values.

The board and the senior management can never neglect the need to focus on their legal and regulatory duties or ignore other key issues like quality delivery, focus on customers and dedication to members, staff, stakeholders, and customers.

While it could be argued that there are common core elements, such as setting strategy/direction and overseeing good governance, that are common to every board of directors, each organisation will also face certain challenges that are unique to the circumstances it operates in. Such challenges must also be addressed in order to promote that organisation's success. With this in mind, it is unsurprising that external organisations look at the performance of boards and evaluate effectiveness.

A final point on effectiveness is to ensure that boards review their performance – internally each year and externally every three to five years. This review should first focus on the proper delivery of the "clunky bits" – that is, all the necessary governance mechanics are in place to meet legal and regulatory requirements are in place. In addition, a review must assess the culture of the organisation and the board and, of course, how well the board focusses on purpose and strategic leadership. Table 1.1 highlights a checklist for board participation:

Table 1.1 *A checklist for board participation*

Key Themes	Description
Constructive approach	Stay positive and provide constructive input
Objectiveness	Remain objective and impartial
Communication	Focus on board matters and be succinct
Integrity	Consider what is right, rather than who is wrong
Preparation	Prepare, prepare, prepare!
Be focussed	Focus on **PURPOSE**

ROLE OF EXTERNAL ADVISORS TO THE BOARD

Board advisors are normally specialist firms or individuals who are appointed to advise the organisation's board members but have no actual authority to make or contribute to the board's formal decision-making nor do they have a vote at the board. Such advisors may have a regular interaction with the Board or be called on infrequently when specific matters arise. The most common external advisors include the following non-exhaustive list: external auditors/accountants, pensions/actuarial consultants, lawyers/legal advisors, health and safety advisors, HR consultants, investment managers, executive search consultants, property specialists, and independent board evaluators. The role of each type of external advisor to the Board will vary depending on the issue and circumstances at hand; however, most commonly the role of external advisors includes reviewing, assessing, assuring, interviewing, monitoring preparation of reports, and recommending courses of action.

It is a requirement that there are no conflicts of interest whereby board members have a personal connection with any individual or firm that is an external advisor to the board. Equally it is considered good governance practice to re-tender the services of external advisors and this should be done in line with the organisation's own policies. However, for certain organisations, known as public interest entities, specific rules exist for external audit services. Public Interest Entities are effectively any of the following: companies whose shares are traded on a UK stock exchange, regulated credit institutions, insurance companies and any large company (annual turnover in excess of £36m, or more than 250 employees), or large charity (annual income exceeding £500,000).

For public interest entities, the rules when making audit appointment decisions derive from: the UK Corporate Governance Code; the Competition and Markets Authority; and the EU Statutory Audit Directive and Regulation. Such organisations are required to rotate their statutory auditor after a maximum period of 20 years, with a mandatory tender at the ten-year midpoint.

INSOLVENCY – WHAT THE BOARD SHOULD KNOW

So, what happens if the company becomes insolvent? Insolvency can be defined as an inability to meet debts as they fall due (the in time or cash flow test), or assessed on a balance sheet basis, where ultimately there are insufficient assets available to meet the liabilities the company in full (the balance sheet test). Many directors will recognise the term – "going concern" this is defined by the Financial Reporting Council (FRC) (Financial Reporting Council: Going Concern And Liquidity Risk, Guidance for Directors of UK Companies 2009) as,

> a fundamental accounting concept that underlies the preparation of financial statements of all UK companies. Under the going concern concept it is assumed that a company will continue in operation and that there is neither the intention nor the need either to liquidate it or to cease trading.

If the cash flow or balance sheet tests indicate a problem and the directors no longer believe the company is a going concern, what is the board's responsibility in this situation?

Taking action is always preferable to doing nothing. A proactive board should be aware of the challenges of the environment their organisation operates in and the associated financial impact and, unless as a result of sudden or unexpected events or circumstances beyond their control, will be aware of a decline in performance. Taking advice sooner rather than later may mean that a formal insolvency process can be avoided. In any event, swift action almost always means that the potential recovery for creditors is better than if the business were run into decline and significant loss before seeking assistance.

When managing a solvent company, the board's responsibility, whether the organisations is in the private, public or charity/voluntary sector, is to the shareholders/stakeholders/members. That focus shifts with an assessment of insolvency, and board directors have a responsibility to ensure that the creditors of the company are not prejudiced (or prejudiced further) until such times as a formal appointment, of an insolvency practitioner (IP) takes place or the company returns to solvency. Directors face the risk of a wrongful trading action at the instance of an incoming liquidator or administrator and being found personally liable to contribute to the company's assets from the time when they knew or ought to have concluded that there was no reasonable prospect that the company would avoid insolvency, unless the court is satisfied that they took every step with a view to minimising the potential loss to the company's creditors that they ought to have taken. They will be judged by the courts based on what would be reasonable in that situation, and the specific skill set, and experience of the individual director. The Finance Director, if they have formal accountancy qualifications, will necessarily be judged differently to the non-finance qualified non-executive director, for example (Legislation. gov.uk, 2013).

Directors may feel very apprehensive when faced with potential company insolvency or using an insolvency procedure; however, there are clear benefits in doing so. An independent, licensed insolvency practitioner (IP) is appointed to take over the running of the business, relieving the directors of the stress and responsibility of doing so. Creditors become bound by the insolvency process, they must rank in statutory priority, and can take no further action against the company thereafter. They participate in a "dividend" to the extent that assets are available, and the balance of their debt is written off. Different insolvency procedures are designed to address different situations and provide different outcomes. Ideally, the board should seek advice specific to their organisation and company structure, but should also be aware that creditors have the right to force a company into a formal insolvency process and be alert to such attempts.

In the event of formal appointment, the insolvency practitioner is under a statutory obligation to review the conduct of any individual who was a director in the three-year period prior to the IP's appointment (Legislation.gov.uk, 2015). The definition of director in this instance is wide and encompasses those acting in an executive and non-executive capacity, de facto, de jure, and shadow directors (Legislation.gov.uk, 2020) and directors with a contract for or of service. Resigning as a director in the period leading up to an insolvency will not relieve the insolvency practitioner of their obligation to the examine the conduct of the individual.

All directors of an insolvent company will be reported to the Insolvency Service in terms of the prevailing statute (GOV.UK, Sep. 2019). Where an IP forms the opinion that the conduct of the director makes them unfit to be involved in the promotion, formation or management of a limited company and to enjoy the privilege of limited liability, then a report on their individual conduct will be prepared and submitted to the UK Government Insolvency Service's Director Disqualification Unit. The Unit will review every such report and select referrals for further investigation. This may lead to disqualification proceedings being raised at court against the targeted individual and could result in the director being disqualified in the future for a period of anything from two years (for less serious offences) up to 15 years (reserved for very serious offences such as fraud). The Insolvency Service invariably target disqualification proceedings against directors where there is a public interest in doing so, or where companies have traded at the expense of the Crown, having failed to pay deducted taxes to HMRC and applying the funds instead to working capital. There is also legislative provision to allow the Disqualification Unit to apply directly to court for a personal contribution from a director to the loss suffered by the company's creditors (Legislation.gov.uk, 2015).

Insolvency practitioners may also judge the actions of the Board against the duties of the directors as set out in the Companies Act 2006 (GOV. UK, 2010) and seek financial recompense. For example, failure to pay tax to the relevant authorities may be judged to be a breach of fiduciary duty. Outstanding director loan accounts will be recovered by a Liquidator or Administrator. Specific provisions of the Insolvency Act 1986 (Legislation.gov.uk, 2011) allow a liquidator to recover any sums or assets in the hands of a third party that are properly adjudged to belong to the company.

Formal insolvency is not inevitable. It may be that a short-term cash flow problem or funding requirement can be addressed and rectified, but the board should be clear about any strategy for trading through such a period of difficulty and set clear targets and timescales to monitor and measure their success in doing so. A focus on cash flow is imperative and specialist support in the way of a turnaround and restructuring advisor is always available in the event that the Board does not have the necessary skill set. Turnaround and restructuring advisors can be firms or individuals who specialise in reviewing strategy, operations, and finances, and make recommendations, in cases where cash is fast running out, this can be in a matter of days. Turnaround specialists are sometimes engaged by lenders who want an independent third-party opinion, in such cases, their duty of care is joint to the organisations and the lender.

The Turnaround Management Association UK (tma-uk.org, n.d.) describes turnaround and restructuring advisors as professionals who "offer added value around solutions that boards may have not known about, they have connectivity with stakeholders such as banks and they provide directors with immediate comfort that they are acting responsibly". Equally, in the event that the company's principal funder is approached for financial support, they may make it a condition of extending or restructuring any facility that a turnaround specialist is appointed, their security package is reviewed or extended and/or that personal guarantees are provided by key members of the board in support of new company borrowing, thus ensuring that future risk is shared between the directors and the company's backers. Board members in this situation are always advised to take independent legal advice. Where directors' personal interests pose a conflict of interest to their role on the board, it is imperative they consider their position.

The earlier the Board takes action, the better, in a potential insolvency situation, but what are the "red flags" that the NEDs should look for? As NEDs do not work in the organisation, they may not receive the level of detailed insight that executive directors may have, the following could provide an indication of a serious financial difficulty that requires further investigation:

- Banking covenants breached.
- Payments on account refused due to insufficient funds.
- Build-up of creditor pressure (e.g. court action, legal letters).
- Notification by company that not in a position to pay on time.
- Regular requests for greater debt funding (loans/overdrafts).
- Delays in submitting information.
- Credit insurance refused.
- Difficulty fulfilling orders/contracts.
- Quality/service level deterioration.
- Investment in appearance assets/lack of investment in important equipment.
- Extension to financial year end to submit accounts.
- Increase in staff turnover.
- Management time spent fighting fires rather than managing.
- Difficulties in getting hold of the executive directors or management to answer questions or report.

The above is not an exhaustive list and any of the above can appear temporarily in a solvent and well-run organisation; however, an important aspect of any board member's role is to probe as appropriate especially if similar issues arise over longer periods and with regularity.

WHEN TO RESIGN

People often ask when "When should I resign form a board?"

The answer is, it depends. There are a variety of reasons that may cause a board member to resign before the end of the term in office, some of the common themes, which emerge are as follows:

- Personal Reasons – this may include health (self or family member), relocation, the development of a potential conflict of interests, career/job change where the board role is not permitted/supported by a new employer. Such situations are specific to the individual and have nothing to do with the board itself. In these cases, it is normally acceptable to step down, assuming your exit is tidy. This includes giving the rest of the board plenty of notice, if possible, and an opportunity to find your replacement. For some organisations, the retiral of a board member requires regulatory or stock market notification.

- Fundamental Disagreement over Strategic Direction – this is a complex area as healthy, robust debate is vital to the proper functioning of a board and we have already touched on the divisive issue of "groupthink"; so it is natural to expect that board members will not and should not agree on everything. However, once the vigorous debate has happened and a decision has been made, it is expected that everyone will pull in the same direction. In some cases, you may find yourself unable to support an extremely consequential decision the rest of the board has made. The important decision of whether you can continue on the Board is whether your position is so different to the rest of the board, that it may no longer be productive.
- Severe Unhealthy Boardroom Dynamics – ultimately boards are made up of a collection of people who may or may not behave appropriately, unhealthy cliques might form, debate may be discouraged and your voice may not be valued. At the extreme, although not considered common, it is not unheard of for individual board members to face issues of harassment or bullying. Unreasonable behaviour is not something any board member should be expected to tolerate.
- Financial Difficulties – is a difficult set of circumstances as joining a board is not an endeavour to simply enjoy the good times with a view to flee as soon as any difficulties emerge. There is a fiduciary duty on board members to "do the right thing" in the interests of all stakeholders, even if that means overseeing the winding up of the organisation. As already highlighted, in the event of insolvency, the actions of all board members, even those who resigned up to three years prior to the event, is assessed by the insolvency practitioner. A difficulty may arise, if the organisation

can no longer afford directors' and officers' liability insurance (D&O) leaving directors feeling personally exposed.

- Organisational Scandal – in the aftermath of a scandal, it may be that stakeholders/shareholders and/or regulators may not feel that current boards members have the credibility to reform the organisation; indeed, it may be seen as appropriate for the entire board to resign. In such a situation, resignation might be the best way forward, especially if there are some new directors, untainted by scandal, who have joined the board.
- Intentional Wrongdoing – if, as a board member, you become aware that someone in your organisation may secretly be engaging in intentional wrongdoing, even to the extent of criminal activity, you are duty bound to do something about it. If you have tried to do something about it and not been able to, what are the implications of resigning? There is no one catch all answer, much depends on the specific circumstances and the nature of the wrongdoing and the structure of the organisation, for example if the chair and/other board members are compromised, there might be an avenue to approach shareholders/funders/members/regulators, albeit depending on the nature of the wrongdoing, it may require a report to the police or other authorities such as the Health and Safety Executive. It may not seem obvious to think of a board member as a potential whistle-blower; however, it is a matter of taking an appropriate course of action, doing nothing, other than reigning may be considered wrongdoing or even a criminal act in itself.

The overall view is that, unless the reason is due to a change in personal circumstances, resignation should be viewed as a last resort and it is important to always remember that when you are gone you can no longer have the positive influence you would hope to have so it should not be done lightly nor threatened when you are not prepared to actually leave. It is not the easy option.

You have taken on the legal and moral duty to do the best for the organisation and the first choice should be to stay and sort out any issues. Resigning in such circumstances should be seen as a last resort on the basis that you disagree fundamentally with the direction that the organisation/rest of the board has agreed or if you are concerned over the legality of the course of action being taken and not being listened to so that it becomes impossible for you to stay.

Should you sense poor/unreasonable behaviour of others or being a lone voice on something you feel very strongly about and so on then the first step is to have your objection fully discussed and minuted, and only when all else has been considered and failed should you take the drastic step of resignation.

Remember the importance of minuting concerns cannot be underestimated, because even if you resign from a board, you carry potential liability for a period of time afterwards, this is usually at least three; however, for certain issues it can be longer, albeit this only relates to board decisions taken while you were on board. The board minutes are your risk mitigation.

LEARNING POINT

The relatively new chair of an organisation stepped down after only 18 months in the role.

She felt a lone voice on the board on many issues which were not that important and were not a problem. However, when the issues became major and related to the fundamental strategic future of the organisation, being a "lone voice" was of such concern that the chair felt no choice but to resign.

It has to be a matter of personal conscience to choose to take such a drastic step and often results in much speculation about the organisation by its stakeholders. This is why some boards are reticent to appoint NEDs who are still progressing in their executive careers as a potential conflict may require them to step down early resulting in unwarranted speculation over the governance or health of the organisation.

DIRECTORS AND OFFICERS LIABILITY INSURANCE (D&O)

D&O insurance is not always well understood, some board members believe it covers them for any type of claim made against them by investors, creditors or other parties, if something goes amiss in the organisation. This type of insurance is designed to cover the costs of defending or settling legal or criminal actions brought board members in relation to a claim for breach of duty, negligence, defamation, health and safety legislation or even pollution.

It is important to note that D&O insurance will not provide coverage for what many would consider the worst acts of the directors or officers; dishonesty, fraud, criminal or malicious acts committed deliberately. Personal claims or proceedings against directors or officers can arise from any decision made, or act carried out, in the workplace, however innocuous it may have seemed at the time. Claims made against directors and/or proceedings brought against directors where personal liability may be involved most often fall under the following:

- Claims by investors and shareholders who blame directors personally for their losses.
- Actions brought by liquidators, where they suspect wrongful trading or incorrect payments to creditors.
- Actions brought by HMRC where insolvent trading or misappropriation of tax payments is suspected.
- Health and Safety Executive (HSE) investigations where negligence is suspected.
- Police and Serious Fraud Office investigations where fraud is suspected.

KEY MESSAGES

- Be aware of the importance of good governance, which should not be underestimated; however, it is more difficult to achieve than it sounds and good processes alone are not enough – an engaged, skilled, and curious board of directors who are pulling in the same direction, while not thinking alike is a vital component.

- Know what the board does and should do as well and what it should not do in any organisation and be mindful of the "red flags" of a potential insolvency situation.
- Be aware that there are some differences between how boards are structured between different sectors, but there are many more similarities than differences!
- Be sure that your board is adding value; board evaluations can be a helpful measure of this.

FURTHER READING

Board Assessment tools – www.governanceexpress.com
The National Cyber Security Centre Board Toolkit – link: https://www.ncsc.gov.uk/collection/board-toolkit

REFERENCES

Annual Review of The UK Corporate Governance Code. (2020). [online] Available at: https://www.frc.org.uk/getattachment/53799a2d-824e-4e15-9325-33eb6a30f063/Annual-Review-of-the-UK-Corporate-Governance-Code [Accessed 1 Jan. 2021].

Chen, J. (n.d.). What Corporate Governance Means for the Bottom Line. [online] *Investopedia*. Available at: https://www.investopedia.com/terms/c/corporategovernance [Accessed 27 Feb. 2021].

Commonalities, Differences, and Future Trends Board Chairs' Practices across Countries Contents. (2016). [online]. Available at: https://www.insead.edu/sites/default/files/assets/dept/centres/icgc/docs/board-chairs-practices-across-countries.pdf [Accessed 14 Feb. 2021].

Diligent Insights. (2019). Subsidiary Governance Framework Template. [online] Available at: https://insights.diligent.com/subsidiary-management/subsidiary-governance-framework-template [Accessed 27 Apr. 2021].

Financial Reporting Council. (2018). The UK Corporate Governance Code. [online]. Available at: https://www.frc.org.uk/getattachment/88bd8c45-50ea-4841-95b0-d2f4f48069a2/2018-UK-Corporate-Governance-Code-FINAL.PDF. [Accessed 27 Feb. 2021].

Financial Reporting Council: Going Concern And Liquidity Risk, Guidance for Directors of UK Companies 2009. (n.d.). [online]. Available at: https://www.frc.org.uk/getattachment/079e9ca2-7153-4831-8248-5de419041f6c/Going-concern-and-liquidity-risk-guidance-for-directors-of-uk-companies-093.pdf#:~:text=Going%20concern%20is%20a%20fundamental [Accessed 1 May 2021].

Fink, L. (2015). BlackRock CEO Larry Fink Tells the World's Biggest Business Leaders to Stop Worrying about Short-Term Results. [online] *Business Insider*. Available at: https://www.businessinsider.com/larry-fink-letter-to-ceos-2015-4?r=US&IR=T [Accessed 27 Feb. 2021].

GOV.UK. (Sep. 2019). Reporting Misconduct by Companies, Directors and Bankrupts to the Insolvency Service. [online] Available at: https://www.gov.uk/government/publications/reporting-misconduct-by-companies-directors-and-bankrupts-to-the-insolvency-service [Accessed 30 Apr. 2021].

GOV.UK (2010). Companies Act 2006. [online] Legislation.gov.uk. Available at: https://www.legislation.gov.uk/ukpga/2006/46/contents.

ICAEW Helpsheet. (2016). [online]. Available at: https://www.icaew.com/-/media/corporate/archive/files/technical/financial-services/helpsheets/subsidiary-board-governance-in-groups-helpsheet-apr-15.ashx [Accessed 26 Apr. 2021].

JTC. (Apr. 2018). Subsidiary Boards – A Balancing Act. [online] Available at: https://www.jtcgroup.com/insights/subsidiary-boards-a-balancing-act/ [Accessed 26 Apr. 2021].

Legislation.gov.uk. (2010). Companies Act 2006. [online] Available at: https://www.legislation.gov.uk/ukpga/2006/46/contents. [Accessed 27 Feb. 2021].

Legislation.gov.uk. (2011). Insolvency Act 1986. [online] Available at: https://www.legislation.gov.uk/ukpga/1986/45/contents. [Accessed 30 Apr. 2021].

Legislation.gov.uk. (2013). Insolvency Act 1986. [online] Available at: https://www.legislation.gov.uk/ukpga/1986/45/section/214. [Accessed 3 May 2021].

Legislation.gov.uk. (2015). Company Directors Disqualification Act 1986. [online] Available at: https://www.legislation.gov.uk/ukpga/1986/46/section/7A [Accessed 3 May 2021].

Legislation.gov.uk. (2020). Companies Act 2006. [online] Available at: https://www.legislation.gov.uk/ukpga/2006/46/section/250. [Accessed 30 Apr. 2021].

Lencioni, P., (2002). *The Five Dysfunctions of a Team: A Leadership Fable*. San Francisco, CA: Jossey Bass.

Oecd.org. (2015). G20/OECD Principles of Corporate Governance – OECD. [online] Available at: http://www.oecd.org/corporate/principles-corporate-governance/. [Accessed 16 Feb. 2021].

Thomas, C., Kidd, D., & Fernandez-Araoz, C. (2007). MIT Sloan Management Review. Technology, C. © M.I. of and reserved, 1977-2021 A. rights (n.d.). Winter 2007. [online] MIT Sloan Management Review. Available at: https://sloanreview.mit.edu/issue/winter-2007/ [Accessed 14 Dec. 2021].

tma-uk.org. (n.d.). TMA UK. [online] Available at: https://tma-uk.org/about/what-is-turnaround [Accessed 1 May 2021].

www.cgi.org.uk. (2019). The Future Board: Getting in Shape for Tomorrow's Challenges report. [online] Available at: https://www.cgi.org.uk/knowledge/resources/the-future-board-getting-in-shape-for-tomorrows-challenges [Accessed 14 Dec. 2021].

www.icsa.org.uk. (n.d.). What Is Corporate Governance? [online] Available at: https://www.icsa.org.uk/about-us/policy/what-is-corporate-governance#:~:text=Corporate%20governance%20is%20the%20system. [Accessed 16 Feb. 2021].

CHAPTER TWO

Governance Codes

Carum Basra and Monica Langa

DOI: 10.4324/9781003142850-2

INTRODUCTION

Sitting somewhere between "hard" and "soft" law, a number of corporate governance codes have proliferated in recent years, the principle behind these codes is to demonstrate to shareholders and stakeholders how the organisation is organised and led. The term "corporate" in this case should be taken to mean an incorporated body and therefore applies a broad spectrum of organisations in the public, charity/voluntary, and private sectors.

Such Codes are just one aspect of the overall legal framework that underpins the environment in which an organisation operates. As a board member of any organisation, it's important to understand if you are expected to be complying with a governance code or if not, what constitutes best practice or the "gold standard" in governance for the type of entity you lead. For smaller firms, a code may represent something to aspire to while for the largest companies, compliance with a code may be a regulatory requirement or for voluntary organisations a condition of funding and/or registration. However, it should be remembered that codes are not the be all and end all of governance, as veteran Director Sir John Tusa highlights,

> Observing guidelines and regulations required of a board member will not make you a useful member. A Board which ticks all the boxes of board obligations will not be a good board. All the difficulties that arise in governance fall into the areas of good judgement, personal interaction and human psychology. No rules exist for getting these questions right. That is why good governance is so challenging.

EMERGENCE OF GOVERNANCE CODES

Before proceeding, it may be helpful to understand how corporate governance codes first emerged. The development of the first Corporate Governance Code also known as the Cadbury Code was a response to the corporate scandals of the late 1980s and early 1990s. In the wake of corporate scandals at Polly Peck, BCCI, and Robert Maxwell's Mirror Group, a committee was established in 1992 with Adrian Cadbury at its helm to restore confidence in the UK's corporate governance regime. The Committee's innovation was to pursue the adoption of a voluntary code of best practice rather than changes to the law. The Committee was of the view that "statutory measures would impose a minimum standard and there would be a greater risk of boards complying with the letter, rather than with the spirit, of their requirements". Crucially, an underlying principle of the Cadbury Code was that there was no "one size fits all" approach to governance. Therefore, the Code gave firms the choice to deviate from the Code provided that they were able to explain why they had done so.

The Cadbury Code has been through several iterations in the last three decades and has inspired a multitude of other Codes including those mentioned later in this chapter. Despite their differing scope, these Codes tend to be voluntary taking a "comply or explain" approach (although some notable exceptions take an "apply and explain" approach) and represent best practice. A code of corporate governance can generally be described as "a non-binding set of principles, standards or best practices, issued by a collective body and relating to the internal governance of corporations".

UNDERSTANDING THE ROLE OF GOVERNANCE CODES

In various jurisdictions, Corporate Governance Codes represent best practice not only for private sector organisations but also for civil society/public sector organisations and charities. In some cases, regulatory organisations or grant funders require adherence to a specific governance code such as social housing providers and sports organisations and, in some very specific instances, complying with a code have been enshrined in statute, this will be explored late in the chapter. Applying and being seen to comply with a code not only supports effective governance and leadership but also provides a strong signal to the outside world. Adhering to a Code demonstrates to external stakeholders including potential investors and funders that their interests will be taken into account.

Importantly, codes of best practice have been produced by a number of organisations at both a national and international level. The Organisation for Economic Co-operation and Development (OECD) has developed Principles of Corporate Governance at a multilateral level. At the European level, the European Confederation of Directors' Associations has developed Corporate Governance Guidance and Principles for Unlisted Companies in Europe.

In the UK, the Financial Reporting Council (FRC) maintains both the UK Corporate Governance Code (Financial Reporting Council, 2018), which applies to premium listed companies and the Wates Principles which apply to the largest unlisted companies. Alternative Investment Market (AIM)-listed companies can choose to apply either the FRC's Corporate Governance Code or the Quoted Companies Alliance's Code or to report against any code they have decided to apply, such as the Wates Principles. In the voluntary sector, the Charity Governance Code (for England and Wales) is overseen by a voluntary steering group with additional Codes developed for charities registered in Scotland and Northern Ireland. In the sporting world, the Code for Sports Governance applies to all entities receiving funding from either Sport England, Sport Scotland, or UK Sport.

Other jurisdictions have taken a different approach, for example in South Africa the King Code explicitly "aspires to apply to all organisations, regardless of their form of incorporation" and sets out detailed sector supplements covering municipalities, non-profit organisations, retirement funds, small and medium enterprises, and state-owned entities.

In short, there are a lot of Codes! While it could be easy to be overwhelmed by the plethora of Codes, a first step may be to simply to understand which Code best fits the kind of organisation that you serve on the board of. There may be some overlap or cross-over for example some charities work in areas, such as housing and sport, that have their own sector- specific governance Codes. Sector-specific Codes may well take precedence given that they will be more tailored.

In 2018 ICSA – the Chartered Governance Institute (ICSA, n.d.) published an opinion piece where the "proliferation of published governance codes released for differing sectors, such as charities, sports bodies, housing associations and unlisted companies" was highlighted as a particular challenge. It was noted that some codes are mandatory while some are voluntary, some are based on a "comply or explain" approach while others are based on "apply or explain", with each code using a different language, in terms of applying principles and requirements. Even the number of principles in each code varies considerably for example; the Code for Sports Governance identifies five principles of good governance, the Housing Associations Code has nine principles, and the UK Corporate Governance Code has 18 principles.

The question raised by ICSA is whether a more "integrated way of promoting good governance across all sectors of society and the economy" may be of benefit to all concerned?

It may be helpful to consider Codes that apply in each sector of the UK economy in turn starting with the Corporate Governance Code (the Code), touched on above, which was developed for stock exchange listed companies.

WHY APPLY A CODE?

In some cases, applying a governance Code may be a regulatory requirement or a requirement of an external funder; however, if there is no compulsion to do so why might a board opt to adhere to a particular Code? There are a number of reasons to do so:

- It offers assurance to stakeholders who need to have confidence in your governance arrangements and the long-term sustainability of your organisation.
- Providing the structures and processes for the direction and control of companies, applying a code is seen as a tool to avoid mismanagement, enable companies to operate more efficiently, potentially improving access to capital (debt, equity, grant funding, and/or public funds), and an aid to mitigating risk and safeguarding stakeholders.

REPORTING AGAINST A CODE

Given that one of the primary drivers for choosing to adhere to a Code is to provide assurance to external stakeholders, it makes sense to publicly disclose how you are adhering. Where you report will depend on the type of organisation you sit on the board of. For most organisations, it will make most sense to publish an account in their annual report explaining their use of a particular Code relevant to their work, and report any actions they have taken over the year in respect of following a Code.

GOVERNANCE CODES IN THE PRIVATE SECTOR

The UK private sector is comprised of a variety of type of organisation, the most well know at the public listed companies (PLCs). The Code applies to premium listed companies in other words those listed on the main market of the London Stock Exchange who are included in the FTSE indexes. A premium listing is typically used by large firms looking to benefit from an increased profile and highly liquid market. To maintain a premium listing, companies must meet the UK's highest standards of regulation and corporate governance and pay significant fees.

To add further complexity to the situation, those companies not listed on the main market but on the Alternative Investment Market (AIM), are required by the London Stock Exchange (LSE) to follow and report on a recognised corporate governance code; however, unlike companies with premium and standard listings, AIM companies are not required to comply or explain with the UK Corporate Governance Code. Many AIM companies choose to apply as much of the code as practicable for a company of their size and stage of development, it is not uniformly applied. Since September 2018, the requirement for AIM companies involves a choice of which code to apply. Some argue that it is not helpful that the LSE does not provide a definitive list of recognised codes, albeit it has highlighted the UK Corporate Governance Code (the Code) and the Quoted Companies Alliance Code (the QCA code) as established benchmarks. While the Code is considered to be the "gold standard" of corporate governance, it is understandable that many small and mid-size AIM-quoted companies select the QCA code as a more appropriate code due to their size and stage of development.

An interesting point to note is that with its latest iteration published in 2018 the Corporate Governance Code became "shorter and sharper" with the number of provisions reduced by a third; the Code now consists of 18 principles and 41 provisions.

In comparison, the QCA code establishes ten broad principles and disclosures considered appropriate for small and mid-sized quoted companies.

The 18 principles of the Code are divided into five main categories namely:

- Board Leadership and Company Purpose
- Division of Responsibilities
- (Board) Composition Succession and Evaluation
- Audit, Risk, and Internal Control
- Remuneration

The 2018 Code emphasises the responsibility of board members in not only promoting the long-term success of the company and generating value for shareholders but for contributing to wider society and establishing the values of the company as well as developing strategy and promoting and monitoring a desired organisational culture. Encouraging stakeholder participation and workforce policies and practices that are consistent with the company's values and reporting against this is another aspect being firmly laid out as the responsibility of the board. The introduction of workforce representation on boards, or alternatives, in order to facilitate a have deeper engagement with workforce, is also now part of the Code. Senior management/executive remuneration considerations have also been introduced.

The focus of both the UK Code and QCA code remains on engagement between the company, shareholders, and their stakeholders, demonstrating a commitment towards good corporate governance and ensuring the company has a well-functioning and diverse board. Both codes also highlight the importance of having an appropriate balance between executive and non-executive directors and supporting the board through committees that have the necessary skills and knowledge to discharge their duties and responsibilities effectively.

While the above codes apply to private sector organisations, it is important to note that the UK's private sector also comprises various types of privately owned non-stock market listed companies ranging from small start-up through to very large organisations such as British Home Stores (BHS). It may be of little surprise to learn that the introduction of governance codes for large privately owned organisations has followed scandals in the corporate or civic environment. It was after the collapse of BHS in 2016 that the British government called on the Financial Reporting Council (FRC) to establish a corporate governance code for private businesses. It is worth noting that privately owned (non-stock exchange listed) companies make up the majority of UK business enterprises, while not being subject to FRC regulations that apply to their big listed company counterparts they make up the majority of employers, tax contributors, and providers of workforce pensions.

James Wates, head of family-owned construction company Wates Group, was asked to chair a panel that produced six principles that came into effect in January 2019. In a similar manner to how the UK Governance Code has developed, the Wates Principles also consider broader issues, such as the treatment of staff and other stakeholders such as suppliers. The principles include promoting executive pay structures that contribute to the long-term success of a company, taking into account pay and conditions elsewhere in the business.

"Private companies are a significant contributor to the UK economy, providing tax revenue and employing millions of people", Wates said in a statement. "They have a significant impact on people's lives, and it is important they are well-governed and transparent about how they operate".

The Wates Principles also state, "A board has a responsibility to oversee meaningful engagement with material stakeholders, including the workforce, and have regard to that discussion when taking decisions". This new code came into effect in January 2019 on a so-called "apply and explain" basis, targeting businesses with more than 2,000 staff or turnover above £200 million and a balance sheet of more than £2 billion.

While the Wates Principles were not developed with smaller privately owned businesses in mind, one can argue that the core essence of the "gold standard" Code are translated by the Wates principles into something that small and medium enterprises (SMEs) can apply to ensure more robust governance systems and approaches are in place. It is not unusual to find that when the content of the Wates Principles is read out to groups of directors of large and small firms alike, the principles are seen as very applicable to their own organisations. If the directors are first told that the content is from the Wates Principles, the reaction of smaller company directors is often the opposite.

While privately owned companies may not choose to apply any governance codes, it may become a necessity as soon as external funding (debt or equity is sought) for example it is unusual for private equity investment firms not to insist on a governance framework as a condition of funding and increasingly debt funders are taking a similar approach.

LEARNING POINT

The CEO of a fifth-generation family-owned company sought debt (bank loan) funding for an important renewable energy project, which had the potential to secure substantial revenue for many years to come. The funding was approved on condition of the introduction of an appropriate governance model, based on a recognised governance code. This was implemented and the result was a very successful renewable energy plant, so successful that the debt was repaid in the half the expected time. Importantly, the introduction of a formal governance structure had the benefit of providing for the interests of the wider family owners in the form of a family council and arguably, a far more streamlined and effective executive decision-making process, which has contributed to the success and continued sustainability of the organisation as it prepares for the sixth generation to succeed the fifth.

Increasingly, stakeholders such as clients, suppliers, and debt and private equity funders require adherence to a governance code such as the Wates Principles.

It is also not unusual to find that some clients and potentially suppliers increasingly require assurance of compliance with governance standards in order to secure commercial contracts. This may include compliance with data protection and anti-bribery/corruption regulation; however, a greater emphasis on environmental, social, and governance (ESG) factors inevitably brings a greater focus on good governance. Agencies who support business owners to secure the best price on selling a privately owned company, or advising buyers on the purchase of such an entity, comment that it can take five years to bring an organisation into a suitable state for sale and much of that time is spent introducing robust governance frameworks.

Regulatory authorities have also developed guidance or supervisory statements in terms of appropriate governance and what is expected of board members. This has especially developed in the financial services sector, in part as a result of the financial crash of 2008–2010 and the corporate scandals that emerged. An example is the Prudential Regulation Authority (PRA) which regulates banks, insurers, designated investment firms, building societies, friendly societies, and credit unions. The PRA guidance to member firms is mostly based on the UK Governance Code; however, it has gone one step further by specifying that

> between them the non-executive directors need to have sufficient current and relevant knowledge and experience, including sector experience, to understand the key activities and risks involved in the business model and to provide effective challenge across the major business lines of the firm. The PRA expects to see evidence of effective challenge, particularly in relation to key strategic decisions.

The PRA's sister organisation the Financial Conduct Authority (FCA) also regulates banks, building societies, and credit unions. In addition, it regulates claims management companies, consumer credit firms, electronic money and payment institutions, financial advisors, general insurers and insurance intermediaries, investment managers, life insurers, and pension providers. Like the PRA, the FCA's view of a regulated entity's board is that governance should be based on the UK Governance Code; however, the FCA expects the following.

Regulated entities to be operated and controlled by the board, therefore, boards must show:

- Decision-making capabilities.
- High-quality board documents and management information.
- Allow enough time for debate and challenge.

- Must *demonstrate* "challenge".
- Board members must know what they "sell".

It is worth noting that all board appointments in either PRA or FCA regulated firms is subject to formal approval by the relevant regulator who will test the skills, knowledge, and experience of individuals. While it is noted above that Credit Unions are regulated by the PRA, The Association of British Credit Unions has also issued a Code of Governance for these organisations to comply with (GOVERNING FOR SUCCESS A Code of Governance and Good Practice for Credit Unions in Great Britain, n.d.). This Code takes into account the requirements of regulations and is based on a "comply or explain" approach, the code itself stresses that the

> co-operative and democratic nature of credit unions means that the participation of members in the decision-making processes is a fundamental principle in the running of the organisation. In small credit unions particularly, this aspect of democracy is given little or no priority as the day to day demands of providing a service and complying with the regulator take up so much time.

This code highlights 45 elements of the code, of which 30 are "required standards" and 15 are considered "gold standards". It provides a useful guidance to board members on what is expected of them with a section dedicated to "putting members at the centre" of decision-making.

While the various codes above exist and have arguably had a positive impact of the quality of governance in the UK's private sector, there remains a great deal of criticism that there is no single authority responsible for punishing errant company directors. The UK Investment Association (IA) – the trade body for the investment management industry has been vocal on the what is seen as a fragmented system of company director sanctions. The IA argues that a single body should be established to provide better scrutiny over punishment for rule and code breaches. Andrew Ninian, the IA's director of stewardship and corporate governance commented, "The current system of sanctions is fragmented between many different authorities, and often directors are only sanctioned as a result of investigations after a company goes into insolvency".

All of the above being said, the role played by shareholders in holding listed companies to account against the UK Governance Code is an interesting dynamic. When shareholders take action and vote against the reappointment of board members on the basis of non-adherence to the Code and/or other areas of governance best practice, it has the effect of making board members take notice. It is worth noting that professional investors, such as pension scheme managers also have a code to comply with, namely the Stewardship Code. Following Sir David Walker's 2009 report on the governance of banks and other financial institutions, it was recommended that the FRC should also be responsible for encouraging best practice in stewardship of UK listed companies by institutional investors. Also operating on a "comply or explain" basis, the FRC published the first UK Stewardship Code in 2010 with revised versions being published in 2012 and the most recent iteration coming into effect in 2020 (THE UK STEWARDSHIP CODE 2020 Financial Reporting Council, n.d.). This code not only encourages good governance practices within the institutional investment firms but also encourages professional investors to focus on governance practices in the companies they invest in and to take action to bring about change. The code highlights "collaborating with other investors to engage an issuer to achieve a specific change; or working as part of a coalition of wider stakeholders to engage on a thematic issue". A good example of this is shareholder action on the issue of a lack of gender diversity in listed company boards.

LEARNING POINT

Following the publication of the Davis report, in 2015 on gender diversity on FTSE 350 Boards, progress on meeting voluntary targets was slow. By early 2018 research showed that over 130 FTSE 250 companies had failed to meet the target of 25% female representation on boards, let alone the new target of 33% by 2020, and for FTSE 350 companies the figures were much worse. 27 Investment firms around the world which managed £10.5 trillion of investment assets decided to take action. The most outspoken being LGIM, which started voting against the reappointment of individual board Chairs in 2016 and became more vocal in 2018. Similarly, in 2018, the Coalition of Christian Investors started doing the same against the Chair and members of board Nominations Committees. The result was a rush to action, by September 2020 the vast majority of FTSE350 boards had a 33% female representation (Webber, 2020).

Compliance with governance codes is becoming an important shareholder issue with board members being held personally to account; as a result, compliance has become much less voluntary in nature.

It is important to highlight that at the time of writing the above, the government started a consultation for what some commentators described as the biggest "shake-up of Britain's corporate governance rules in decades", with government ministers putting a renewed focus on targeted negligent auditors and directors found to have been involved in wrongdoing. If adopted the changes would apply to not only premium public listed companies but also AIM listed and large privately owned companies. The Financial Reporting Council (FRC), which has been criticised over a lack of action, would be replaced by the Audit, Reporting and Governance Authority (ARGA), which would have legal powers to claw back bonuses and future payments to directors of failed companies and also personally fine directors found to have been negligent or involved in wrongdoing. These changes are considered in more detail in Chapter 3 (Risk Management in the Boardroom).

Having discussed the impact of governance codes in the private sector, it is helpful to consider codes that apply in other sectors starting with the public sector.

GOVERNANCE CODES IN THE PUBLIC SECTOR

There is recognition that there are many elements of the UK Corporate Governance Code, which are relevant to board members of public bodies, as there are a number of similarities between the public and private sectors in terms of corporate governance principles, it is not always possible to draw a direct parallel between the two. Public bodies may face many similar challenges as private organisations; there are also important areas of difference, so a number of principles and codes have been developed specifically for this sector.

It is important to note that there are various types of organisation in the public sector ranging from parliamentary boards to non-departmental public bodies. A non-departmental public body (NDPB) is generally thought of as an organisation that delivers a public service, is not a government department and operates to a greater or lesser extent at arm's length from Ministers. It is worth differentiating between NDPBs and other bodies that receive all or much of their funding from public funds. The latter includes some bodies deemed to be public such as colleges of further education but also organisations set up as trusts or by company law or charity law, such as art bodies and sports bodies. In governance terms, it is interesting to note that governments are increasingly using Codes of Conduct to control the standards of these bodies. This could be for a couple of reasons – governments want to ensure that their funds are being properly managed and also governments want to be able to demonstrate to electorates and regulators that they are being careful with their disbursement of public money. It could be argued that this is a response to governance failures but is it also a signal that the role of board members in ensuring the proper conduct of their organisations is being increasingly recognised. Public bodies also include the NHS, Local Authorities, Police Forces as well as a variety of cultural (museums), heritage (Heritage England, Scottish National Heritage), and regulatory (Human Medicine Commission) organisations.

NOLAN PRINCIPLES

The UK government established a Committee on Standards in Public Life in 1994. The committee, chaired by Lord Nolan, made recommendations aimed at improving the standards of behaviour in public life. The committee established seven principles known as the "Nolan principles". These seven principles are seen as the benchmark of expected behaviours in public life, including the charity sector. The seven principles are:

1. Selflessness – Holders of public office should act solely in terms of the public interest. They should not do so in order to gain financial or other benefits for themselves, their family or their friends.
2. Integrity – Holders of public office should not place themselves under any financial or other obligation to outside individuals or organisations that might seek to influence them in the performance of their official duties.
3. Objectivity – In carrying out public business, including making public appointments, awarding contracts, or recommending individuals for rewards and benefits, holders of public office should make choices on merit.
4. Accountability – Holders of public office are accountable for their decisions and actions to the public and must submit themselves to whatever scrutiny is appropriate to their office.
5. Openness – Holders of public office should be as open as possible about all the decisions and actions they take. They should give reasons for their decisions and restrict information only when the wider public interest clearly demands.
6. Honesty – Holders of public office have a duty to declare any private interests relating to their public duties and to take steps to resolve any conflicts arising in a way that protects the public interest.
7. Leadership – Holders of public office should promote and support these principles by leadership and example.

In addition to the above in the Scottish Government added a further two principles:

8. Duty – Public Service
9. Respect – for others in all dealings

The Nolan principles focus on behaviour and culture. By practicing accountability, integrity, and leadership, public money will be spent wisely and the services for beneficiaries will meet their needs. By being selfless and honest, decisions will be made which are in the interests of the organisation rather than for personal interest or gain. Charitable organisations that are open and involve multiple stakeholders tend to be more successful and relevant.

The UK Government/Parliament and each respective devolved administration also operate a system of governance similar to that which one might expect to see in organisations or corporations. To that end, the Cabinet Office and HM Treasury have produced a Corporate Governance Code for Central Government Departments (Corporate Governance in Central Government Departments: Code of Good Practice, 2017). The code covers six areas namely:

- Parliamentary accountability.
- Role of the board.
- Board composition.
- Board effectiveness.
- Risk management.
- Arm's length bodies.

This code is very closely aligned with the UK Governance Code, albeit it specifies that development of ministerial and government policy lies exclusively with ministers and relevant advisors, NOT the board. It does specify the make-up of any such board as comprising,

the department's lead minister, who should chair, other departmental ministers, the permanent secretary, the finance director, who should be professionally qualified, other senior

officials and at least four non-executive board members,
the majority of whom should be senior people from the
commercial private sector, with experience of managing complex
organisations.

The Scottish Government, or as it was previously called, the Scottish
Executive, took the Nolan Committee recommendations one step
further with the introduction of the Ethical Standards in Public Life
(Scotland) Act 2000, which brought in a statutory Code of Conduct
for Board Members of Devolved Public Bodies and set up a Standards
Commission for Scotland to oversee the ethical standards framework
(www.gov.scot, n.d.).

Some of the key points that are emphasised for board members relate
to a code of conduct such as taking care when expressing views to avoid
compromising one's position as a member of a public body. The duty
of all public bodies to publish a Register of Board Member Interests
is highlighted as well as board member PERSONAL responsibility
to ensure that their entries to the register, which is published online,
are current.

The code goes on to specify that

> Board members must declare financial and non-financial interests
> which might be perceived to influence their contribution to a
> discussion or decision in Board proceedings. This requirement also
> applies to interests held by your close family, friends and business
> associates. The test on making a declaration is whether a member of
> the public, with knowledge of the relevant facts, would reasonably
> regard the interest as so significant that it is likely to prejudice your
> discussion or decision making.

A responsibly to ensure that the reputation of a public body is
not damaged by the receipt by board members (or provision) "of
inappropriate gifts and hospitality" is also highlighted in great detail.
Nevertheless, there have been a number of high-profile reports and
inquiries in Scotland highlighting inadequacies in the governance

of public bodies. One example is the Code of Good Governance for Scotland's Colleges (Code of Good Governance for Scotland's Colleges, n.d.). The Welsh colleges apply a similar code (Code of Good Governance for Colleges in Wales, n.d.) as English do Colleges in England and the same in Northern Ireland (Guide for Governors of Northern Ireland Further Education Colleges, 2019).

LEARNING POINT

In 2015 a number of newspapers reported on the removal of the Chair and entire Board of directors at Glasgow Clyde College. The Education Secretary, at the time, referred to the Board's mismanagement of the college's budget, repeatedly ignoring warnings about management failings, and alienating student representatives by excluding them from decision-making. Various aspects of the Code of Conduct for Board Members of Devolved Public Bodies were considered to have been breached and a replacement Board was put in place.

Board members of public bodies face the same levels of responsibility as those in private sector listed companies with potentially even greater public scrutiny, this emphasises the importance of following the relevant code(s).

2019 also saw the introduction of the NHS Scotland Blueprint for Good Governance (Mclaughlin, n.d.). NHS Board members in Scotland were already subject to the Model Code of Conduct, this Blueprint was developed to help Boards ensure they were abiding by the Code. The Blueprint recognised that "NHS Boards across the UK operate in an increasingly demanding environment". It points to the need for good governance as being essential in "addressing the challenges the public sector faces and providing high quality, safe, sustainable health and social care services depends on NHS Boards developing robust, accountable and transparent corporate governance systems". The foreword to the document is striking with the comment: "Governance issues are increasing in the public sector, as is the public interest in governance problems being experienced by public bodies".

This Blueprint specifically refers to the UK Governance Code and draws key themes from it while also highlighting that the Independent Commission on Good Governance in Public Services has added a view on effective governance also influencing "good management, good performance, good stewardship of public money, good public engagement and ultimately good outcomes". Five functions of good governance are contained in the Blueprint:

- Setting the direction, clarifying priorities, and defining expectations.
- Holding the executive leadership team to account and seeking assurance that the organisation is being effectively managed.
- Managing risks to the quality, delivery, and sustainability of services.
- Engaging with stakeholders.
- Influencing the board's and the organisation's culture.

GOVERNANCE CODES IN THE CHARITY/VOLUNTARY SECTOR

The charity/voluntary sector is no less complex than the private and public sectors and that includes from a governance codes view point. Organisations, may find they are subject to more than one overlapping governance code, including those issued by regulatory organisations, much depends on the activities and/or geographic spread of activities, for example registered charities with operations in England and Wales are subject to regulations by the Charities Commission (England and Wales); however, if those charities also operate in Scotland, the operations in Scotland become subject to regulations of the Office of the Scottish Charity Regulator and likewise operations in Northern Ireland are subject to the regulations of the Charity Commission (Northern Ireland). The good news is that the regulatory requirements do not contradict each other; however, there are some differences.

The devolved nations in the UK have each developed Governance Codes (Charity Governance Code, n.d.), which are voluntary codes of practice. The codes offer a set of principles as a guide to governance behaviour and practice. Below is an example of the kind of principles being adopted as per the Charity Governance Code.

PRINCIPLE 1. LEADING OUR ORGANISATION

We do this by: Agreeing our vision, purpose, mission, values, and objectives making sure that they remain relevant; Developing, resourcing, monitoring, and evaluating a plan so that our organisation achieves its stated purpose and objectives; Managing, supporting, and holding to account staff, volunteers, and all who act on behalf of the organisation.

PRINCIPLE 2. EXERCISING CONTROL OVER OUR ORGANISATION

We do this by: Identifying and complying with all relevant legal and regulatory requirements; Making sure there are appropriate internal financial and management controls; Identifying major risks for our organisation and deciding ways of managing the risks.

PRINCIPLE 3. BEING TRANSPARENT AND ACCOUNTABLE

We do this by: Identifying those who have a legitimate interest in the work of our organisation (stakeholders) and making sure there is regular and effective communication with them about our organisation;

Responding to stakeholders' questions or views about the work of our organisation and how we run it; Encouraging and enabling the engagement of those who benefit from our organisation in the planning and decision-making of the organisation.

PRINCIPLE 4. WORKING EFFECTIVELY

We do this by: Making sure that our governing body, individual board members, committees, staff and volunteers understand their: role, legal duties, and delegated responsibility for decision-making; Making sure that as a board we exercise our collective responsibility through board meetings that are efficient and effective; Making sure that there is suitable board recruitment, development, and retirement processes.

PRINCIPLE 5. BEHAVING WITH INTEGRITY

We do this by being honest, fair, and independent; understanding, declaring, and managing conflicts of interest and conflicts of loyalties; and protecting and promoting our organisation's reputation.

In 2017, the Charity Governance Code Steering Group published a governance code for the charity/voluntary sector for England and Wales. The steering group includes Association of Chief Executives in Voluntary Organisations (ACEVO); the Association of Chairs, ICSA; The Chartered Governance Institute; National Council for Voluntary Organisations (NCVO); the Small Charities Coalition; and Wales Council for Voluntary Action (WCVO) with the Charity Commission in the role of observer. Importantly, this code was written not only for registered charities, but it was designed to apply to other not-for-profit organisations delivering a public or community benefit/social purpose regardless of size or activities.

The code is presented as seven principles:

- Organisational purpose – linked to board clarity of not only the organisation's aims but that they are delivered with sustainability in mind.

- Leadership – delivered by an effective board with a focus on strategic matters that match the organisations aims and values.
- Integrity – in how the board acts and in the values, it adopts and culture it creates. Creating a culture which help achieve the organisation's charitable purposes. Understanding the "importance of the public's confidence and trust in charities, and trustees undertake their duties accordingly".
- Decision-making, risk, and control – with processes that are "informed, rigorous and timely and that effective delegation, control and risk assessment and management systems are set up and monitored".
- Board effectiveness – collective team responsibility for working together effectively and a responsibility to ensure the right mix of "skills, experience, backgrounds and knowledge to make informed decisions".
- Equality, diversity, and inclusion – to support decision-making and effectiveness.
- Openness and accountability – transparency and accountability throughout the organisation and all its work "unless there is good reason for it not to be".

The authors of the Code highlight that although it is derived from the Charity Commission's (for England and Wales) guidance it "is fundamentally different" as it is principles-based and intentionally aspirational in nature. Helpfully, the authors of the Code have developed a diagnostic tool for large charities and one for small charities, which can help in board members in the practical implementation, this can be found in the further reading section at the end of the chapter. There is no one definition of a "small" charity; however, the Small Charities Coalition defines small charities as those with an annual income under £1m while large charities are those with an income above £1m per annum. Interestingly, the Charities Commission went as far as actually removing its previous guidance around good governance (CC10 the hallmarks of an effective charity) and instead encourages charities to use the Code. It should be noted, however, that guidance for Charity Trustees (Board members) (GOV. UK, n.d.) remains in place. This guidance explains the key duties of all trustees of charities in England and Wales, and what trustees need to do to carry out these duties competently, it considers topics such as who can and who cannot be a trustee, the importance of governing documents how to recruit and appoint trustees as well as key statutes that affect running of such organisations.

The Office of the Scottish Charity Regulator (OSCR) regulates registered Scottish charities as well as the Scottish operations of Charities based in other parts of the UK. Board members are subject to the Charities and Trustee Investment (Scotland) Act 2005 (the Act) and just as in all parts of the UK, those charities which are also companies, must comply with the Companies Acts. The guidance (www.oscr.org.uk, n.d.) for trustees/board members covers:

General Duties – complying with the Act and putting the interests of the organisation and the beneficiaries first.

Specific Duties – ensuring the charity's details are on the regulator's register, submitting annual reports to the regulator, ensuring financial records are kept, having oversight of the approach to fundraising activities, and providing information of the organisation's registration number to the public and a copy of the governing document to anyone who requests it. In terms of governance codes, Scotland's Third Sector Governance Forum (2019) developed a Scottish Governance Code for the Third Sector, which was published in 2019. It highlights the core principles of good governance for the boards of charities, voluntary organisations, and social enterprises in Scotland. The authors of the Code stress that it was written by practitioners in the sector with five core principles as follows:

- Organisational Purpose – A well-run board is clear about the purpose and values of the organisation and how it will achieve its aims.
- Leadership – A well-run board is clear about its role and responsibilities, and provides strategic direction in line with the organisation's purpose, vision, and values.

- Board behaviour – A well-run board, both collectively and individually, embraces and demonstrates mutual respect, integrity, openness, and accountability.
- Control – A well-run board will develop and implement appropriate controls to direct and oversee progress and performance of the organisation.
- Effectiveness – A well-run board understands its role, powers and duties, and works collectively and proactively to achieve its organisational purpose.

In Northern Ireland, the Charity Regulator has produced a governance code directly itself (The Code of Good Governance, 2016). The Code includes five principles namely:

- An effective board will provide good governance and leadership by understanding its role and responsibilities.
- An effective board will provide good governance and leadership by working well both as individuals and as a team.
- An effective board will provide good governance and leadership by ensuring delivery of organisational purpose.
- An effective board will provide good governance and leadership by exercising appropriate control.
- An effective board will provide good governance and leadership by behaving with integrity and by being open and accountable.

In the UK, Higher Education Institutions (HEIs) – (universities) – might be considered hybrid organisations as they are companies, registered charities, and receive funding from the public sector in the form of government funding in addition to other sources of income. They could also be described as commercially driven organisations; however, universities are legally established as charities regulated by charity regulators as well as being subject to university-specific and other higher education providers are regulated and universities may be considered public bodies for some purposes. A UK-wide voluntary Higher Education Code (The Higher Education Code of Governance,

2020) is designed for each institution to decide how best to implement it and "adopt a governance model which is proportionate and effective for their set of circumstances".

It is also noted that university institutions in the devolved nations have to consider this code alongside their own legislative and regulatory environments. For example, Scottish universities are subject to the Scottish Code of Good Higher Education Governance, which has behind it the Higher Education (Scotland) Act (2016). The authors of the Code recognise that it,

> applies in a complex context of other regulatory and legislative requirements with which HEIs must comply. These include not only Scottish and UK laws relating specifically to higher education, but also (among others): charities law and regulations overseen by the Office of the Scottish Charity Regulator (OSCR); the requirements of the Scottish Funding Council, including those laid down in its Financial Memorandum and Accounts Direction; the Statement of Recommended Practice for Further and Higher Education (SORP2015); relevant company law; equality law and associated duties; legislation on health and safety and on the protection of children and vulnerable adults; Freedom of Information and Data Protection legislation; procurement law; complaints handling requirements overseen by the Scottish Public Sector Ombudsman; the requirements of professional bodies and other regulators relevant to the wide range of HEIs' activity.

It could be argued that this is quite onerous for board members to contend with.

In particular, the Scottish Code highlights the importance of the role of the senior board member, in other words the chair of the board (or court), in some cases called the rector. The interesting aspect of the Higher Education (Scotland) Act is that it requires that before any Chair can be appointed, following an appropriate recruitment process, at least two candidates must stand for election by the student body, staff, and other board members.

LEARNING POINT

Since the implementation of the Higher Education (Scotland) Act (2016), a number of Scottish universities have faced considerable challenges in making chair appointments. Suitable candidates have been known to be "put off" by what is perceived as a rather public facing election campaign. Where two suitable candidates have been selected for the election process, and one subsequently withdraws, universities courts have discovered that they effectively have to restart the recruitment process (albeit the remaining candidate can remain in the process without going through fresh interviews, until at least one other candidate can be added to the election stage). On the basis that chairs of university courts are appointed for a maximum of two terms of three or four years, the election requirement has added an extra and onerous challenge for the sector.

Well-intentioned governance requirements to give a "voice" to stakeholders is a positive step; however, when options on implementation are limited, unintended challenges can arise.

In a similar vein, English universities are also subject to the Public Interest Governance Principles (part of the ongoing conditions of registration with the Office for Students) and

Welsh universities are subject to the Welsh Governance Charter. Overall, as mentioned at the start of this section, compliance with the Code is voluntary; its adoption is a valuable source of assurance to stakeholders who need to have confidence in the governance arrangements of HEIs.

As highlighted above, there are many organisations in the charity/ voluntary sector are covered by additional regulatory codes such as those issued by the National Housing Federation (NHF) which governs housing associations and Sporting regulatory bodies such as UK Sport, Sport England, Sport Scotland, and the equivalent bodies in Wales and

Northern Ireland. While there are housing associations and sporting bodies, which are no in the charity sector, the majority are not-for-profit or non-profit distributing organisations so they have been grouped in this section.

The NHF Code was updated in 2020 and changed from eight requirements to include four principles with a greater focus on stakeholder engagement in decision-making as well as equality, inclusion, and diversity:

- Mission and values
- Strategy and delivery
- Board effectiveness
- Control and assurance

LEARNING POINT

In 2019 the Charity Commission published its report into Oxfam's sex scandal in Haiti and a key criticism of the Board of Trustees and the broader leadership was what it described as a "culture of tolerating poor behaviour" and that the governance of the organisation had "repeatedly fallen below standards expected". In short, governance failings were at the heart of numerous systemic, cultural, and control-related failings.

Since news of the first allegations became public, Oxfam lost many thousands of regular donors, worth in excess of £14m, and government bodies cut tens of millions of pounds in funding.

Having touched on Housing Associations, let us turn our attention to sporting bodies, from a governance codes perspective; this is an unusual sector in that organisations may be required to comply with the UK Code for Sports Governance plus an individual nation version. An interesting aspect of the codes of governance in the sporting sector is that while they are voluntary in nature, compliance becomes compulsory for any sporting body seeking public funding for sport and physical activity. For the UK Code for Sports Governance, this has been the case since 2017 (Uksport.gov.uk, 2017). The Scottish, Welsh, and Northern Ireland administrations also issued codes of governance for the sports sector. The UK Code has been described as a "gold standard" of governance and considered to be among the most advanced globally. It also applies to organisations seeking National Lottery funding. The UK Code has been designed with three tiers so that it can apply proportionally to any organisation seeking funding from Sport England or UK Sport, regardless of size and sector; this includes national governing bodies of sport, clubs, charities, and local authorities. The Code has a focus on:

- Increased skills and diversity in decision-making, with a target of at least 30% gender diversity on boards.
- Greater transparency, for example publishing more information on the structure, strategy, and financial position of the organisation.
- Constitutional arrangements that give boards the prime role in decision-making.

The Sport Scotland Sports Governing Bodies (SGB) Governance Framework (sportscotland SGB GOVERNANCE FRAMEWORK, 2015.) has 12 principles and closely references the Nolan Principles and the UK Corporate Governance Code, the principles are:

- Commitment to implementing the Nolan Principles.
- Commitment to continuous improvement.
- Strategic planning framework.
- Appropriate composition.
- Succession planning.
- Effective performance management systems.
- Clear roles and responsibilities.
- Legally compliant.
- Effective control environment.
- Appropriate operational structure.

- Positive relations and partnerships.
- Proactive GB and home country engagement.

The Sports Governance Guide for Northern Ireland (Sports Governance Guide, n.d.) includes five principles:

- Understanding roles and responsibilities.
- Working as an individual and a team.
- Delivery of organisational purpose.
- Exercising appropriate control.
- Behaving with integrity.

Welsh Sport's National Governing Bodies (NGBs) have been encouraged to sign up to the Governance and Leadership Framework since it was launched in 2015 (GOVERNANCE AND LEADERSHIP FRAMEWORK FOR WALES: BUILDING ON SUCCESS by the Sport Sector, for the Sport Sector, n.d.) under each principle it also provides examples of positive behaviours and those to be discouraged, it contains the following seven principles:

- Integrity – acting for the future of the Sport, recreation, activity or area.
- Defining and evaluating the role of the Board.
- Setting visions, mission, and purpose.
- Balanced, inclusive, and skilled board.
- Standards, systems, and controls.
- Accountability and transparency.
- Understanding, engaging with, and embracing the sporting landscape.

Having considered the large number of codes that apply to organisations in different sectors it may be helpful to summarise the codes, the issuing body and which organisations, and indeed which nations within the UK they apply to.

Table 2.1 lists some of the Governance Codes discussed in the chapter by sector and nation.

Table 2.1 *Governance codes by sector and nation*

Private Sector

Code	Issued By	Applies To	Nation
UK Corporate Governance Code	Financial Reporting Council	Premium Listed Companies	UK-wide
Wates Principles	Financial Reporting Council	Companies with more than 2,000 employees; OR a turnover of more than £200 million, and a balance sheet of more than £2 billion.	UK-wide
QCA Corporate Governance Code	Quoted Companies Alliance	Tailored for small and mid-size quoted companies in the UK	UK-wide
PRA Supervisory Code	Prudential Regulation Authority	PRA-regulated firms, including, banks, insurers, designated investment firms, building societies, friendly societies and credit unions	UK-wide
Governing for Success	Association of British Credit Unions	Credit Unions	UK-wide

Public Sector

Corporate governance code for central government departments	Cabinet Office and HM Treasury	Central government and its departments	UK
Statutory Code of Conduct for Board Members of Devolved Public Bodies	Ethical Standards in Public Life etc. (Scotland) Act 2000	Scottish Public Bodies	Scotland
Nolan Principles (1995)	The Nolan Commission	All public sector bodies	UK-wide
A Blueprint for Good Governance (2019)	NHS Scotland	Health Boards and Special Health Boards	Scotland

(Continued)

Private Sector

Code	Issued By	Applies To	Nation
The Code of Good Governance for English Colleges (2019)	Association of Colleges	Further Education Colleges	England
Code for Good Governance for Colleges in Wales (2016)	Colleges Wales	Further Education Colleges	Wales
Guide for Governors of Northern Ireland Further Education Colleges (2019)	Department for the Economy	Further Education Colleges	Northern Ireland
A Code for Good Governance Scotland's Colleges (2013)	The Post-16 Education (Scotland) Act 2013	Further Education Colleges	Scotland

Charity/Voluntary/Non-profit Distributing Sector

The Charities Governance Code	The Charity Governance Code Steering Group Charity Commission	Registered charities	England and Wales
Guidance for Charity Trustees	Charity Commission	Registered charities	England and Wales
Guidance for Trustees	Office of the Scottish Charity Regulator and Charities and Trustee Investment (Scotland) Act 2005	All Scottish registered charities (including non-Scottish charities with operations in Scotland),	Scotland
Scottish Governance Code for the Third Sector	Scottish Good Governance Forum	Registered charities, voluntary organisations, and social enterprises	Scotland

Private Sector

Code	Issued By	Applies To	Nation
The Code of Good Governance	Charity Commission Northern Ireland	Registered charities and voluntary and community organisations	Northern Ireland
Higher Education Code of Governance (2020)	Committee of University Chairs	Universities	England and Wales
Scottish Code of Higher Education Governance (2016)	The Higher Education (Scotland) Act 2016	Universities	Scotland
A Code for Sports Governance	Sport England and UK Sport	All organisations who receive funding from Sport England or UK Sport	UK-wide
Governance and Leadership Framework for Wales	Sport Wales and the Sport and Recreation Alliance	Sport governing bodies in Wales	Wales
SGB Governance Framework	Sport Scotland	All Scottish sporting organisations in receipt of public money	Scotland
Sports Governance Guide for Northern Ireland	Sport Northern Ireland	Sporting bodies and associations	Northern Ireland
Code of Governance: Promoting board excellence for housing associations (2020)	National Housing Federation	Housing Associations	UK-wide

The above is a non-exhaustive list of codes in existence in the UK by sector and nation.

Having touched on the sheer number of governance codes in existence, and the above is not an exhaustive list, board members may feel concerned, especially those on board in highly regulated organisations, that they may fall foul of one or more complex provisions. While not every board has access to a board/company secretary/clerk to the board, those which do, can count on the support of a valuable resource in guiding them through the complexity that compliance with multiple governance codes can present.

SUPPORT ON GOVERNANCE CODE COMPLIANCE

As good governance becomes more prominent in the private, public, and charity/voluntary sectors and governance codes are updated and added, it can become an area of concern for board members that they may not be experts in every nuance of every code that may apply to their organisation(s). Some governance codes are very detailed and some are supported by statute; however, this is one of the important areas that the company secretary, or in the public sector often called the board secretary, can provide support to board members as the "resident expert" of the governance codes that apply to the organisation. As explored further in Chapter 6 (The Role of the Company Secretary), only certain organisations, such as listed companies are required to have one and it is worth noting that the Corporate Governance Code specifically states that "All directors should have access to the advice of the company secretary, who is responsible for advising the board on all governance matters". Some public sector codes also highlight the requirement for a company secretary for example the Code of Good Governance for Scotland's Colleges requires colleges to appoint a board secretary, it specifies who they report to and emphasises their independence from the senior management team. A similar provision exists in the equivalent Code for English colleges where the role is called clerk to the board, the Welsh equivalent goes as far as describing the role as clerk/governance officer.

KEY MESSAGES

- Good governance is based around dynamic decision-making, values, and attitude, and adapted to the environment and circumstances of the organisation rather than a static "box ticking" exercise.
- Although mainly voluntary in nature, governance codes are gaining in profile and importance and board members are being expected to adopt increasingly higher standards of good practice and governance using governance codes that have become increasingly principle-based rather than rules-based.
- Board members need to be aware of all the relevant codes affecting their organisation(s) especially as some of codes are legally enforceable, a board/company secretary is a good source of information and can support the board in ensuring compliance with the governance codes which apply.
- Many board members have found it to their benefit to apply a governance code either because key clients/suppliers have demanded it as a condition of transacting business or when external funding (debt or equity) has been sought.
- Owners of private companies have found that a better price can be commanded, for selling a business when robust governance controls are in place and have found that governance codes provide a useful framework for this.

FURTHER READING

https://www.charitygovernancecode.org/en/pdf

https://cdn.ymaws.com/www.iodsa.co.za/resource/collection/684B68A7-B768-465C-8214-E3A007F15A5A/IoDSA_King_IV_Report_-_Web Version.pdf

REFERENCES

Charity Governance Code. (n.d.). Download the Code. [online] Available at: https://www.charitygovernancecode.org/en/pdf [Accessed 31 Mar. 2021].

Code of Good Governance for Colleges in Wales. (n.d.). [online]. Available at: https://www.gllm.ac.uk/governance/downloads/4294967333.pdf [Accessed 24 Feb. 2021].

Code of Good Governance for Scotland's Colleges. (n.d.). [online]. Available at: https://collegesscotland.ac.uk/briefings-and-publications/publications/792-code-of-good-governance-for-scotland-s-colleges-august-2016/file [Accessed 24 Feb. 2021].

Corporate Governance in Central Government Departments: Code of Good Practice. (2017). [online]. Available at: https://assets.publishing.service.gov.uk/government/uploads/system/uploads/attachment_data/file/609903/PU2077_code_of_practice_2017.pdf [Accessed 7 Feb. 2021].

Financial Reporting Council. (2018). The UK Corporate Governance Code. [online]. Available at: https://www.frc.org.uk/getattachment/88bd8c45-50ea-4841-95b0-d2f4f48069a2/2018-UK-Corporate-Governance-Code-FINAL.PDF. [Accessed 7 Feb. 2021].

GOVERNANCE AND LEADERSHIP FRAMEWORK FOR WALES: BUILDING ON SUCCESS By the Sport Sector, for the Sport Sector. (n.d.). [online]. Available at: https://www.sport.wales/files/0a26509a4b1cbd61460824c823653507.pdf [Accessed 21 Feb. 2021].

GOVERNING FOR SUCCESS A Code of Governance and Good Practice for Credit Unions in Great Britain. (n.d.). [online]. Available at: https://ldn.coop/wp-content/uploads/2015/03/Code_of_Governance_for_Credit_Unions-1.pdf [Accessed 21 Feb. 2021].

GOV.UK. (n.d.). The Essential Trustee: What You Need to Know, What You Need to Do. [online] Available at: https://www.gov.uk/government/publications/the-essential-trustee-what-you-need-to-know-cc3/the-essential-trustee-what-you-need-to-know-what-you-need-to-do. [Accessed 11 Fe. 2021].

Guide for Governors of Northern Ireland Further Education Colleges. (2019). [online]. Available at: https://www.swc.ac.uk/swc/media/Documents/Discover/Public%20Documents/Guide-for-Governors-of-NI-FE-Colleges.pdf?ext=.pdf [Accessed 24 Feb. 2021].

ICSA. (n.d.). Britain Should Consider a United Code of Governance. [online] www.icsa.org.uk. Available at: https://www.icsa.org.uk/knowledge/

governance-and-compliance/indepth/comment/guest-comment/uk-united-governance-code. [Accessed 5 Feb. 2021].

Mclaughlin, C. (n.d.). [online]. Available at: https://www.sehd.scot.nhs.uk/dl/DL(2019)02.pdf [Accessed 13 Feb. 2021].

Sports Governance Guide. (n.d.). Home. [online] Available at: https://www.sportsgovernanceni.net/ [Accessed 21 Feb. 2021].

sportscotland SGB GOVERNANCE FRAMEWORK. (n.d.). [online]. Available at: https://sportscotland.org.uk/media-imported/1480369/governance-framework-web-final-feb-2015.pdf [Accessed 21 Feb. 2021].

The Code of Good Governance. (2016). [online]. Available at: https://www.nicva.org/sites/default/files/d7content/attachments-articles/revised_code_of_good_governance.pdf [Accessed 11 Feb. 2021].

The Five Core Principles – Scotland's Third Sector Governance Forum. (2021). [online] Available at: https://goodgovernance.scot/governance-code/the-five-core-principles/ [Accessed 11 Feb. 2021].

The Higher Education Code of Governance. (2020). [online]. Available at: https://www.universitychairs.ac.uk/wp-content/uploads/2020/09/CUC-HE-Code-of-Governance-publication-final.pdf [Accessed 8 Feb. 2021].

THE UK STEWARDSHIP CODE 2020 Financial Reporting Council. (n.d.). [online]. Available at: https://www.frc.org.uk/getattachment/5aae591d-d9d3-4cf4-814a-d14e156a1d87/Stewardship-Code_Dec-19-Final-Corrected.pdf.

Uksport.gov.uk. (2017). A Code for Sports Governance | UK Sport. [online] Available at: https://www.uksport.gov.uk/resources/governance-code. [Accessed 11 Feb. 2021].

Webber, A. (2020). FTSE 350 meets female board representation target. [online] *Personnel Today*. Available at: https://www.personneltoday.com/hr/ftse-350-meets-female-board-representation-target/ [Accessed 7 Feb. 2021].

www.gov.scot. (n.d.). On Board – A guide for Board Members of Public Bodies in Scotland (April 2015) – gov.scot. [online] Available at: https://www.gov.scot/publications/board-guide-board-members-public-bodies-scotland-april-2015/pages/55/ [Accessed 8 Feb. 2021].

www.oscr.org.uk. (n.d.). OSCR | Charity Trustee Duties. [online] Available at: https://www.oscr.org.uk/guidance-and-forms/guidance-and-good-practice-for-charity-trustees/charity-trustee-duties/ [Accessed 11 Feb. 2021].

CHAPTER THREE

Risk Management in the Boardroom

Vicky Kubitscheck

DOI: 10.4324/9781003142850-3

INTRODUCTION

This chapter focusses on the oversight and management of risks – one of the key areas underpinning effective corporate governance. After setting the scene with a brief review of the concept of risk management and its rise in stature in the boardroom, we will discuss the key principles of good risk management practices and their role in strengthening the resilience and viability of organisations. By focussing on principles, our discussion is transferable between sectors and industries. These principles can be applied proportionately to the nature, size, and complexity of the organisation in the private, public, and charity/voluntary sectors alike.

To help bring these principles to life, we will draw on key lessons from case studies before reflecting on steps for future proofing our governance of risks. While it is outside the reach of this chapter to make the reader an expert in risk management, it aims to equip the reader with a practical approach and a fresh look to managing risks in the boardroom in a new order of governance.

UNDER THE SPOTLIGHT

Risk management as a discipline has grown in stature over the last two decades, rising to new heights after the global financial crisis of 2008. Boards were reminded of the fragility of their organisations particularly where the approach to managing risk had not been as well developed or integrated as required for effective oversight of the business – from top to bottom, consistently and consciously.

So as not to waste a good crisis, governments and regulators responded without exception across sectors and jurisdictions to raise the bar for more effective and conscious risk management in organisations, placing that responsibility squarely on the shoulders of the governing body – the board of the company. This new order of governance reinforces the stewardship role of the board in ensuring that the culture of the company as well its business strategy and operating model are developed with a composure that is (more) risk-aware. To reinforce the point, the UK financial services regulators, the Prudential Regulatory Authority and Financial Conduct Authority have perhaps gone one step further through their Senior Management and Certification Regime, which gives the regulators the power to hold organisations as well as individuals to account. Individuals can potentially be held personally liable, sanctioned, and fined by the regulators. Such a regime is expected to be adopted more widely as the UK Government consults on material reforms to corporate governance in the UK. This is discussed further later in this chapter.

Through regulatory developments, fuelled by high-profile corporate failures along the way, we are reminded of the case for more effective risk management in organisations. Good stewardship is now expected to incorporate sensible risk-taking in the pursuit of profit or financial health in a more transparent and responsible way than ever before with regard to the welfare of all stakeholders. This is equally being emphasised in the National Commission's Report[1] for the public sector as well as the roadmap for refreshing the Charity Governance Code.[2] In a diverse board, directors do not each need to be an expert in risk management. However, having a good grasp of the principles is regarded a fundamental skill for operating in the boardroom.

The UK Companies Act (2006) stipulates that all directors – whether executive or non-executive – have an overall duty "to promote the success of the company" (s.172) and "to exercise reasonable care, skill and diligence" (s.174). Additionally, directors are governed and guided by sector specific regulatory authorities including the Financial Reporting Council. Furthermore, prevailing standards of governance present obligations on the board as the governing body to provide entrepreneurial leadership of the company; these obligations are reflected at the highest level in one of the key principles set out in the Financial Reporting Council's Corporate Governance Code:

> to establish procedures to manage risk, oversee the internal control framework, and determine the nature and extent of the principal risks the company is willing to take [that is, its risk appetite] in order to achieve its long-term strategic objectives.

(2018, Section 4, Principle O)

This principle underpins the board's responsibility for assessing the on-going viability and going concern of the organisation.

Managing risks to the successful delivery of an organisation's strategic goals therefore is an integral part of directors' fiduciary duties and the board process. To this end, the board is responsible for ensuring an appropriate framework for risk management is established and operates effectively. This includes ensuring that a competent chief executive is in place to embed and execute the board's risk culture and risk management strategy. These obligations are applicable in principle whether we are dealing with boards in the private, public or third sectors as the need to protect the interests of stakeholders – economically and socially – is fundamental to exercising responsible stewardship in the boardroom.

In the rest of this chapter, we will discuss the practical implications for directors in the proper discharge of their obligations regarding the management of risks that could threaten the success and viability of their organisation.

THE CONCEPT OF RISK MANAGEMENT

The concept of risk management has probably been obscured by jargon and terminology overload. This has been fuelled by regulations and "risk professionals" eager to assist and inadvertently creating a new language and an air of mystery (or misery as some might say). Terminology is not helped by the negative overtones associated with the word "risk" which is commonly perceived to be all downside. I recall many early risk management implementation programmes beginning with the need to overcome these barriers by aligning the risk vocabulary with that of the organisation's corporate language. Terminology is inevitable, peculiar to each sector and industry but the principles of risk management can fortunately be jargon free and applicable across sectors and industries.

In reality, risk management is a long-established discipline in business – at least as early as the mid-18th century when the word "entrepreneur" (which describes a person who starts a business and is willing to risk loss in order to make money) first appeared in the French dictionary. In brief, anticipating, assessing, and managing risk is intuitive and an integral part to making informed decisions.

The decision-making that is integral to the risk management process consists of two elements – the likelihood of the outcome and the impact or magnitude of the outcome. In other words, managing risk is probabilistic in nature and the term "risk" is generally defined as a possible event with an outcome that could be favourable or unfavourable. This is important as there is a tendency to focus on the negative or "downside" of a risk when the avoidance of a risk could be less favourable – a missed opportunity; for example, avoiding the risks of entering a new market can also mean foregoing strategic diversification benefits. Instead, the risk of taking an action should be weighed against the risk of inaction and the potential reward or loss arising.

This simple example illustrates the importance of considering the "downside" and "upside" risks for making balanced and risk informed decisions. Indeed, good stewardship by the board is not about avoiding risk but about understanding the risks in order to decide on how much risk-taking makes sense for growing and sustaining a healthy business. As Warren Buffet says, "risk comes from not knowing what you are doing" (Sydner 2017).

Conscious risk-taking involves conscious risk assessment, control or mitigation and reliable assurance. Risk and control are two sides of the same coin. A simple analogy is the top designed speed of a car (the risk) and specification of the brakes (the control). The faster we wish a car to be driven safely, the better the brakes will need to be. Borrowing the much-quoted words of Theodore Roosevelt "risk is like fire: if controlled it will help you; if uncontrolled it will rise up and destroy you".

Creating value through sensible risk-taking and sound management of risks clearly lies at the heart of effective risk governance in our modern organisations although this is easily overshadowed by process and regulatory compulsion. The notable increasing cost of compliance is driving organisations to seek more strategic value from the process. This topic is often raised by boards in my discussions with them.

Risk management operates with three main differences in the 21st century:

- the management of risks is required to take a more enterprise-wide approach that covers both financial and non-financial aspects of the business; this involves recognising the varied interests of an organisation's stakeholders (in a "triple-bottom-line"[3] way that covers economic, social, and environment issues or the "3P's" – profit, people, planet) within an integrated governance framework (which has evolved more recently to include a fourth "P" to cover the "principles of governance" and a fifth to cover "purpose") (Bullivant, 2016);
- managing risk and assurance over its efficacy needs to be more conscious, explicit, and transparent; and
- value creation is as important as value protection.

Some refer to this broadening of approach as the "professionalisation" and maturation of risk management which has led to the rise and formal recognition of the role of "risk managers" and "chief risk officers" since the late 1990s and particularly after the 2008 financial crisis. It provided impetus to broadening the role of professional bodies such as the Institute of Risk Management (IRM) and the publication of risk management standards. Corporate failures have served to remind us that in "professionalising" the risk management process we must focus on the quality of risk-informed decision-making rather than the glossiness of the documentation of risk policies, procedures, and organisation charts. The significance of the human factor in risk management is profound and can be obscured by an excessive focus on compliance rather than outcomes of policies.

Progressive theories of late have awakened the heart of risk management from building resilient to "anti-fragile"[4] organisations, which are capable of learning from shocks and transforming into stronger enterprises with highly regenerative qualities (characterised by "corporate honeybees"[5]). We see the focus of more mature risk management practices on the purpose of the organisation and the safe-guarding of its values and integrity (the human aspects of an enterprise). Some organisations have sought to differentiate themselves from traditional profit-centric models by formalising their commitment to creating value for all stakeholders including non-shareholding stakeholders such as employees, local communities, and the environment through certification as "B Corporations".[6]

With environmental risks topping global risk surveys, real actions are replacing mere ideologies. As momentum increases to deliver the Paris Agreement commitment for the EU to be climate-neutral by 2050, every board is expected to understand how their businesses should be evolving in a low carbon economy to remain relevant to its market. In response, business-led communities such as Chapter Zero ("The Director Climate Forum") have emerged to help boards navigate the climate risk landscape and implement best practice. Corporates, through investor behaviours, are also recognising the positive correlation between market performance and strategies which are committed to environmental, social, and governance ("ESG") principles. These qualities are being reinforced by UK regulatory agendas, which signal a marked and irreversible change in their approach to regulating companies in a deeper, more integrated and substantive way than ever before.

In summary, conceptually, risk management is:

- integral to the governance and decision-making process across the enterprise;
- probabilistic in nature with both upside and downside outcomes;
- achieved through complementary controls and risk mitigation;
- most effective when implemented in a joined-up, non-silo way across the enterprise and supported by a conscious approach to gaining assurance;
- a discipline which if applied effectively can help build more resilient and anti-fragile organisations that create as well as protect value.

These concepts will underpin the discussions in the rest of this chapter.

THE KEY PRINCIPLES OF RISK MANAGEMENT

As introduced above, risk management is integral to the decision-making process in the boardroom and while the board is not expected to have day to day responsibilities for managing risks, it is required to lead and direct the organisation's strategy for managing risks (the "risk strategy"). This involves defining a framework for managing risks and the acceptable risk-taking behaviours (the "risk culture") as well as making risk-informed decisions when discharging its duties. To be fit for purpose, the design of the framework should be proportionate to the nature and complexity of the activities of the organisation.

Most risk management frameworks adopt a "three lines of defence" model where the first line of defence refers to line management who are responsible for managing risks relating to areas under their control, the second line to those functions in an advisory and monitoring capacity such as the risk functions and the third line to independent assurance activity such as internal audits.

The way the board discharges their risk governance responsibilities is dynamic and is evident in the boardroom when the board is:

- defining its "risk appetite" as to what risks are acceptable in the pursuit of value; this sets the tone for risk-taking behaviours and the risk culture of the organisation;
- identifying the potential risks in the form of threats ("downside risks") and opportunities ("upside risks") to the business/organisation arising from internal and external factors, including "known unknowns";
- assessing or measuring the risk which includes determining the likelihood of occurrence as well as the potential impact (both upside and downside effect) of the risk;
- monitoring and reporting the reasonableness and outcomes of its decisions which includes determining the level of independent assurance required.

These processes reflect the core components of any board's risk management framework; they are iterative, dynamic, and integral to the board process that serve to inform and sharpen risk decisions and strategies. The way the framework is implemented will drive the actual risk culture of the organisation. In other words, risk culture reflects the behaviours, values, and attitudes to managing risks exhibited beyond the written rules and risk policies espoused by an organisation. We summarise these elements in Figure 3.1 followed by an outline of each core component process.

DEFINING THE BOARD'S RISK APPETITE

Intrinsic to any decision-making within an organisation is its attitude to risk-taking or more generally its risk culture and underlying corporate values. In the absence of any steer from the

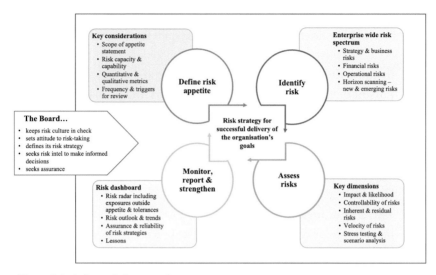

Figure 3.1 *A dynamic framework.*

board, the vacuum will be filled by individual decision makers and their personal appetite and tolerances. When this happens, surprises occur in the boardroom. In extremis, organisations fall apart. The root of many catastrophic failures can be found in a corporate culture that encouraged excessive or blind risk-taking. The significance of a board's risk appetite statement (or policy) in an organisation's risk management armoury is yet to be fully understood. As recently as 2012, the Committee of Sponsoring Organizations of the Treadway Commission published a comprehensive paper on understanding and communicating risk appetite, which their framework defines as,

> … the amount of risk, on a broad level, an entity is willing to accept in pursuit of value. It reflects the entity's risk management philosophy, and in turn influences the entity's culture and operating style. … Risk appetite guides resource allocation. … Risk appetite … [assists the organisation] in aligning the organization, people, and processes in … [designing the] infrastructure necessary to effectively respond to and monitor risks.

(p. 3)

Attitude to risk-taking is manifested in one of three actions – to avoid or accept the risk as perceived, or to contain it within tolerable impact limits. Where there is no appetite for a risk, a board can choose to avoid it altogether. In practical terms, this means that the organisation will not engage in activities that could pose such a risk, for example, risks associated with doing business in certain markets in which the company has no expertise or experience. Conversely, and using the same example, to accept such a risk would mean a board tolerating the consequences that could arise from allowing such activities to be undertaken. This decision happens where the board believes the likely reward will exceed the expected costs. Alternatively, and remaining with the same scenario, a board could accept the risk and manage it actively to optimise the result. For example, the board could limit the number of products and the speed at which they are offered to new markets in order to allow experience to build through a "test and learn" process and to contain negative consequences at more manageable levels. Some risks can be transferred to some extent, for example, property damage risks by purchasing building insurance.

Determining risk appetite is a function of two closely related elements – the capability and capacity for risk-taking. Capability refers to the ability to manage a risk while capacity refers to the ability to absorb the impact should the risk materialise. Such considerations were evident in many governments' lockdown strategies during the COVID-19 pandemic of 2020. Taking the UK scenario, the speed at which the UK's pandemic risk capability was assembled through its top epidemiologists and virologists was unprecedented. The potential for the UK to suffer over 500,000 COVID-19–related deaths (and 2.2 million in respect of the US) without any mitigating actions according to widely reported scientific simulations far exceeded the UK government's (or any reasonable person's) appetite or impact tolerance. The risk of overwhelming the country's health system was clear.

The fluid nature of the risks presented by the COVID-19 pandemic required dynamic decision-making at government level, which were greatly influenced by the capacity and capability of the NHS, in particular, the number of available critical care beds and ventilators as well as doctors, nurses, paramedics, and care workers. The risk of exceeding the capacity of the NHS at the peak of the pandemic "within weeks" was managed by a number of actions which included the installation of the "Nightingale hospitals" at record speed across the country and the redirection of clinicians within the NHS to supporting respiratory patients as well as the re-engagement of retired medical staff. Efforts to strengthen the capability of the NHS include accelerated research and development of diagnostic tests, treatment options, and vaccines which contributed to the UK becoming the first country to approve and roll out a vaccination programme. As the UK sought to maintain risks within its tolerances, real-time decision-making based on "the data" (information on infection and death rates as well as from risk modelling) and economic/people impact were evident through the easing or tightening of lockdown measures.

To direct and guide management decision-making across the organisation consistently, the board ensures its appetite for taking risks is defined and communicated, for example, in a risk appetite statement. This is similar to drawing lines in the sand outside of which is regarded to exceed the board's appetite. Having such clarity guards against inconsistencies and surprises. Each board will articulate its appetite in its own style but there are three guiding principles or questions for defining a board's risk appetite:

- Scope – what risks should be covered?
  As the overall aim of any risk appetite statement is to guide consistent decision-making, a board should articulate its appetite and tolerances to cover key types of decisions involved in managing the spectrum of risks inherent in the organisation's business model. For example, appetite/tolerance for reputation damage, operating in certain markets and financial loss (See next section on identifying the risk spectrum).

- Description – how should risk appetite be described?

  As decision-making involves judgement and since not all risks are readily quantifiable, for example, customer service risks, it makes practical sense for risk appetite to be described in both quantitative (scale) and qualitative (nature) terms. Financial risks tend to be easier to quantify and their risk appetites are usually expressed in quantitative terms, for example, tolerable limits of investment losses or deviation from planned revenue. At the other end of the spectrum are operational risks which tend to be less readily quantifiable. Risk appetites for such risks are expressed both qualitatively and quantitatively as far as possible. For example, the risk appetite for customer service risks could be expressed with a tolerable limit for the number of certain types of complaint (quantitative) and potential impact on the reputation of the organisation (qualitative).

  Risk tolerances should be set to facilitate timely escalation of risk reporting and mitigating actions as "early warnings" before the "cliff edge" limits are reached and the situation becomes either intolerable or irrecoverable for the organisation. It is important to ensure that any cushion or buffer built into risk tolerances avoids inadvertent lock-in of capacity that could result in sub-optimal use of the organisation's resources.

- Frequency – how often should the board's risk appetite be defined?

  Risk appetite and related limits and tolerances tend to remain stable once they are set. However, as risk appetite is an intrinsic part of the decision-making process, its review can be triggered by material events and decisions that challenge the current risk tolerance, for example, in response to the UK leaving the European Union, opportunities may arise to operate in new jurisdictions that are currently outside the board's appetite.

  In the absence of any material trigger events in the intervening period, the board's risk appetite, limits, and tolerances should be reviewed at least once a year to allow for refinements arising from new perspectives and lessons from previous decisions as well as changes in the business environment and plans.

LEARNING POINT

In summary, the board defines its attitude to risk-taking and implicitly its risk culture through its risk appetite statements. These statements enable the board to better guide decision-making across the organisation. Furthermore, the process of determining the board's attitude to risks enables better understanding of the organisation's capacity and capability for absorbing and managing risks. Surprises in the boardroom are also minimised.

IDENTIFYING RISKS

The ability to identify threats and roadblocks to the successful delivery of an organisation's strategic goals – the principal risks – is crucial to creating and protecting value for the organisation and its stakeholders. It is about collecting risk intelligence for the board's risk radar. As a process, it involves three key considerations:

- a forward-looking and sharp focus on the firm's strategic goals;
- an approach that is enterprise wide and covers all aspects of the organisation and its business model. Good boardroom practice includes a systematic consideration of risks to the business strategy as part of any proposal put forward to the board for decision; and
- timing of risk recognition which is critical for being on the "front foot". By installing a methodical approach, the board ensures it is "scanning the horizon" regularly to take advantage of opportunities ("upside risks") and avert threats ("downside risks"). By also encouraging active listening, the board ensures that risk intelligence is being gathered in real time.

The author would argue for a fourth dimension that is beyond any process – imagination; without it, potentially catastrophic or highly disruptive but plausible scenarios will not be contemplated. To expect the unexpected is forearming. This openness to thinking beyond the unthinkable is analogous to being aware of rare but possible events such as "black swans",[7] "gray rhinos"[8] and "dragon kings".[9] For example, immediately after 9/11 in 2001, US President George W. Bush famously stated that "nobody in our government at least, and I don't think the prior government, could envisage flying air planes into buildings" (Kuntz and Seifter 2004). This failure to imagine the possibility and the magnitude of the terrorists' ambitions (together with the lack of sharing and joining the dots of intelligence between agencies) probably led to "tepid responses" to earlier signs or attacks.

Taking an enterprise-wide approach to identifying risks means consideration is given to all parts of the organisation, its entities, and business lines. This enables full appreciation of the spectrum of risks relevant to running the business. Some common categories of risks in the spectrum include:

- strategic and business risks: these cover risk factors that impact the overall mission, strategy and business model of the organisation such as changes in the operating market arising from competition, customer behaviours, and industry developments.
- financial risks: these cover a broad range of risk types relating to the financial management of the organisation. Depending on the nature and type of the business, this category could cover sub-risk types such as credit risk, market risk, investment risk, liquidity risk, and insurance risk.
- operational risks: these refer generally to potential losses that could arise from inadequate or failed processes, people, and systems. Specific examples include customer risk, people risk, compliance risk, technology and cyber/information security risk, safety risk, environmental and legal risk.

Reputation risk cuts across all these risk types arising as a consequence of other risks materialising. It is likely to appear on every board's risk radar.

LEARNING POINT

Two practical tips for identifying risks effectively involve the board:

- scheduling time for "horizon scanning" and reviewing the changing risk profile of the organisation with a critical and strategic lens. Recognising that the enterprise risk picture is dynamic, some boards integrate such discussions into their strategy sessions. It is also worth stating that time spent on identifying potential threats including "known unknowns" is more important than debating where a risk should be categorised in the risk register;
- focussing on "big ticket" issue for the board's risk radar rather than on the number of issues or whether they are immediately measurable; awareness of the principal risks that make or break the organisation's business model is the goal. A laundry list of risks that is crowded with secondary level risks can deflect and dilute attention from the risks that affects the bottom line or the viability of the organisation.

ASSESSING RISKS

The assessment of a risk involves understanding the nature and behaviour of the risk. The process entails the consideration of four key characteristics of a risk:

- the likelihood of the risk (upside or downside) materialising;
- the size or impact of the risk should it materialise, bearing in mind that some impacts are easier to measure and describe than others; it is however more important to understand the potential magnitude of a risk than trying to quantify precisely its impact which by its very nature is uncertain. Risk impact can be

expressed as "gross risk" or "net risk" which refers to the residual level of risk after taking into account the effects of any risk mitigation or control;

- the controllability of the risk, which recognises those aspects of the risk:
  - that cannot be controlled by the organisation, such as geopolitical, economic factors or competitor actions that are "inherent" to operating in certain commercial environments;
  - that can be controlled. As there is a cost to implementing controls, understanding whether to fully control or accept a residual level of the risk is essential to the decision-making process.
- the velocity or speed of crystallisation, which helps assess the available "runway" or lead time and the options available for risk mitigation before the board's risk appetite is exceeded.

The techniques for assessing risks have been evolving and strengthening over time and it is now common to find the following approaches in our toolbox:

- scenario analysis, which is a proactive approach to considering potential risk events with the aim of assessing the sufficiency of a company's existing resources (capability and capacity for managing such risks should they materialise) and informing risk mitigation plans;
- stress testing, which refers to "strength testing" the company's capacity for absorbing certain risks;
- reverse stress testing, which combines the techniques of scenario analysis and stress testing of events to determine the "breaking point" that could sink the organisation. These extreme but plausible analyses help inform recovery and resolution plans which may include adjustments to the business model. The process of analysis is usually deemed more valuable than the output as it is highly effective in alerting an organisation to its vulnerabilities.

The board (or a sub-committee of the board) is expected to have oversight of these analyses which includes challenging the robustness of the scenarios and the results of the analyses where appropriate. On an on-going basis, risk assessments are undertaken to inform the strategies for managing risks, the trade-offs between risk and reward (for different stakeholders) including any tactical actions required to deliver goals and to avoid exceeding the board's risk tolerances. More robust and anti-fragile solutions can be developed as a result. The approach and regularity for conducting risk assessments should be documented in the organisation's risk management framework and reviewed periodically by the board.

MONITORING AND REPORTING OF RISKS

The monitoring of risks which the board has identified as potential threats to its strategic goals is an essential part of the board's oversight process. It completes the feedback loop required for the board to re-evaluate the soundness of previous assessments and decisions. This feedback loop is integral to the board risk assurance process. It follows that the board's risk dashboard and monitoring of "key risk indicators" and related frameworks should include:

- the status of the assessments of the risks on the board's risk radar;
- the "risk outlook", which considers the trends and anticipated outcomes of the risks;
- any risks or exposures exceeding the board's risk tolerances, which include near-misses;
- any potential changes to the risk radar including new and emerging risks as well as potential latent or incubation risks which could erupt without warning;
- periodic independent assurance of the efficacy of the risk management framework including the organisation's risk culture.

The volume of reportable information is significant. Getting "decision grade" board papers which provide enough detail for supporting effective decision-making without hindering oversight is a common challenge for most boards. This calls for good teamwork between management and the board for maintaining a shared and sharp focus on what is really important to inspire confidence in the boardroom. An action taken to inspire confidence is "assurance".

In practice, many boards face an additional challenge when it comes to receiving risk reports from different sources within the organisation. Invariably, organisations operate a "three lines of defence" model where each line of defence will offer their perspective and context in the risk management and reporting process. Management in the first line of defence will report on specific risks affecting their areas of control which may (or may not) be corroborated by reports from the second and/or third lines of defence.

Consequently, the board needs to ensure that the management information and resulting assurance it receives is holistic and represents the "one truth" of the risk picture; where a limited view is provided, this should be made explicit. Furthermore, in smaller organisations constrained by resources the lines of defence can be blurred; the limitations of the resulting framework should be taken into account by the board in its oversight. Having a healthy scepticism of the information it receives and to seek assurance over the integrity of the processes and systems used in the preparation of the information is integral to being an effective board.

Boards cannot take risk assurance for granted. This is underscored by lessons from corporate failures and emerging governance reforms (covered in the next section). Boards today are required to take a more conscious approach to seeking assurance over the efficacy of their organisations' systems of risk management and internal control which includes timely escalation of risks that are or likely to exceed the board's appetite. Understanding the stakeholders in the "assurance food chain" (illustrated in Figure 3.2) and mapping of the quality of risk assurance

Figure 3.2 *The assurance food chain.*
Source: *Integrated Assurance: Risk Governance Beyond Boundaries* (Kubitscheck 2014, Figure 6.4)

being received from each line of defence is a step towards ensuring that assurance gaps and overlaps are identified, and efforts to strengthen risk management strategies are optimised. These are core tenets of "integrated assurance" as described by Kubitscheck (2014).

Integrated assurance and the mapping of risk assurance is a growing discipline across sectors. For example, NHS Providers and Baker Tilly (2015) published a "Board Assurance Toolkit" featuring the mapping process to help the boards of all health and social care services provider organisations in England,

> to ensure there is an effective and comprehensive process to identify, understand, monitor and address current and future risks … [which] extends to include a board assurance framework being in place, which is assessed by the board, reflecting risks in the initiatives in the strategic plan.
>
> (p. 5)

The toolkit was designed to meet the HM Treasury (2012) Guidance on Assurance Frameworks for supporting accounting officers and boards in central government departments.

Even more important than receiving the information is what the board does with it; how a board responds to information including what it ignores can send a strong signal to the executive as to its true values. A board which challenges appropriately the adequacy of the assurance it receives and signals the importance of root-cause analyses and identifying lessons of issues for fine-tuning risk strategies and previous judgements will enable the development of more agile and adaptive organisations. Without this learning, the board could be regarded impotent.

LEARNING POINT

We have so far discussed the principles and key components of a board's risk management framework.

The key takeaway message about risk management is that it is inherently uncertain, multi-dimensional and dynamic, and that effective boards require the support of risk and assurance frameworks that are enterprise-wide yet integrated in their approach.

In the next section, we draw on some practical examples and events to help bring the key principles we have discussed to life and to encourage self-reflection for enhancing our board practice.

PITFALLS AND LESSONS: WHY ORGANISATIONS FAIL …

The governing body at the helm of an organisation – whether it is the board of a company or the central government of a nation is accountable when things go right and particularly when things go wrong. Its conduct and policies are scrutinised and questioned. Had the risks been managed competently? Who was responsible? Could the risk event have been avoided? Where was risk management?

The number of crises and corporate failures seems to outweigh successes. This may perhaps be a function of media interest and the complexity of running organisations successfully. To quote Mickey Rooney: "You always pass failure on the road to success"; I would add the words of Mary Kay Ash, only if you "fail forward to success".

Successful organisations cannot avoid risks but they are committed to learning and building on their experiences to become more responsive, agile, stronger, and therefore less fragile. There is seldom one specific cause of failure but a number of factors that combine to accelerate the path to breaking point or to magnify the failure. When distilled, the root causes of many corporate failures can be attributed to at least one of the following issues in an organisation's risk defences:

- Destructive risk culture

  A board (and consequently its organisation) has an unhealthy or destructive risk culture where behaviours and attitude to risk-taking give no regard to the organisation's capacity or capability to handle a risk. A board in such a state is unsustainable, putting the welfare of the organisation and its stakeholders at risk. Destructive risk cultures arise when there are:
  - a lack of competent or accountable leadership for ensuring effective systems of risk governance are in place; these include a culture of openness, active learning from past experiences, continual and constructive challenge of assumptions and decisions, and reward systems that are consistent with the strategic goals of the whole organisation; and
  - greed, hubris, value displacement, and myopic risk strategies – characteristics of highly toxic risk cultures usually found in dramatic corporate failures.
- Risk blindness

  A board is regarded to be "risk blind" when its risk radar is off. It is unable to recognise potentially material threats to or within its organisation, strategy or business model which leads to blind risk-taking. Risk blindness and blind spots can arise and prosper as a result of:
  - inadequacies or breakdowns in the organisation's risk management processes;
  - insufficient skills or experience to identify emerging risks or to keep up with the changing risk picture, for example as complexity of the business increases; and

- group-think, complacency, and blind trust in people and processes arising, for example, from a lack of objective and robust assurance and debate.

We will draw on five key events to illustrate these issues. The multi-billion-dollar bail-out of the global American Insurance Group Inc. (AIG) and the devastating Beirut explosion represent spectacular examples of risk blindness. The dramatic collapse of Carillion and scandals of abuse at Oxfam illustrate a toxic mix of poor risk culture and risk blindness. The final event discussed is a positive example of risk awareness within the global Coca-Cola group.

The dramatic collapse of corporate giant AIG in 2008 was a classic example of risk blindness, exacerbated by group-think and blind trust. AIG, a company with assets of $1trn and $95.8bn in shareholders' equity reported losses totalling $90bn and required a $182bn bail-out by the US Federal Reserve. The US-based National Association of Insurance Commissioners (2008) was blunt in its conclusion that AIG went bankrupt because it did not understand either the nature or the size of the risks it was taking stating that

> The AIG financial holding company took on more risk than they could handle when investing in collateralized debt instruments, such as credit derivative swaps on mortgage-backed securities. It is important to note that these types of investments are financial products, not state-regulated insurance products [which is where AIG's core expertise laid]. When the U.S. housing markets experienced a downturn, these risky investments lost lots of money for the AIG financial holding company.

AIG's collapse was related to the sub-prime mortgage debacle which triggered the credit crunch and banking financial crisis of 2008. AIG was selling credit default protection to banks engaged in the sub-prime mortgage market on the assumption that they would never go into default. These credit derivative swaps were characterised as "free money" or "gold". This assumption was not challenged by the AIG Board; it was unsurprising. The AIG Board comprised prominent former politicians and government officials "hand-picked" by the CEO for prestige of the board rather than for their expertise or sector knowledge; group-think was inevitable and prevalent. AIG was effectively underwriting the potential credit defaults of banks – blindly. When the credit crisis broke, AIG had already accumulated exposures of over $60 billion in credit default swaps.

On 4 August 2020, the capital of Beirut was devastated by what was reported to be one of the largest non-nuclear explosions in history. At the time of writing, investigations are in progress; early reports indicated that the incident resulted in at least 200 deaths, 5,000 injured and some 300,000 being made homeless with economic losses potentially amounting to $15bn. Immediately after the incident, Lebanon's prime minister, Hassan Diab, stated that the explosion was caused by the unsafe storage of 2,750 tonnes of ammonium nitrate in one of the port's warehouses. Port officials were held under house arrest. Experts estimated the blast to be equivalent to a tenth of the intensity of the nuclear bomb dropped on Hiroshima in 1945. A week after the incident, the prime minister and the cabinet resigned.

The incident questions at least two aspects of risk-blindness which may have contributed to the catastrophe. First, whether the full implication of the risk of storing a large amount of ammonium nitrate in a warehouse located within a densely populated area was recognised or taken seriously enough. It was thought that the ammonium nitrate ended up in one of the port's warehouses in 2013 when a Moldovan-flagged ship carrying the cargo suffered technical faults while docked in Beirut enroute to Mozambique was abandoned by its owners after it was banned from leaving under court order. Seven years on, the chemical had not been disposed of or resold as expected, putting the people in the capital city at risk. The risk was being incubated. Second, whether the changing nature of the risk was recognised so as to ensure that safety measures were being observed and the risk was monitored? Experts state that ammonium nitrate is safe if stored appropriately but can over time accumulate moisture to change from fine crystals to a rock which intensifies the chemical reaction when ignited. Maintenance works to the warehouse had taken place hours before the explosion.

In a study by Cass Business School (2011), which included 23 major risk events around the turn of new Millennium, risk blindness was found to be a common cause of breakdowns in the risk governance of high-profile organisations such as Arthur Andersen (2001), Enron (2001), Firestone (2000), Northern Rock (2007), UK Passport Agency (1999), BP Texas Refinery (2005), Independent Assurance (2001), EAD Airbus (2006), Cadbury Schweppes (2007), and Railtrack (2000–2002) to name a few.

Such pitfalls and lessons are not unique to the private sector. In 2016, the charity regulator Fundraising Standards Board found failings in four household charities in their oversight of telemarketing activities which resulted in several breaches of the regulator's fundraising code that included the use of pressurising techniques and exploitation of vulnerable people. The British Red Cross, Macmillan Cancer Support, NSPCC, and Oxfam together with GoGen, a third-party telephone fundraising agency, breached industry standards eroding public trust and support. All four charities took remedial steps to strengthen their oversight of what is essentially a core activity and lifeline of any charity. GoGen shut down shortly after the investigation.

LEARNING POINT

The CASS Business School study (2011) and the failings found by the charity regulator (2016) highlighted two key lessons for the board to discharge their risk oversight duties effectively:

- the critical need for board members and in particular non-executive directors to ask more challenging questions about the underlying risks and to seek appropriate assurance over the organisation's risk management systems;
- that organisations and boards can delegate or outsource their responsibilities but not their accountabilities.

The next event illustrates the catastrophic combination of risk-blindness and poor risk culture that exposed underlying weaknesses of the UK system of governance and regulation at the highest level. It can be described as a magnificent case study, rich in lessons and learning points for directors and central government. For this reason, we have elaborated on the case somewhat.

When Carillion, a UK listed multi-national construction and facilities management company, entered into compulsory liquidation in January 2018, it hit the headlines with liabilities of nearly £7bn, a pension debt of around £2.6bn and just £29m in cash. It employed around 43,000 people worldwide with over 18,000 in the UK. It was thought to be the largest trading liquidation in the UK at the time. The implications of the collapse were wide reaching not least because Carillion was a material service provider to the UK Government. According to the National Audit Office (2018) Carillion was the central government's sixth largest supplier in 2017. At the time of its collapse, it had around 450 public service contracts. Public sector contracts accounted for 33% of Carillion's total revenue and 45% of its UK revenue. It was involved in strategic projects including the HS2 high-speed rail line (£1.2bn joint venture contract), Battersea Power Station Redevelopment (£400m), hospital constructions in the Midlands and Liverpool (totalling some £700m, which doubled in cost following the collapse) as well as maintenance of 50 prisons. The collapse triggered multiple parliamentary inquiries and investigations. The big questions raised related to the UK Government's handling of Carillion, the conduct of Carillion's Board, and the role of Carillion's auditors and regulators including the Pensions Regulator, Financial Conduct Authority, and the Financial Reporting Council.

The UK Parliamentary 2018 joint inquiry ("the Inquiry") by the Business, Energy and Industrial Strategy and Work and Pensions Committees on Carillion found failings in every aspect of the system of governance within Carillion stating that

Carillion's rise and spectacular fall was a story of recklessness, hubris and greed. Its business model was a relentless dash for cash, driven by acquisitions, rising debt, expansion into new markets and exploitation of suppliers.

(p. 3)

The real surprise was not that Carillion collapsed but that it lasted as long as it did which the inquiry attributed to the Government's lack of "decisiveness and bravery" to reform the "feeble and timid" regulatory regimes as already recommended by previous cabinet inquiries into earlier corporate failings.

The risk culture of the Board of Carillion was at best one of blind optimism rather than of strategic or operational expertise, and at worst, complicit in the "rotten culture" through its "chronic lack of accountability and professionalism". The problems did not lie in a few rogue contracts but in a "deliberate, naïve and hubristic strategy". The directors of Carillion (most of whom were also shareholders) approved year on year increases in dividends since the company was formed in 1999 regardless of cash flows and ballooning losses and debts masked by new contracts and some creative accounting. In short, the Board of Carillion paid "scant regard for long-term sustainability or the impact on employees, pensioners and suppliers".

The tone of Carillion's risk culture set by the Board trumped any system of risk management or internal control that might have been in place. The concept of risk oversight was non-existent in practical terms. The Board was effectively endorsing behaviours of blind risk-taking by not challenging the conduct of the executive or management and by the approval of high salaries and bonuses while debts and losses were mounting. In also approving the use of "big name firms as badges of credibility in return for lucrative fees" without receiving the objective assurance it required, the Board had practically abandoned its duties to govern risks. For 19 years (and £29m in fees), KPMG as the company's auditors signed off the "directors' increasingly fantastical figures" without exercising the expected level of professional scepticism; Deloitte (£10m in fees since its appointment in 2010) as the company's internal auditors and independent assurance providers over the company's risk management and internal control failed to raise red flags. On the day before Carillion collapsed, £6m was paid to its professional advisors as its Board pleaded for a bailout from taxpayers. Carillion thought it was "too big to fail" (Bank of England 2016).

The Inquiry painted a picture of a total breakdown in Carillion's system of governance and risk management, which was allowed to thrive by an ineffective regulatory and legislative environment:

- The Pensions Regulator was described as being "feeble" in their response to Carillion's persistent underfunding of its employee pension schemes but with limited legal powers, scheme members were left with little choice other than to accept reduced pensions. As it stands, the Pensions Protection Fund (and its levy payers) will pick up the bill.
- The Financial Reporting Council (FRC) whose "tick-box" approach to regulating listed companies was "passive" and "toothless" in identifying and investigating failings in the disclosures of Carillion's annual reports. The changes required for the FRC to be effective laid more in its outlook and culture than in increased legal powers.
- Of the role of the Government, the Inquiry concluded that the Crown Representative system was deficient in providing early risk warnings over Carillion as a key strategic supplier. The focus on the delivery on price and volume over service and value risked reinforcing the wrong behaviours. The National Audit Office (2018) confirmed that the UK Government had monitored Carillion as part of its risk management system for strategic suppliers but criticised the Government "for not identifying that Carillion was financially struggling long before its January 2018 collapse", saying its traffic light system of warnings was "too slow and clunky". The scale of Carillion's losses was a surprise to the Cabinet although Carillion's financial struggles and red flags could have been traced back some five years earlier to 2013. The Government's risk radar was off.

In response to the inquiry, a path for reform which could be described as "once in a life-time" transformation is being carved by the UK Department for Business, Energy and Industrial Strategy (2021) in their consultation paper "Restoring trust in audit and corporate governance". The reforms that will transform the UK legal and governance structures covering no less than 150 recommendations from three independent government studies: Kingman's 2018 review of the FRC, the Competition and Market Authority's 2019 Statutory Audit Services Market Study and the Brydon's 2019 review into the quality and effectiveness of corporate audit.

A range of measures are already in train. These include the FRC's transition to become the new regulator, the Audit, Reporting and Governance Authority (ARGA), the operational break-up of the "Big Four" audit firms as well as an overhaul of the Government's approach to overseeing public sector strategic suppliers. The spectacular fall of Carillion has sharpened focus on the importance of long-term corporate accountability that is supported by an effective regulatory and legal regime. Disclosure under section 172 of the Companies Act has since 2019 been extended substantially to require directors to state the consequences of long-term decisions on the company and its stakeholders including employees and third parties. Increased transparency will be a central pillar in the reforms which will see resilience statements that include the impact of distributions to shareholders and capital maintenance as well as sustainability reports and audit and assurance policies being disclosed.

The broader implications of the reforms could see the professionalisation of directors, creation of a US equivalent of the Sarbanes-Oxley Act ("UK SOX") as well as the adoption of the UK financial services Senior Management and Certification Regime which gives regulators the power to hold organisations and individuals to account, including banning individuals from being directors and application of malus and clawback requirements in remuneration policies. The reforms would be momentous in effecting change to non-financial institutions in the way the Walker Review did for the financial services sector. Organisations most affected at the outset include premium listed and larger private companies as well as those regarded to be "public interest entities".

The next case illustrates how risk blindness and poor culture can prosper under passive risk governance. The Charity Commission's inquiry in 2019 into gross sexual misconduct by Oxfam staff in Haiti and Chad dating back to 2006 exposed serious breakdowns in Oxfam's safeguarding governance and incident management with devastating impact on those the charity was set up to serve and protect.

The inquiry was triggered by media reports of serious events in Haiti as part of the Oxfam relief programme in 2011 just as an earlier inquiry was being concluded over disclosures of numerous investigations within Oxfam of safeguarding allegations involving senior staff. While recognising that Oxfam, a global network consisting of some 19 non-governmental organisations is a large and complex charity, the inquiry concluded that the trustee board had failed to exercise sufficient oversight. The inquiry found that there was a culture of tolerance of poor behaviour in Oxfam in Haiti at the time; early warning signs from 2010 were ignored which when combined with poor accountability allowed some individuals to take advantage of the situation. Systems of risk management at Oxfam were rendered ineffective by defects in the oversight of the trustee board. For example, the under-reporting of "safeguarding serious incidents" to the Charity Commission and pattern of persistent issues were not spotted or followed up. While aware of the need to strengthen the organisation's safeguarding standards, the trustee board had not ensured that resources and capabilities adequately matched the risks faced by the organisation. It also failed to seek sufficient assurance of the actions required to resolve the issues and to challenge and hold the executive management to account. The inactions of the trustee board had the same effect as being risk blind; by allowing risks to be taken outside appetite, they were engendering a culture that did harm rather than safeguard its people and beneficiaries. Oxfam under new leadership accepted all 79 recommendations of the inquiry.

For a positive illustration of risk appetite and risk recognition, one can look to the PR fiasco of Coca-Cola when it launched its bottled water line "Dasani" in the UK in February 2004 only to withdraw it within five weeks. Dasani was an already established and successful bottled water brand in the US (since 1999) and the multi-million-dollar launch in the UK coincided with a rising demand for bottled water and a wider European marketing campaign. Dasani was launched on 10 February 2004 with marketing exuberance but rapidly attracted controversy, characterised by the words of columnist at *The Independent* Matthew Beard:

> A company takes ordinary mains water, puts it into fancy blue bottles, slaps on an exotic name and sells it for thousands of times more than it cost out of the tap. It sounds like an idea dreamt up in a boardroom that was too outrageous to implement, or a far-fetched plot of a television comedy. But the idea is, with a few modifications, behind Coca-Cola's latest drink, bottled water called Dasani.

(quoted in IBS Centre for Management Research, 2015)

Dasani was tap water bottled in Sidcup in Kent, courtesy of Thames Water. Each bottle was sold for 95p against cost of the (tap) water of 3p. The problem was a lack of transparency. To justify its price, an additional purification process, claimed to be "perfected by NASA", was introduced which not only offended the public and Thames Water but created a health hazard. Illegal levels of the cancer-causing compound Bromate were found in the bottles. Around 500,000 bottles were recalled immediately. Coca-Cola threw in the towel and rapidly exited Dasani from the UK and Europe. Some commentators believe that this swift action reflected Coca-Cola's low risk appetite for reputation damage and that it prioritised its reputation over income. Coca-Cola's loss of the bottled water market in the UK and Europe was estimated to be in the millions and possibly much more as the sale of bottled water overtakes cola. However, demonstrating its ability to learn and adapt – characteristics of a resilient model. Coca-Cola bounced back in 2008 with the purchase of UK-based bottled water company Abbey Well, and a successful launch of another water brand "Glaceau Smartwater" in 2015 with no PR faux pax.

LEARNING POINT

The risk events discussed above and especially the spectacular collapse of Carillion and the rescue of AIG serve to remind us that no organisation is too big to fail.

Organisations fail when those entrusted to lead are unfit to do so, sleep walking instead into catastrophic risks while stuffing their pockets and putting the welfare of the organisation, its employees and other stakeholders at risk.

The case of Oxfam reminds us that a passive approach to the governance of risks can have the same effect as being risk blind. The human factor is the weakest link in any risk management strategy. The events also remind us that, while the value of diversity (skills, background, and experience) in the boardroom for supporting the quality of discussions (challenge) and to minimise group-think is accepted as a concept, it is generally underdelivered.

In brief, an unhealthy risk culture and risk blindness is a toxic mix which leads organisations to self-destruct – the only uncertainty being the scale and timing of failure.

FUTURE PROOFING: FOREWARNED IS FOREARMED

As we progress through the 21st century, the scene is set for a period of transformation greater than ever imagined. Against a web of geopolitical events, trade wars, climate change crises, technology/cyber risks, the COVID-19 pandemic and other potential pandemics fanning the global fires of activism and civil unrest and fear of resulting recessions, navigating the risk landscape in the boardroom will be the greatest challenge yet for many boards. The COVID-19 pandemic in particular has been highly effective in disrupting every aspect of society by accelerating mega risk trends and magnifying known issues in our economic, social, and environmental policies and infrastructures. Together, the known unknowns are many and complex at a domestic and global scale.

Nearly a year on after the WHO declared the spread of COVID-19 as a pandemic in March 2020, three risks – business disruption, pandemic threats, and cyber incidents (dubbed the "pandemic trio") – dominated global risk surveys, such as the Allianz Global Risk Barometer 2021. In its annual Global Risks Report 2021, the World Economic Forum (WEF) indicated the top most likely risks to arise over the next decade were environmental risks (relating to extreme weather, climate action failure, and human-led environment damage) alongside digital power concentration, digital inequality, and cybersecurity failure. Impact wise, infectious disease was rated the highest of the next decade followed by climate action failure and other environmental risk as well as weapons of mass destruction, livelihood crises, debt crises, and IT infrastructure breakdown.

Additionally, as the UK moves into a new sphere of operating outside the European Union, the "fog" of economic uncertainty and geopolitical risks is expected to linger for some time in a prevailing weather of fractious international relations, intense divisiveness within national politics and economic slowdown. These headwinds are exacerbated by the global COVID-19 pandemic, serving as a reminder of the threat societies pose to themselves unless a more global and holistic approach to governance in the interest of all stakeholders is adopted.

Resilience has become the new watch word for boards. The strength and leadership of boards together with their risk strategies are being tested. Those boards and organisations that have been operationally prepared and armed for a severe business disruption event found themselves being able to maintain near normal levels of service during the pandemic. According to the Deloitte Third-party risk management Global Survey 2020, those organisations that had prioritised and invested in business disruption defences including the effective oversight of third-party risk management fared better than others that had not. Some agile organisations who were able to rapidly adapt their businesses to the new operating environment, for example transforming their restaurants to take-outs with delivery services managed to reduce the impact and to avert a total shut down. The pandemic did however disarm many organisations' risk mitigation strategies in industries such as the airlines, hotels, and restaurants – those industries which rely on footfall and for which social distancing is near impossible.

Against this risk horizon, progressive risk management strategies that aim to build not only resilient but more regenerative corporate systems are emerging in the 21st-century boardroom. They exhibit the following key characteristics:

- they exist in organisations with a clear purpose and understanding of the impact they have on their stakeholders including shareholders/financial sponsors, employees, third parties, and society in the short and longer term – that is, an environment that is conducive to developing a healthy risk culture where values of the organisation become value;
- they are led by people who have the appropriate skills and knowledge and who operate with principles expected of stewards, officials or custodians of an organisation entrusted by all stakeholders;
- they have embedded understanding of the organisation's risk appetite for supporting informed risk-based decisions across the organisation;
- they operate a risk radar that reflects the changing risk profile of the organisation, its activities and operating environment, and is dynamic and prepared with integrity;

- they recognise the benefits of healthy scepticism through conscious assurance that guards against "group-think" and blind trust;
- they encourage active listening and learning from experiences because it supports development and innovation;
- they have a reward system that drives value contribution to the organisation while discouraging myopic and excessive risk-taking for short-term gains.

Together, these characteristics reflect organisations and operating models that are not only resilient but strengthened in their risk capability and capacity to become less fragile or anti-fragile. To help future-proof our organisations and sense-check the maturity of our risk management strategies and approaches against these characteristics, we set out a short list of questions for reflection:

STRATEGIC RISK ALIGNMENT

- Do we, as a board, have a common understanding of our organisation's purpose and the value we aim to create for our internal and external stakeholders?
- Is our purpose and risk strategy fit for the future by supporting value creation and the sustainability agenda?
- Is our risk radar switched on to the things that could "break us" in the near as well as longer term? Are we too internally focussed?
- Do we consciously and periodically challenge our approach (while being alert to group-think) to horizon scanning and formulating our risk strategies? Do we have blind spots?

OPERATING PRINCIPLES OF OUR RISK STRATEGY

- Do we have a culture and behavioural qualities that support informed risk-taking to maintain (or grow) the reputation of the organisation?

- Are diversity and related principles (such as equal opportunities, gender pay gap, Modern Slavery Act) embedded in our resourcing and operating policies?
- Do we seek sufficient "checks and balances" (assurance) and "one truth" of the risk picture?
- Have we communicated the importance of "speaking up" and responded to events positively and with integrity?

RISK APPETITE AND TOLERANCES

- Has the board defined and communicated its appetite for risks in particular reputation damage, new strategic initiatives, change, and third-party risks?
- Do we give/have given mixed messages through our decisions and actions?
- Have there been surprises in the boardroom due to differing attitude to risks and tolerances?
- Do we strength-test our risk assessments and strategies for "anti-fragile" and regenerative qualities, for example, with the help of scenario analyses and sensitivity tests?

LEARNING CULTURE

- Have we embedded our attitude to active listening and learning from our experiences (negative and positive) including near-misses?
- Do we set aside time in the board agenda to review past decisions and lessons learnt?
- Do we invest enough time and resources into developing our people at all levels including the board in line with our evolving strategy and goals?

The "master question" that underpins all these suggested questions is "what can we do better?" Resilience across the "5 Ps"[10] is being reimagined by many boards. Forewarned to be forearmed through self-challenge is the essence of future proofing our systems of governance and risk management. However, as events have illustrated, the human factor remains key to effective risk management as it is people who can compensate for broken processes and make them work; conversely, they can also wilfully circumvent well-designed processes. A focus on the quality of leadership and key decision makers must therefore be central to any board's risk management and governance strategy.

KEY MESSAGES

- Managing risk is an integral part of the decision-making process regardless of size, complexity, or nature of activity of any organisation. In the absence of any guidance or a defined framework for delivering the goals of the organisation, surprises in the boardroom are more likely to occur. The risk management vacuum will be filled by individual intuition, approach and appetite for risk-taking.
- Risk management is dynamic. It involves an iterative process between surveying the risk horizon, collecting and evaluating risk intelligence, and strength-testing risk strategies and adjusting decisions with a sharp focus on delivering the organisation's purpose and strategic objectives. Many corporate failures can be attributable to a toxic mix of risk blindness and poor risk culture which has been left unchecked in the boardroom. Assurance cannot be taken for granted.
- The board is the ultimate role model. It is accountable for engendering a healthy risk culture and embedding joined-up conscious risk-taking behaviours that aim to protect and create sustainable value for its stakeholders. Progressive boards avoid sleepwalking into evolving risks and future-proof their approaches by setting aside time to reflect and ask, "what can we do better?" and "are we optimising value for our stakeholders?"
- Progressive risk management approaches seek authenticity and doing the right thing for all stakeholders in the pursuit of resilience and

sustainability – financially and environmentally. Organisations benefit from recognising the positive correlation between performance, stakeholder advocacy and strategies which are committed to environmental, social and governance ("ESG") principles.

- The human factor is significant in making or breaking any system of risk management and control. At the heart of governance failures, near misses or successes are accounts of either poor culture, hubris, incompetence, or high standards of probity and accountability for the wellbeing of the organisation and its stakeholders.

FURTHER READING

ARMIC. *Explained Guides on Risk and Managing Risk*, https://www.airmic.com/sites/default/files/technical-documents/Airmic%20Explained%-20Guides-Risk%20and%20managing%20risk_v9_FINAL.pdf

Chapter Zero Board Toolkit (To help non-executive directors ensure their businesses have the strategic plans in place to respond to climate change), https://www.chapterzero.org.uk/toolkit/.

FRC. *Guidance on Risk Management Internal Control and Related Reporting*, https://www.frc.org.uk/getattachment/d672c107-b1fb-4051-84b0-f5b83a1b93f6/Guidance-on-Risk-Management-Internal-Control-and-Related-Reporting.pdf

FRC. *Guidance on Board Effectiveness*, https://www.frc.org.uk/getattachment/61232f60-a338-471b-ba5a-bfed25219147/2018-Guidance-on-Board-Effectiveness-FINAL.PDF

NOTES

1 The National Commission's report (2019) refers to the King Committee's "four meaningful outcomes of good governance" – ethical culture, good performance, effective control, and legitimacy.

2 The Charity Governance Code Steering Committee (Charity Governance Code, 2020) identified a wide-reaching roadmap for enhancing the code

which includes financial governance and resilience, environmental and sustainable issues, as well as risk management.

3 Triple-bottom-line refers to an accounting framework which goes beyond the traditional measures of profits, return on investment and shareholder value to include environmental and social dimensions (Elkington, 1994). The term is commonly referred to as the 3P's – profit, people, and planet for developing sustainable business models.

4 Taleb (2012) states that "anti-fragility is beyond resilience and robustness" which occurs when things strive and grow from shocks and stresses. The concept encompasses flexibility, agility as well as the exploitation of opportunities.

5 Elkington (2004) defines four corporate types ("caterpillars", "locusts", "butterflies", and "honeybees") based on their regenerative or degenerative qualities. Key characteristics of "corporate honeybees" include a sustainable business models based on ethics and constant innovation, with a capacity to moderate the impacts of corporate caterpillars in its supply chain, to learn from the mistakes of corporate locusts and to boost the efforts of corporate butterflies.

6 Kim et al. (2016) identify "B Corporations" as organisations committed to a broader set of stakeholder values, unlike traditional business models which are focussed on shareholder value. Examples of "B Corporations" include Ben & Jerry's and Patagonia.

7 A "black swan" refers to any event that "seems to us, on the basis of our limited experience, to be impossible" (Taleb, 2007).

8 A "gray rhino" refers to a "highly probable, high impact yet neglected threat … Gray rhinos are not random surprises, but occur after a series of warnings and visible evidence". Examples include the bursting of the housing bubble and financial crisis in 2008, Hurricane Katrina and other natural disasters including pandemics where the event is a matter of "when, not if" (Wucker, 2016).

9 A "dragon king" refers to "extreme events that do not belong to the same population". They lie outside a power-law distribution, sometimes known as "extreme outliers" and appear as a result of amplifying mechanisms that are not necessary fully active for the rest of the population (Sornette and Ouillon, 2009).

10 The "5 Ps" refer to purpose, the principles of governance, profit/prosperity, people and planet.

REFERENCES

Allianz, 2021, *Global Risk Barometer 2021*, https://www.agcs.allianz.com/news-and-insights/reports/allianz-risk-barometer.html, accessed 29 January 2021.

Bank of England Speech, 2016, *Ending Too Big to Fail: How Best to Deal with Failed Large Banks*, England.

Brydon, D, 2019, *Independent Review into the Quality and Effectiveness of Audit*, https://assets.publishing.service.gov.uk/government/uploads/system/uploads/attachment_data/file/852960/brydon-review-final-report.pdf, accessed 20 December 2019.

Bullivant, J. 2016, *The New Integrated Governance Handbook 2016: developing governance between organisations (GBO)*, Final report. [online] Available at: https://www.good-governance.org.uk/wp-content/uploads/2017/04/The-new-Integrated-Governance-Handbook-2016.pdf.

Cass Business School and AIRMIC, 2011, *Roads to Ruin – A Study of Major Risk Events: Their Origins, Impact and Implications, Executive Briefing*, England.

Charity Commission, 2019, *Charity Inquiry: Oxfam GB*, England.

Charity Governance Code Steering Committee, 2020, *Refreshing the Charity Governance Code: Summary of Consultation Responses*, England.

Committee of Sponsoring Organisations of the Treadway Commission (COSO), 2012, *Enterprise Risk Management – Understanding and Communicating Risk Appetite*, Durham, NC.

Competition and Markets Authority, 2019, *Statutory Audit Services Market Study*, https://www.gov.uk/government/news/cma-recommends-shake-up-of-uk-audit-market, accessed 20 December 2019.

Deloitte, *Third-Party Risk Management Global Survey 2020*, https://www2.deloitte.com/uk/en/pages/risk/articles/third-party-risk-management-survey.html, accessed 10 August 2020.

Department for Business, Energy and Industrial Strategy, 2021, *Restoring Trust in Audit and Corporate Governance: Consultation on the Government's Proposals*, https://assets.publishing.service.gov.uk/government/uploads/system/uploads/attachment_data/file/970673/restoring-trust-in-audit-and-corporate-governance-command-paper.pdf, accessed 18 March 2021.

Elkington, J, 2004, Enter the Triple Bottom Line, Chapter 1 in Henriques, A, & Richardson, JA, *The Triple Bottom Line: Does It All Add Up? – Assessing the Sustainability of Business and CSR*, Earthscan, London, England.

Financial Reporting Council, 2018, *UK Corporate Governance Code 2018*, Section 4, Principle O, London, England.

Fundraising Standards Board, 2016, https://fundraising.co.uk/2016/05/11/frsb-rules-gogen-four-national-charities-breached-telephone-fundraising-standards/, accessed 18 September 2020.

Good Governance Institute, 2016, *The New Integrated Governance Handbook*, https://www.good-governance.org.uk/wp-content/uploads/2017/04/The-new-Integrated-Governance-Handbook-2016.pdf, accessed 3 August 2020.

H.M. Treasury, 2012, *Guidance on Assurance Frameworks*, London, England.

IBS Centre for Management Research, 2015, *Coca-Cola's Dasani in the UK: The Public Relations Fiasco*, https://www.icmrindia.org/casestudies/catalogue/Marketing/Coca-Cola%27s%20Dasani%20in%20the%20UK.htm, accessed 6 August 2020.

Kim, S, Karlesky, MJ, Myers, CG, Schifeling, T, 2016, Why Companies Are Becoming B Corporations, *Harvard Business Review*, https://hbr.org/2016/06/why-companies-are-becoming-b-corporations, accessed 6 August 2020.

Kingman, J, 2018, *Independent Review of the Financial Reporting Council*, https://assets.publishing.service.gov.uk/government/uploads/system/uploads/attachment_data/file/767387/frc-independent-review-final-report.pdf, accessed 9 January 2019.

Kubitscheck, V, 2014, *Integrated Assurance: Risk Governance Beyond Boundaries*, Gower, England.

Kuntz and Seifter, 2004, *Media Looked Past 9–11 Commission Documentation of Bush Administration Fabrications*, https://www.mediamatters.org/george-w-bush/media-looked-past-9-11-commission-documentation-bush-administration-fabrications, accessed 2 November 2020.

National Association of Insurance Commissioners, News Release September 2008, *AIG: Conversation Should Stay Focused on the Facts*, http://www.naic.org/Releases/2008_docs/AIG_facts.htm, accessed 22 October 2011.

National Audit Office, 2018, *Investigation into the Government's Handling of the Collapse of Carillion*, England.

The National Commission's Report, 2019, Modern Governance in the Public Sector (The First Report from the National Commission on the Future of Governance in the Public Sector): A Framework of Enquiry. [Online], https://www.good-governance.org.uk/wp-content/uploads/2019/11/GGI-NatComm-Phase1-FrameworkReport-201119-Final-1.pdf.

NHS Providers and Baker Tilly, 2015, *Board Assurance: A Toolkit for Health Sector Organisations*, https://nhsproviders.org/media/1182/board-assurance-a-tool-kit.pdf, accessed 9 April 2021.

Sornette, D, and Ouillon, G, 2009, *Dragon-Kings: Mechanisms, Statistical Methods and Empirical Evidence*, https://arxiv.org/ftp/arxiv/papers/1205/1205.1002.pdf, accessed 8 July 2020.

Sydner, B, 2017, *7 Insights from Legendary Investor Warren Buffet*, para. 4, https://www.cnbc.com/2017/05/01/7-insights-from-legendary-investor-warren-buffett.html, accessed 24 June 2020.

Taleb, N, 2007, *The Black Swan: The Impact of the Highly Improbable*, Penguin, London, England.

UK Parliament, 2006, *Companies Act*, England, s171, s174.

World Economic Forum, 2021, *Global Risk Report 2021 16th Edition* https://www.weforum.org/reports/the-global-risks-report-2021, accessed 29 January 2021.

Wucker, M, 2016, *The Gray Rhino: How to Recognize and Act on the Obvious Dangers We Ignore*, St Martin's Press/Macmillan, New York, US.

CHAPTER FOUR

Environment, Social, and Governance (ESG) and Sustainability

Sital Cheema and Monica Langa

DOI: 10.4324/9781003142850-4

INTRODUCTION

Environment, social, and governance (ESG) requirements together with climate change and sustainability are topics that boards need to be aware of. The legal, regulatory, and reporting requirements in relation to climate change and sustainability are changing. Going forward, boards will increasingly require the skills to ask the "right" questions, in order to do so the collective knowledge and understanding of directors will need to increase or organisations may choose to add specialist knowledge by making new appointments to the board. We will aim to demystify a topic which is often wrapped up in scientific jargon and is seen as so big and so global, that there is significant room for misunderstanding.

ESG and sustainability are key themes that are being discussed at board-level and there are benefits, to organisations, of incorporating ESG into the core of how they operate. The regulatory and legal implications of compliance with sustainability goals, as set by government policy and which types of organisations are directly affected by changes in reporting requirements are also important. ESG risk-proofing your organisation and how this area is being approached in the private, public, and charity/voluntary sectors.

Not forgetting the much-used term "Building Back Better", which is based on a UK Government policy paper and considers approaches that organisations might adopt in a post Coronavirus Disease 2019 (COVID-19) rethink of how they operate with long-term sustainability in mind.

First, it is important to consider ESG and what it actually means and why it has become much spoken about in boardrooms across the UK.

DEFINING ESG AND WHY IT HAS INCREASED IN IMPORTANCE

ESG stands for environmental, social, and governance, and refers to three central factors in measuring the sustainability of an investment. It was derived from the "Triple Bottom Line", also known as the "People, Planet, and Profits" (PPP), a concept introduced in the 1990s. It argued that organisations should focus on each of the three "P's" and not just on "Profits", since they were equally important for any commercial enterprise to be sustainable. An early example is that of high street retailer Marks and Spencer PLC (M&S) realising that climate change and other environmental factors might affect its ability to secure the quality and quantity of cotton supplies that it may require many years into the future, it started to plan for and mitigate this risk at the very beginning of the 21st century to ensure its longer-term sustainability as a business. This concept evolved into the focus of ESG, which is a term, initially perhaps best known in the investment management industry, as it has become a key aspect of sustainable and responsible investing (SRI). It has developed and become a topic that every type of organisation should be aware of as the implications spread beyond the investments made by private individuals, large private pension schemes, local government pension schemes (LGPS), and charity investment portfolios. Whether or not your organisation is driven by a profit-making focus, its long-term sustainability is inextricably linked with the sustainability of the planet and the people living on that planet; the people making up the workforce, supply chain, customer base, investors, and beneficiaries.

Looking at ESG through an investment lens, there is at its root a simple idea that companies are more likely to succeed and deliver strong returns if they create value for all their stakeholders – employees, customers, suppliers, and wider society including the environment – and not just the company owners/beneficiaries. Consequently, ESG investment analysis considers how companies serve society and how this impacts their current and future performance. ESG analysis is not just about what the company is doing today, it takes into consideration a variety of future trends, which are critically important and should inherently include disruptive change that can have significant implications for a company's future profitability or its very existence. Developing this theme beyond the view of investment returns, one can see how this approach can be applied to every type of organisation, whether or not it is commercially driven, has a charitable focus or is a provider of public services. One could argue that ESG factors are so central to securing the long-term future of every type of organisation that it should be a core aspect of every board's core strategy, the first step in this is to understand it better. For a greater understanding of ESG, it is worth breaking down the term into its component parts:

E FOR ENVIRONMENT IN ESG

Environmental criteria examine how a business contributes to and performs on environmental challenges and includes very important issues such as waste management, pollution, greenhouse gas emissions (GGE), deforestation, irreversible depletion of marine ecosystems, use of scarce resources, and climate change. It is important to recognise that issues surrounding climate change and ecosystem degradation have a key impact on sustainability in its broadest sense, in other words sustainability of life; however, in this chapter we concentrate on the sustainability of organisations. A simple example of this involves companies that might rely on a single source of supply for key products reducing social and environmental risks is even more critical to ensuring access to those resources. For example, a supplier with poor water management practices could face unexpected shortages and cause delays in sourcing. Managing these risks helps companies meet the demands of their customer bases, thereby protecting their market share, and controlling their costs.

A summary of environmental issues, as they pertain to ESG, and potential solutions is presented in Table 4.1.

Thinking in terms of a circular economy and the fact that we are embedded within "our one planet boundary", consider how you as a member of a board, can change/influence your organisation's strategy and inspire your board, employees, and other stakeholders to contribute on an industry/sectoral level, at an organisational level and on an individual basis.

Table 4.1 Environmental, social, and governance issues and potential solutions

Issues	*Potential Solutions*
Global warming; natural disasters	Reduce carbon footprint; climate change mitigation and adaption: reduce GHG gas emissions; increased use of EVs; switch to clean renewable energy; switch to a regenerative diet; regenerative farming; afforestation to increase biodiversity of land; increase protected seas which prohibit commercial fishing from current insignificant 1% of the ocean surface.
Sea level rises and physical risk to buildings and infrastructure	Climate-resilient buildings, roads, bridges, replacement of outmoded sewage systems via use of biotechnology; circular economy – reuse, reduce, recycle, regenerate, reconfigure
Plastic pollution on land makes its way into our oceans into our food chains and bodies	Stop using plastic! Do not use single-use plastic; use "social" recycled plastic, not "virgin" plastic.
	Innovation and technology to reduce 40% wasted by-catch. Forty-six per cent of plastic pollution in the sea is due to fishing nets and only 0.03% is due to plastic straws (Seaspiracy, 2021); reduce fish intake.
	Regenerate the land via bioremediation (using living organisms to break down hazardous substances, strengthening soil by recycling soil nutrients), and phytoremediation (using plants such as vetiver grass to detoxify soils and water contaminated by heavy metals and excess minerals).
Water scarcity	Use local, innovative, climate resilient, and cost-effective solutions for localised problems. Vertical farming; regenerative farming; converting humidity into water (Magic water); convert to recycling water within your operations ("dry factory" concept introduced by L'Oreal); household recycling "dry" water systems introduced by the Dutch Water Alliance; regenerate our top soils to avoid desertification
Food scarcity	Reduce soil desertification via regenerative farming; tax "ocean fishing" to reduce the unsustainable rate of overfishing of our natural fisheries by charging for this unidirectional externality. Switch to a regenerative highly plant-based, low-fish, and low-meat diet to shift demand away from unsustainable commercial fishing and industrial farming.

(*Continued*)

Issues	*Potential Solutions*
Zoonotic global pandemics such as COVID-19	Reduce our ecological footprint; stop deforestation and further fragmentation of ecosystems leading to transmission of zoonotic diseases; invest in afforestation; increase biodiversity; increase sea and land conservation areas which are managed properly.
Soil desertification	Regenerative farming; regenerative diets; land use change; stop tilling; stop ploughing; stop use of pesticides, herbicides, fungicides, insecticides; stop using synthetic fertilisers.
Waste disposal	Circular economics – reduce, reuse, recycle, reconfigure. Convert all human and animal waste into useful substances such as compost, biofuels, pure core phosphorous. Biomimicry is the key – by imitating nature's own recycling processes we avoid stumbling on future technological disasters.
Water sanitation	Use local innovative technologies or biotechnology such as membrane technology (which emulates the natural process by which our small intestines filter water using aquaporins).

S FOR SOCIAL IN ESG

The "S" in ESG relates to the social aspect of how an organisation is run and how it interacts with stakeholders and the communities it affects. A number of social factors can affect an organisation's sustainability, including financial performance; these include how it deals with social trends and its workforce. A focus on these topics can increase profits and corporate responsibility. How the organisation treats its people, its approach to workplace diversity and equal opportunities, the work conditions and health & safety are all important aspects. One could argue this is really another term for human capital management (HCM), which is defined (Gartner, n.d.) as "a set of practices related to people resource management. These practices are focussed on the organisational need to provide specific competencies and are implemented in three categories: workforce acquisition, workforce management and workforce optimisation". Importantly, this aspect takes into consideration the values, ethics, and social conscience of the organisation and relates closely to areas such as its tolerance for bad practices such as product mis-selling.

As with all ESG factors, it applies to any type of organisation in any sector. One notable example relates to the charity/voluntary sector, which experienced this very situation when scandals around questionable fundraising practices came to light in 2015. At the time, the Charity Commission's chairman, William Shawcross, commented that

> Poor fundraising practice, inappropriate data sharing, damaging commercial relationships [and] the high-profile collapse of Kids Company, have all combined to knock the public's confidence in charity.... The public wants to see charities account better for how they spend their money, they want to see ethical fundraising, and they want to know that charities are making a positive difference to their causes.

It is perhaps of no surprise that many organisations in the sector experienced a marked decrease in donations as a result and took the opportunity to review their approaches to fundraising, and other matters through a social responsibility lens.

G FOR GOVERNANCE IN ESG

Unsurprisingly the "G" in the context of ESG relates to how an organisation is governed and extends to how well it complies with governance codes that it may be subject to but also important areas such as its approach to executive remuneration, tax practices, and strategy, ensuring the absence of corruption and bribery, regulatory compliance, the structure and diversity of the board, and the appropriateness of its governance policies and controls. It is also important to think about governance in terms of how it applies to and supports the E and the S in ESG. Good governance is, of course, a vital aspect of preventing corruption and fraud. While these can happen in any sector or type of organisation, in the public sector, an attack from those who would undertake corruption or commit fraud creates a loss to the taxpayer and reputational risk to the organisation, and undermines trust in government. Good governance practices and controls are vital. One could argue that the UK Government suspended some of its normal governance practices in the area of procurement, in the early days and weeks of the COVID-19 pandemic to secure much needed supplies of personal protective equipment and virus-testing kits. While there were examples of good decision-making processes too, in respect of the more "relaxed" approach to procurement of much needed medical supplies, the results one could argue were mixed and not in all cases seen as value for public money spent.

The corporate ratings agency S&P Global (www.spglobal.com, n.d.) highlights a number of criteria that may allow an objective view of how well an organisation does when considering the "G" in ESG:

Codes of business conduct – does the organisation take business seriously?

Risk and crisis management – are practices in the organisation effective? Is the risk management function independent from business lines?

Supply chain management – when outsourcing production, services, or business processes, an organisation also outsources its own corporate responsibilities and its reputation. Are appropriate strategies in place to manage the associated risks and opportunities posed by their supply chain?

Tax strategy criteria – does the organisation have a clear policy on its approach to taxation issues and an awareness of the extra-financial risks associated with the company's tax practices.

Materiality score – can the organisation identify the sources of long-term value creation, understand the link between long-term issues and the business case, develop long-term metrics, and transparently report these items publicly?

ESG AND SUSTAINABILITY

ESG and sustainability includes the area of climate change mitigation, especially as the need for a global transition to a low-carbon economy becomes ever more apparent. Climate change continues to be high on the corporate and public agenda as social issues and human capital management continue to gain in prominence. It is safe to say that ESG considerations are moving mainstream.

Climate change mitigation – as we transition to legally binding Net Zero Carbon Emissions by 2050. It is very important to ascertain what pathway your organisation's operations, products, and services are on? Is it sustainable at current levels of global warming? How will you seek to sustainably transition your organisation to comply with legal requirements? In order to reach the requirement for "net zero" carbon emissions by 2050, the UK must cut emissions by 78% by 2035. How about your stakeholders? Are they "climate proof"? This includes suppliers, customers, shareholders, and funders. The UK Climate Change Committee (CCC) has stated that the 2020s must be the decisive decade of progress and action on climate change. By the early 2030s, every new car and van, and every replacement boiler must be zero-carbon; by 2035, all UK electricity production will be zero carbon.

Climate adaptation – managing the physical risks of adverse weather conditions – floods, drought, sea-level rises, heat morbidity, storms, typhoons, earthquakes, and tsunamis. What will happen to your coastal based production sites if the sea level rises? Where are your suppliers located – inland, on an island, on the coast? How will this affect your output? What are your contingency plans for differing scenario analyses for extreme weather patterns and the increased physical costs of maintaining your buildings, offices, factories, and plants?

Increase in global pandemics such as COVID-19 and Ebola transmitted via zoonotic diseases (spread from animals to humans often resulting from the fragmentation of the edge an ecosystem such as a forest) due to a loss of biodiversity. What scenario planning has your organisation, your industry/sector completed in terms of keeping your people healthy and safe? Is working from home the only way? Do you need to adapt your operating environment? Have you considered you organisation's strategy to support increased biodiversity? What risk metrics do you use, do these include science-based targets, and analysis? What is your board's audit policy?

Circular economy – the need for your organisational strategy to consider "reduce, reuse, recycle, regenerate" with respect to not only reducing greenhouse gas emissions and water use but also waste conversion into biofuels or compost to ensure healthy soils and avoidance of famines.

Preserving and restoring biodiversity of our natural habitats – fisheries, marine life, mangroves, coral reefs, and tropical forest ecosystems to ensure that our earth is itself, self-sustainable and "a going concern" for many generations to come. There is an urgent need to increase protected sea areas that are well-managed and monitored to prevent illegal fishing with by-catch of endangered species (dolphins, turtles, sea birds) and sea floor damage. The natural movement of particularly larger marine species sequesters substantial amounts of CO_2. Global warming is a direct result of overfishing. An ocean tax should be introduced to pay for this unidirectional external cost to our planet and used to reduce "sea piracy".

Regenerative farming; regenerative diets; increased use of biotechnology, bio-sequestration, and "biomimicry"; land use change to avoid soil desertification, water scarcity, and "climatimigration" of billions of people. The UN says the global population will increase from the current 7.7bn in 2021 to10.5bn by 2050. This increase in population combined with rising global temperatures, increasing soil desertification, declining natural capital (water, fisheries, timber) and increasing pollution (CO_2 emissions, commercial fishing nets, plastics, pesticides) is expected to lead to political and social unrest and eventual annihilation of humankind ....by humankind.

SUSTAINABILITY AND CLIMATE CHANGE

Sustainable development was defined in 1987 by the Brundtland commission as:

> *development that meets the needs of the present without compromising the ability of future generations to meet their own needs.*

The Dasgupta Review on the Economics of Biodiversity (the Review) was published in February 2021 (GOV.UK, Feb. 2021.). The Review builds on the idea of sustainability by showing that "inclusive wealth" (the combination of production capital, human capital, and *natural capital*) is a much better measure of the world's productive base compared to traditional economics which does not measure the value of nature.

We are however embedded and fully rely on our one and only planet. This "one planet boundary" concept is a very important factor in measuring whether we are living sustainably and in harmony on Earth. Ecologists have shown that until quite recently, the beginning of the Anthropocene Period in 1950, we were living within our "natural capital means" of 1 planet Earth (Figure 4.1).

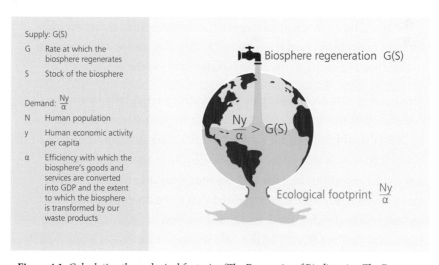

Figure 4.1 *Calculating the ecological footprint (The Economics of Biodiversity: The Dasgupta Review, Feb 2021.).*

However, an ecosystem will depreciate if it is "harvested at a greater rate than it is able to regenerate itself".

The ecological footprint is calculated using the formula as presented above of $Ny/\alpha = G(S) > 1.6$ this is explained as follows; essentially, the global stock of supply of the biosphere is equal to one planet Earth and is a function of how quickly the Earth is able to regenerate or self-sustain itself – as a going concern.

The anthropogenic demand we place on our ecosystem is the sum of our global GDP reduced by the efficiency (technology) with which we convert the Earth's goods and services into GDP and the extent to which the biosphere is transformed by our waste products. According to the Global Footprint Network we were over utilising our planet by 1.7 times up until 2019. According to Dasgupta this has reduced to 1.6 times our planet's capacity to provide due to the reduced demand we have placed on Earth due to the global lockdowns forced by the COVID-19 pandemic. Over the years we have been able to increase our efficiency through significant technological advancements that have reduced our global ecological footprint. Since the Anthropogenic period began in 1950 until 2019, the global population has risen from 2.5bn to 7.7bn as medical advancements have increased our average lifespan over this period from 43 to 73. This has meant an increasing population is placing a much greater demand on the biosphere.

This present rate is obviously *not sustainable* particularly if we consider that the UN has estimated a rise in our population to 10.5bn by 2050 (World Population Prospects 2019 Data Booklet, 2019). If we continue on this path, we will leave future generations with less than the productive base that we ourselves inherited across our various demographics. It is suggested that if we do not act now our unsustainable development, and the obsession of focusing on Gross Domestic Product (GDP) as the only measure of success, it may lead to the 6th mass extinction event of our planet's 3.8bn year history. Greta Thunberg, the young climate activist, alluded to this in her speech at the UN in 2019.

The Review thus defines sustainability as follows:

> Inclusive wealth is the measure of an economy's productive capacity. If the inclusive wealth per capita we bequeath to our descendants is greater than the inclusive wealth per capita we ourselves inherited, we would be leaving behind a larger productive base for each of our descendants.

The University of Alberta (University of Alberta, 2013) defines sustainability as,

> Sustainability means meeting our own needs without compromising the ability of future generations to meet their own needs. In addition to natural resources, we also need social and economic resources. Sustainability is not just environmentalism. Embedded in most definitions of sustainability we also find concerns for social equity and economic development.

When appraising long-term investment projects, such as preventing further fragmentation of forestland (and thereby reducing the likelihood of future global pandemics such as COVID-19 via zoonotic transmission), we should measure the net present values (NPV) of the benefits received during the lifetime of the project (not just GDP but actually accounting for depreciation is important). The appraisal of a project therefore whether "green" or not is a measure of the flow of social benefits, net of costs, in terms of accounting values of goods and services.

LEARNING POINT

As an extension of the Dasgupta Review, boards should consider themselves not as the leader of their own organisation acting with respect to maximising their own organisation's financial position, but as a global citizen leader, managing their organisation with the goal of maximising global inclusive wealth (people, planet, and profit).

The objective is to increase your "inclusive" balance sheet assets over time – financial capital, human capital (investment in training your employees) and natural capital (investment in preservation and restoration of biodiversity and climate change mitigation by planting trees).

It is not possible to discuss sustainability without giving consideration to climate change. Climate change is defined (Shaftel, 2019) as "a long-term change in the average weather patterns that have come to define Earth's local, regional and global climates. These changes have a broad range of observed effects that are synonymous with the term".

Climate change threatens agricultural production, an increase in "unfriendly disease- bearing" insects causing global pandemics and an increase in the occurrence and severity of natural disasters. Ultimately, such events have the potential to negatively affect every organisation in small ways such as impact on the supply chain to the very significant detrimental effects to the air we breathe and to the very continuation of life on the planet!

In June 2019, the UK became one of the first major economies to pass laws to end its contribution to global warming by 2050. Under the UK Climate Change Act, the UK must reach Net Zero Greenhouse Gas emissions by 2050. The Act also requires the Government to set a new Carbon Budget every five years, following the advice of the Climate Change Committee. The Sixth Carbon Budget must be legislated by June 2021. The target requires the UK to bring all greenhouse gas emissions to net zero by 2050. The UK has already reduced emissions by 42% while growing the economy by 72% and has put clean growth at the heart of its modern Industrial Strategy. This could see the number of "green collar jobs" grow to two million and the value of exports from the low carbon economy grow to £170 billion a year by 2030 (Green Finance Strategy Transforming Finance for a Greener Future, 2019).

Together, Scotland, Wales, and Northern Ireland cover a fifth of UK emissions. They have an integral role in delivering the UK's Sixth Carbon Budget on the path to Net Zero. The Committee is liaising with Welsh ministers on Welsh emissions targets as well as the Scottish Government and Northern Ireland Executive to provide further advice on setting and meeting climate targets. It is worth noting that the Scottish Government has set targets to achieve net zero emissions by 2045.

The CCC's recommended Sixth Carbon Budget includes emissions from international aviation and shipping (IAS). Its recommended UN nationally determined contribution (NDC) to the UN does not include emissions from international aviation and shipping, in line with the UN convention. It is worth noting that UK emissions in 2019 were 42% below 1990 levels.

Going forward, as we move closer to the 2050 "net zero" target, all boards will need to consider their own organisation's operations, products, and services transition within a sustainable net zero economy and price carbon risks into their financial accounts.

We have considered the UK's position on sustainability; however, it is important to note that the UK will not be a lone actor in what is after all a global issue. To set some international context, it is useful to consider the United Nation's Sustainable Development Goals.

SUSTAINABILITY GOALS

Sustainable development and sustainability goals must operate on an international stage to have a global impact and the lead has been taken by the United Nations. In 2015, the United Nations General Assembly convened with the 196 member countries, including the UK and came to an unprecedented agreement on an Agenda for Sustainable Development, to be achieved by 2030. The 17 Sustainable Development Goals (UN SDGs) below with 169 underlying socio-economic targets were proposed. The first 6 SDGs were quantitative targets or end goals that were to be globally pursued. Goal 7 (Affordable and

Clean Energy), goal 8 (Decent Work and Economic Growth), goal 9 (Industry, Innovation, and Infrastructure) and goal 17 (Partnerships for the Goals) outlined how the nations intended to work together to attain their global of No Poverty, Zero Hunger, Good Health and Well Being, Quality Education, Gender Equality and Clean Water and Sanitation for all. Goal 13 Climate Action was the precursor to the Paris Agreement, signed later that year in December 2015. The UN SDGs (Neshovski, 2018) are presented below (Figure 4.2):

Please note; the content of this publication has not been approved by the United Nations and does not reflect the views of the United Nations or its officials or Member States.

A key requirement for participating nations in the quest for a more sustainable social, environmental, and economic future is to develop national strategies for their sustainable development. The UK Government bases its vision of sustainable development on four broad objectives:

- Social progress which recognises the needs of everyone;
- Effective protection of the environment;

Figure 4.2 *The UN SDGs (Neshovski, 2018).*

- Prudent use of natural resources; and
- Maintenance of high and stable levels of economic growth and employment.

The UK Sustainable Development Strategy recognises that everybody has the right to a healthy, clean, and safe environment. This can be achieved by reducing pollution, poverty, poor housing, and unemployment. Global environmental threats, such as climate change and poor air quality must be reduced to protect human and environmental health. The use of non-renewable resources such as fossil fuels should not be stopped overnight, but they must be used efficiently and the development of alternatives should be used to help phase them out. Finally, everybody has the right to a good standard of living, with better job opportunities. Economic prosperity is required if the UK is to prosper. For this, we need a workforce equipped with suitable skills and education within a framework to support them.

The UK Sustainable Development Strategy was published in 2018 and recognises the need for a new, more environmentally sound approach to economic development, especially with regard to transport, energy production, and waste management. The UK Government has stated its aim to support economic growth in a more sustainable way, to ensure that the costs of growth do not result in excessive environmental deterioration or social injustice.

It could be argued that the COVID-19 pandemic has offered an unexpected opportunity for policy-makers and numerous organisations to take a proactive step in adopting sustainable approaches using a post-pandemic "Building Back Better" approach.

ESG IN THE BOARDROOM

ESG has evolved over the last 30 years. We have developed methods of measuring each of the three "non- financials" or "intangibles" – Environment, Social, and Governance via numerous quantitative and qualitative models and assessments. They are becoming increasingly relevant, visible, and impactful; having "triple materiality" – not only on our financial balance sheet but on our society and natural capital reserves. In other words, all UK boards have to be mindful of their "Triple Bottom Line" – the 3 P's – profit, people, and planet as the pressure increases from legislators, regulators, stakeholder activism, customers, and suppliers – a green and circular supply chain is being demanded. Those organisations ignoring this "sea change" are likely to suffer reputation risk, brand "demonisation", and leadership challenges.

The implications of the above translate into the following for directors:

- Disclosure of climate finance assumptions and integration of scenario analysis into financial accounts or public budgets to prove they are both financially viable and climate resilient and thereby sustainable going concerns.
- A need to be aware of the increased ESG governance (enhanced stewardship) that is required by shareholders, stakeholders, and providers of debt funding (now across corporate bonds, government bonds, and private equity as well as listed equities issued).
- The cost of capital for organisations will fall relative to their industry sector or other national governments if the board moves towards a "green strategy" for the issue of its corporate or government bonds, public and private equity as demand for clean, green finance increases.
- Boards will want to ensure that the Local Government Pension Assets or Private Institutional Pension assets of their employees are increasingly invested in green sustainable companies that will meet Net Zero legal requirements to avoid write-offs in relation to stranded climate assets within their organisation or pension fund.
- Boards "with green strategies" and on course for net zero sustainable transitions of their operations, services, and products are likely to meet the increasingly stringent stress testing being undertaken by insurers pricing in both climate and sustainability risk factors into the cost of providing insurance.

ESG CONSIDERATIONS NO LONGER A "NICE TO HAVE" BUT A MUST

The need to understand prevailing ESG, sustainability and global thematics is equally relevant and all-encompassing for all board directors – we share the same planet and breathe the same air! However, given the rapidly evolving landscape with increased credible scientific evidence, stakeholder "movements" are demanding change now.

The World Economic Forum (World Economic Forum, 2018) suggested that 8 of the 10 top global risks are related to ESG. As boards have the primary oversight role, they also have a legal duty to act in good faith and in the best interests of the organisation and its stakeholders. Boards must understand how their risk oversight role specifically applies to ESG-related risks.

By identifying ESG risks such as ecosystem degradation and opportunities such as clean tech, boards can consider how best to integrate values, goals, and key performance indicators (KPIs) into strategic plans to mitigate ESG risks and inform decisions that are aligned with their fiduciary duties and the values of the organisation.

Legal environment – the UK requirement to achieve Net Zero Carbon Emissions by 2050 is combined with the European Union (EU) Sustainable Finance Disclosure Reporting (EU SFDR) requirements which came into force in March 2021. The Task Force on Climate-related Financial Disclosures (TCFD) have become legally enforceable between 2021 and 2025 for certain types of organisations. The types of organisations that will be required to disclose their financial exposure to climate change include:

- Listed commercial companies.
- UK-registered large private companies – meaning two of the following criteria: turnover of more than £36m; balance sheet total of more than £18m; more than 250 employees.
- Banks and building societies.

- Insurance companies.
- Asset managers.
- Life insurers and FCA-regulated pension schemes.
- Occupational pension schemes.

Whilst in 2021, the TCFD reporting requirements only applied to the above list, it will be interesting to see how quickly these, or similar requirements extend to other types of organisations – perhaps one that you sit on the board of.

The timetable for compliance (Anthesis Report, 2020) is shown in Table 4.2 below.

It is important to stress, that while the above Task Force on Climate-related Financial Disclosures (TCFD) framework is designed to drive climate action in the private sector, there is growing interest in its relevance for guiding public sector climate action. There is some concern, however, of the limitations of the TCFD when applied to the public sector, this is therefore still under consideration. Similarly, it is not being applied to the charity/voluntary sector other than to the

Table 4.2 Mandatory Task Force on Climate-Related Financial Disclosures (TCFD) (2020)

Year	Organisation Type
2021	Bigger pension schemes (above £5bn) and financial institutions – banks building societies, insurance companies and all premium listed Financial Conduct Authority (FCA) regulated firms.
2022	Smaller pension schemes (above £1bn), the largest UK FCA-regulated asset management firms, life insurers, FCA-regulated pension providers and all UK public listed companies (PLCs).
2023	Other UK-authorised asset management firms and life insurers and FCA-regulated pension providers.
2024–2025	Other occupational pension schemes.

Anthesis, (2020). UK Government to Implement Mandatory TCFD Climate Risk Reporting. [online] Available at: https://www.anthesisgroup.com/mandatory-tcfd-climate-risk-reporting/.

pension schemes of charity employees and the investment firms that manage charity investment assets.

Regulatory environment – while not every type of organisation falls under an industry regulator, those that do are finding increasing requirements to demonstrate an understanding of and compliance with ESG requirements. For example, financial institutions such as banks, building societies, credit unions, and a number of non-profit-distributing savings and insurance societies are regulated by the Prudential Regulation Authority (PRA), since 2020, the PRA has required the boards of all the organisations it regulates, to demonstrate that ESG implications are discussed and documented at board meetings. It could easily be argued that this is a trend that may well expand to many other types of organisations.

Increasing collective shareholder activism. Any organisation, which holds investments, such as in pension schemes and charity funds, or which is a public listed company, should be aware of the Institutional Investors Group on Climate Change (IIGCC). The IIGCC is the European membership body for investor collaboration on climate change and the voice of investors taking action for a prosperous, low-carbon future. IIGCC has more than 250 members, mainly pension funds and asset managers, across 16 countries, with over €33 trillion (as at 2021) in assets under management. The IIGCC has demanded that any organisations its members invest in, *financial fully integrate and price in both transition and physical climate risks into accounts.* Since 2021, the Big 4 Auditing firms (PwC, KPMG, EY, and Deloitte) have agreed to ensure that, as part of the audit process, financial accounts are assured not only for financial resilience but climate resilience and hence a sustainable going concern.

Gen Z economics – younger generations value not only financial wealth but increasingly demand that we assess inclusive wealth (production capital, human capital, and natural capital) into our business decision-making – governance and culture, strategy alignment, risk metrics, and impact analysis as well as transparent consistent outcomes-based reporting.

LEARNING POINT

In early 2021, Robeco Institutional Asset Management, the Dutch fund management firm, persuaded the Board of Italian energy company Enel to affect a change in its board composition. Robeco worked with the Italian asset managers' association Assogestioni and the Climate Action 100+ initiative to have a former wind power executive added to Enel's board. It was part of an effort to move the company towards renewables and away from fossil fuels.

This demonstrates the power and value of investor engagement, voting, and progressive ESG focussed asset stewardship.

Members of Gen Z – loosely, people born from 1995 to 2010 – could be described as "true digital natives". From their earliest youth, they have been exposed to the internet, to social networks, and to mobile systems. It is argued that they mobilize themselves for a variety of causes to improve the world and they make decisions and relate to institutions in a very different way to other generations. Even consumption of goods, services, and the causes and brands they associate with is as a matter of ethical concern. Whereas traditional financial economics is grounded in the individual increasing personal GDP on an "egotistic" basis, Gen Z are more inclined to value social well-being ("social scarcity value" of people and planet).

ESG RISK-PROOFING

For boards seeking to build company resilience to ESG related risks, guiding principles include:

- Assess which ESG risks the company is most exposed to and seek advice from specialists on how to mitigate these risks.
- Evaluate whether monitoring of ESG risks is adequately delegated to management and is properly resourced.

- Within the evaluation board process, conduct yearly ESG skills audits on directors and impart required ESG training to the directors.
- Initiate an annual affirmation process on ESG compliance and by the directors as well as an ESG risk assessment matrix.
- Encourage high-quality ESG reporting and proactive disclosures.
- Promote engagement with all stakeholders on ESG related issues.
- Consider establishing a specialist ESG and sustainability committee which reports to the main board.

To support implementation of the above principles, it is useful to be aware of the Sustainability Accounting Standards Board (SASB), it is a non-profit organisation, founded in 2011, to develop sustainability accounting standards. SASB has developed a financial materiality map, this tool helps organisations to identify industry-specific sustainability issues that are likely to affect their financial condition or operating performance.

While SASB is a set of international accounting standards, a number of large UK private sector organisations adopt them such as Barclays PLC and Diageo PLC.

As social and environmental issues continue to affect consumer and investor behaviour and capital is re-allocated towards those enterprises with clear ESG strategies, boards must adapt to a more "conscious capitalism" where ESG – when adopted effectively – can limit risk and contribute to improved returns. In its report (ESG: A View from the Top, Sept. 2018.) KPMG highlighted enhanced corporate reputation, improved operational efficiency, and better risk management are the main benefits of ESG integration. It can be argued that to not only sustain but to thrive in this new era of accelerating transformation and stakeholder activism, organisations should embrace ESG as a strategic organisational imperative.

While one might not hear arguments that there are any disadvantages to adopting ESG principles, there are some barriers. Board directors may have limited knowledge or insufficient expertise to adequately address ESG issues. Other perceived barriers include short-term performance pressures and a possible view that ESG issues are not considered to have a significant impact on the organisation they are on the board of. The continuing trend of greater regulation and higher stakeholder expectations is likely to keep momentum on ESG issues building.

Another organisation that seeks to support ESG reporting is Gallup, which has a global workplace data pool of 100 million employees, across 140 countries – the biggest workplace data pool in the world – and through meta-analytics, Gallup scientists found a handful of metrics that benchmark a company's current state of ESG from the perspective of the employees.

Gallup (Clifton, J. Apr. 2021) points to the importance of employee commitment to the success of the ESG journey, starting from the Board and the CEO's office as commitment to any cause cascades throughout any organisation from the top and through its managers. Gallup identified five items that map to environmental, social, and governance reporting standards:

Environmental – "My organisation makes a positive impact on people and the planet".
Gallup argue that *"Employees know better than anyone if their company makes the world a little better or a little worse"*.
Social – "At work, I am treated with respect".
Gallup commented that discerning between diversity, equity and inclusion is very difficult and suggests treating each employee with 100% respect is a more helpful measure.
"My organisation cares about my overall wellbeing".
"There is someone at work who encourages my development".
Governance – "If I raised a concern about ethics and integrity, I am confident my employer would do what is right".

(1–5)

Gallup highlights that "The employees always know".

Employees are the first to know if any widespread bad practice is taking place, the reality of how customers and suppliers are treated or if there is a culture of sexual harassment, discrimination and unfairness. Gallup makes the point that most often it is the employees who know what the board and investors do not.

One could at this stage, become overwhelmed, simply despair, and turn to the next chapter. Please do not! *It is still considered likely that our people-made problems are possible to be reversed and board members have an important role to play!* Boards in every type of organisation in the private, public, and charity/voluntary sectors are increasingly hearing about ESG and sustainability, so it may be helpful to touch on the approaches to ESG, at board-level in the 3 sectors.

APPROACHES TO ESG IN THE 3 SECTORS (PRIVATE, PUBLIC, AND CHARITY/VOLUNTARY)

We have considered the importance of ESG to board members generally, it is worth noting that often the topic is seen as being of importance to specific types of organisations such as oil producers or investment firms; however, it is of equal importance to all organisations and their boards. Let us consider the different approaches taken in each sector.

PRIVATE SECTOR

As with other sectors, the private sector is large and diverse. Public listed companies and the largest privately owned companies are likely to be directly affected, not only by the regulations already highlighted in this chapter so far but by the new Audit Reporting and Governance Authority (ARGA), which is set to replace the Financial Reporting Council (FRC). It is proposed that ARGA will have a greater oversight function, making it a requirement for larger companies to make annual "resilience statements" detailing risks to the business, including climate risks. Importantly, ESG compliance will be expected to form part of the criteria for awarding executive bonuses. It is likely that these rules will apply to all public listed companies and privately owned companies with either more than 2,000 employees; a turnover of more than £200 million, or a balance sheet of more than £2 billion.

While there is less regulatory pressure on companies that are smaller than those highlighted above, the increasing focus on ESG by private equity and debt funders as well as by clients and suppliers mean that the issues are gaining in importance across the private sector.

LEARNING POINT

The publication, Shares Magazine (www.sharesmagazine.co.uk, Jan. 2020) ranked UK consumer goods giant Unilever top of the FTSE100 companies for ESG, partly due to the near 50/50 gender representation at senior management level, plus the fact it sends zero waste to landfill in the top 21 countries it operates in. It also has the lowest levels of energy consumption per employee among firms in the index. This publication also quoted Alexandra Mousavizadeh, economist and partner at Tortoise Intelligence, as calling for FTSE 100 firms to start a "race to the top". She commented, "The appetite from consumers, clients and shareholders for irresponsible corporate behaviour is diminishing. It is two minutes to midnight and we need this index to identify the gap between PR talk and real action".

The Board Directors of those organisations who have the foresight to integrate Economic, Environment, Social, and Governance (EESG) factors into their business strategy will be the leaders in their industry and be better able to anticipate, mitigate, and adapt to future risks and opportunities delivering long-term sustainable outperformance.

PUBLIC SECTOR

It could be argued that Public Sector companies, which are part or fully owned by government still have a very long way to go in terms of sustainability reporting. Many public sector organisations, such as the NHS are very large and can have a proportionally large impact; however, their annual reporting does not yet adhere to guidelines and expectations from annual reporting that have been highlighted for the largest private sector organisations. It should also be noted that many public sector bodies donate a very large amount of money and resources towards social, albeit this is not systematically measured.

While the sector can be commended for a number of "green" initiatives to become low carbon internally, it is not clear to what extent ESG has become corporate strategy or how much it is discussed in board rooms. Maybe the board thinks it's not relevant and not worth their time. At the same time, the public sector does invest substantial amounts, not only in terms of public sector pensions, which increasingly must be based on ESG factors, but at a policy level the UK Government and the devolved administrations have also committed to a low-carbon approach. The Climate Change Act 2008 legally committed the UK to significantly reducing its carbon emissions to "Net Zero" by 2050. More importantly, the Act committed the UK to generating a significantly higher percentage of its energy from renewable sources by 2020. A non-partisan, House of Commons committee on climate change was established to study and recommend ways of meeting the country's obligations. The committee

---

LEARNING POINT

2020 saw the launch of the Scottish National Investment Bank (the "Bank"). It is a development finance company established by the Scottish Government under the Scottish National Investment Bank Act 2020. The Bank is a public limited company wholly owned by the Scottish Ministers.

> As a public sector company, the organisation is a **mission-led** development investment bank providing patient capital to build a stronger, fairer, more **sustainable** Scotland. The organisation's mission is based on three main goals:
>
> - Supporting Scotland's transition to net zero by 2045.
> - Building communities and promoting equality by 2040.
> - Harnessing innovation to enable our people to flourish by 2040.
>
> This is another example of ESG and sustainability considerations shaping the use of public sector finance.

highlighted that traditional sources of capital for investment in green infrastructure could not provide even half that amount by 2025; there would be a funding gap that needed to be covered by the state budget. As a result, the Green Investment Bank was established by the UK government in 2012 as the first institution of its type in the world. In 2017, the organisation was acquired by Macquarie Group Limited, creating one of Europe's largest teams of dedicated green infrastructure investors, and now operates under the name Green Investment Group PLC.

When thinking about ESG approaches in the public sector, in addition to the development of infrastructure investment, as outlined above, one might also think of the sector as being a large pensions provider, which means the sustainability of the investments for which public sector employees' future pensions rely, is of vital importance.

Over and above public sector pensions, it is also important to note that the public sector is a highly influential procurement organisation which procures vast sums of goods and services. Since January 2021, it has been a mandatory requirement to evaluate key environmental, social. and governance ("ESG") related themes in all UK central government procurement. A "social value model" has been used to make assessments in this regard. While it may be argued that the figure should be higher, a minimum weighting of 10% must be given to ESG objectives in each procurement. The "social value model" is divided into five broad themes, each containing one or more policy outcomes to be achieved that must be evaluated expressly through specific ESG objectives as listed below:

- *COVID-19 recovery* – helping local communities to manage and recover from the impact of COVID-19.
- *Tackling economic inequality* – create new businesses, new jobs, and new skills and increasing supply chain resilience and capacity.
- *Fighting climate change* – effective stewardship of the environment.
- *Equal opportunity* – reducing the disability employment gap and tackling workforce inequality.
- *Wellbeing* – improving health and wellbeing and improving community integration.

CHARITY/VOLUNTARY SECTOR

While it could be argued that no single sector has exactly the same approach to ESG, it is interesting to note that in late 2020, the charity voluntary sector was criticised (Andy Ricketts, Oct. 2020) due to many organisations having a "reactive and fragmented" approach to addressing environmental, social, and governance.

Research conducted by the business consultancy C&E Advisory for its annual Corporate-NGO Partnerships Barometer report, which assesses the state of partnerships between companies and charities, indicates that many voluntary sector organisations do not have a holistic approach to ESG issues. The report comments that

> *From identifying and mitigating risks, and leveraging opportunities, to helping organisations to fully live their stated values, the benefits of taking a holistic approach to the planning and delivery of ESG practices have been well demonstrated.*

It is a matter of concern that a number of well-known development organisations and charities have been caught up in scandals relating to poor safeguarding, environmental, supply chain, and other practices. A key criticism of the sector is that is does not appear to take a holistic approach to tackling ESG issues – or that organisations poorly communicate practices in this regard. Manny Amadi, chief executive of C&E Advisory commented that many organisations could be leaving themselves open to serious risks, as well as justifiable criticism in the future.

"While many non-profits have clear, core social and environmental missions to which they dedicate resources and on which they often demonstrate laudable results, it is often not evident how effectively such organisations perform on other ESG issues", he said.

It is also important to add that there are numerous examples of very good practice and innovative partnerships with the private sector in relation to ESG such as the partnership between Tesco and WWF-UK, which aims to halve the environmental footprint of the average UK shopping basket. This innovative partnership has a goal of halving the environmental impact of the average shopping basket, in order to achieve this, Tesco needed to better understand and track its entire "food value chain", from food production (farming, fishing, and manufacturing) and food delivery (transportation, packaging, and stores) right through to food consumption (food waste and dietary choice). This has resulted in a pioneering industry measure of the environmental impact of the average UK shopping basket, based on key foods and ingredients. WWF-UK commented that it aims to help UK consumers to eat more sustainably by making it easier for people to make healthy choices from sustainable sources. Restoring nature in food production by producing food within a thriving farming sector that protects the natural resources it depends on. The partnership is working on eliminating deforestation from imported products like palm oil, soy, timber, and cattle, and to reach a 100% sustainable seafood range. Eliminating food waste and unnecessary packaging is another key theme.

Additionally, various umbrella bodies that represent the charity/ voluntary sector are taking the lead in supporting the sector. For example, in April 2021 the Scottish Council for Voluntary Organisations (SCVO) announced a new project to support the voluntary sector to positively contribute to Scotland's plan to reduce its carbon output by 2045. SCVO has started gathering information on how the sector is responding to climate change targets and has started surveying organisations on their environmental policies and to what extent they consider environmental sustainability to be part of the board's remit.

LEARNING POINT

The 2019 Newton Charity Investment Survey, which was conducted among leaders and decision-makers in the UK charity sector, and which received 102 responses as published by Civil Society (www.civilsociety.co.uk, n.d.), highlighted that investment decisions are increasingly influenced by issues such as climate and sustainability, as they start to see the financial benefits of engaging with companies on environmental, social, and governance (ESG) factors. The media profile gained by Extinction Rebellion, Greta Thunberg and others in 2019 had the effect of making charity board members think very carefully about climate change and how any investment portfolios are managed in light of this.

Equally important to note, is that the same survey found 80% of respondents, as opposed to 73% the previous year, stating it is better to engage with businesses which scored less well on ESG criteria. The survey suggested that charity trustees had an increased belief in pressurising poor-scoring companies to change rather than be simply excluded from charity investment portfolios. This is perhaps a strong example of how board members from the sector can influence the behaviour of other organisations in relation to sustainability, climate change, and ESG.

The importance of ESG in the sector from a governance perspective was further brought into sharp focus in April 2021, when it was announced that Ministers had suspended aid grants to Oxfam again over further allegations of sexual exploitation against the charity, in the Democratic Republic of Congo. This follows a period where Oxfam was only just authorised, in March 2021 to bid for UK aid funds again, having been barred after a sexual exploitation scandal in Haiti exposed in 2018. A Government spokesman said:

> All organisations bidding for UK aid must meet the high standards of safeguarding required to keep the people they work with safe. Given the most recent reports which call into question Oxfam's ability to meet those standards, we will not consider any new funding to Oxfam until the issues have been resolved.

TAKING THE LEAD – POST-COVID-19

The COVID-19 pandemic and related "lockdowns" in the UK and across much of the world as well as changes in travel patterns, and working environments and the varying effects felt by many sectors, gave a "pause for thought" to many boards. Following a vaccination programme, as the UK economy and its population started to emerge from tight restrictions and businesses started to reopen, the UK Government Treasury department published its "Build Back Better: our plan for growth" policy paper (GOV.UK, Mar. 2021) which sets out the government's plans to,

> support growth through significant investment in infrastructure, skills and innovation, and to pursue growth that levels up every part of the UK, **enables the transition to net zero**, and supports our vision for Global Britain.

From a board perspective it is interesting to note that looking at COVID-19 pandemic from a distance, one could argue that the something was accomplished that the human race had previously struggled to do – reducing global carbon emissions by a record figure of c. 7% in a single year! As pointed out by Board Agenda (Board Agenda, 2021) – "The planet we live on remains very much in the grip of climate change, and the pandemic has only underscored the destructive consequences of our war on nature".

Business Journal – Board Agenda (Board Agenda, 2021) highlights six action points for boards to consider in order to "build back better" as highlighted in Table 4.3 below:

Table 4.3 *Guidance for boards to build back better*

Board Actions	Questions to Ask
Revisit organisation statements of purpose	What does value creation mean to your organisation? Are your organisation's efforts consistent with current sustainability demands and principles? Are they in line with the UN Sustainable Development Goals? Does your organisation have a comprehensive view of how the world is changing as a result of the coronavirus pandemic and of its role in these changes? How is your organisation supporting societal progress? Does your corporate culture encourage participation?
Schedule a meeting of the entire board with the sole purpose of discussing sustainability	Ask the CEO to provide all pertinent data on the organisation's sustainability progress. Compare leading sustainability practices of benchmark organisations with yours. Discuss in detail the process by which your organisation identifies risks and opportunities in the medium- and long-term, does it consider the possibility of systemic risks and shocks (like pandemics)? How will gaps be filled? Does the organisation have existing strategies for reaching goals and strategies needed for future development?
Audit board members' sustainability expertise and mindset	Which sustainability archetype predominates on your board? Do the directors have sufficient expertise and interest to embed sustainability thinking in their processes, risk management, and investment decisions, including mergers, acquisitions, and innovation? Does the board need to recruit new members, perhaps those with specialist sustainability expertise?

(Continued)

Board Actions	Questions to Ask
Organise the board in such a way that it can effectively oversee sustainability	How should the board's membership evolve to make sustainability a priority?
	Which board committees should concern themselves with sustainability?
	Should there be a dedicated ESG committee? If so, how will it report to the main board?
	Does the board have a process to plan and act in accordance with a range of events on different timescales, including in times of crisis?
	Would it help for an independent expert panel to scrutinise the board's actions and progress?
Evaluate the information provided to the board on sustainability	What information does the board currently have and what further information does it need?
	Does the board regularly receive benchmark data used to judge its performance and that of competitors?
	Has the board established suitable key performance indicators (KPIs) for management?
	Does the board need additional resources to better understand or investigate the firm's sustainability performance?
	Is there a suitable balance between attention to efficiency and resilience?
	If the company received government support during the pandemic, evaluate the fundamental economic reasons for this support and prioritise them in evaluating strategy going forward.
Does the board need to hear from its critics more directly?	Explore how the firm engages with, and learns from, its critics.
	Determine and prioritise common denominators in the "build back better" sentiment among key stakeholders.
	Study potential ESG litigation and policy developments in the geographies the organisation operates in and stress test current governance approaches against them.
	In the event of any corporate restructuring, should the organisation allocate funds to expedite or intensify ESG efforts?

Board Agenda, (2021). How boards can steer companies to "build back better". [online] Available at: https://boardagenda.com/2021/02/04/how-boards-can-steer-companies-to-build-back-better/

Sustainability and ESG are global issues, although on an organisation-by-organisation level, it can be affected most directly by board members giving this important topic due consideration. Putting ESG considerations at the centre of each organisation's strategy and values not only has a positive effect on the organisation's long-term sustainability and financial performance but on the stakeholders and the wider communities in which organisations operate.

KEY MESSAGES

- ESG is not a "nice to have", but an *absolute must for every organisation.*
- Board members must develop their knowledge of ESG and sustainability, or add directors with sufficient knowledge to "ask the right questions".
- Net Zero" will be a legal requirement – think Net Zero!
- Financial returns are inextricably linked with sustainability and climate change.
- Start with what you can measure, keep it simple. Benchmark employees first.
- Every day you delay is a day lost in reaching ESG targets – act now!

FURTHER READING

https://materiality.sasb.org/

https://www.sasb.org/standards/download/

UNEP (2020), Building Back Better: The Role of Green Fiscal Policies (Policy Brief) https://wedocs.unep.org/handle/20.500.11822/32923

UNEP, and PRI (2019), Fiduciary Duty in the 21st Century https://www.unepfi.org/publications/investment-publications/fiduciary-duty-in-the-21st-century-final-report/#:~:text=A%20new%20report%20from%20UNEP, 2019%20at%20an%20investor%20roundtable.&text=Through%20the%20programme%2C%20UNEP%20FI, fiduciaries'%20duties%20to%20their%20beneficiaries.

UNFPA (1995), 'Program of Action of the 1994 International Conference on Population and Development (Chapters I–VIII)', Population and Development Review, 21(1), 187–213. https://www.unfpa.org/publications/international-conference-population-and-development-programme-action

UNU-IHDP and UNEP (2014), Inclusive Wealth Report 2014. Measuring Progress Towards Sustainability (Cambridge: Cambridge University Press). https://assets.cambridge.org/97811071/09629/frontmatter/9781107109629_frontmatter.pdf

REFERENCES

Andy Ricketts. (n.d.). Charities Warned Over "Reactive and Fragmented" Approach to Environmental, Social and Governance Issues. [online]. www.thirdsector.co.uk. Available at: https://www.thirdsector.co.uk/charities-warned-reactive-fragmented-approach-environmental-social-governance-issues/management/article/1697155 [Accessed 4 Apr. 2021].

Anthesis. (2020). UK Government to Implement Mandatory TCFD Climate Risk Reporting. [online]. Available at: https://www.anthesisgroup.com/mandatory-tcfd-climate-risk-reporting/.

Board Agenda. (2021). How Boards Can Steer Companies to "Build Back Better." [online]. Available at: https://boardagenda.com/2021/02/04/how-boards-can-steer-companies-to-build-back-better/ [Accessed 3 Apr. 2021].

Clifton, J. (Apr. 2021). Gallup Does Capitalism Need a Soul? [online]. Available at: https://www.gallup.com/workplace/347156/capitalism-need-soul-transplant.aspx?utm_source=workplace&utm_medium=email&utm_campaign=workplace_newsletter_test_a_apr_04282021&utm_term=newsletter&utm_content=discover_cta_1&elqTrackId=d5407cc821184826950433dbfe4fa16f&elq=b8ae17658fa7438e923f323283efbd14&elqaid=6433&elqat=1&elqCampaignId=1346.

ESG: A view from the top. (Sept. 2018). [online]. Available at: https://assets.kpmg/content/dam/kpmg/cn/pdf/en/2018/09/esg-a-view-from-the-top.pdf.

Gartner. (n.d.). Human Capital Management (hcm). [online]. Available at: https://www.gartner.com/en/information-technology/glossary/hcm-human-capital-management#:~:text=Human%20capital%20management%20(HCM)%20is.

GOV.UK. (Mar. 2021). Build Back Better: Our Plan for Growth. [online]. Available at: https://www.gov.uk/government/publications/build-back-better-our-plan-for-growth [Accessed 3 Apr. 2021].

GOV.UK. (Feb.2021). Final Report – The Economics of Biodiversity: The Dasgupta Review. [online]. Available at: https://www.gov.uk/government/

publications/final-report-the-economics-of-biodiversity-the-dasgupta-review [Accessed 3 Apr. 2021].

Green Finance Strategy Transforming Finance for a Greener Future. (2019). [online] Available at: https://assets.publishing.service. gov.uk/government/uploads/system/uploads/attachment_data/ file/820284/190716_BEIS_Green_Finance_Strategy

Neshovski, R. (2018). United Nations Sustainable Development. [online]. United Nations Sustainable Development. Available at: https://www.un.org/ sustainabledevelopment/.

royalsociety.org. (n.d.). Royal Society Climate Change Briefings | Royal Society. [online]. Available at: https://royalsociety.org/topics-policy/ projects/royal-society-climate-change-briefings/?gclid=EAIaIQobChMI_ Ji71bfd7wIVRKOyCh19LA81EAAYASAAEgKYEfD_BwE [Accessed 1 Apr. 2021].

Shaftel, H. (2019). Overview: Weather, Global Warming and Climate Change. [online]. Climate Change: Vital Signs of the Planet. Available at: https:// climate.nasa.gov/resources/global-warming-vs-climate-change/.

www.civilsociety.co.uk. (n.d.). Stephanie Smith: Charities Are Seeing the Benefits of ESG Engagement for Investments. [online]. Available at: https:// www.civilsociety.co.uk/finance/stephanie-smith-charities-are-seeing-the- benefits-of-esg-engagement-for-investments.html [Accessed 7 Apr. 2021].

www.sharesmagazine.co.uk. (Jan. 2020). Ranking the FTSE 100 on Its Commitment to ESG | Shares Magazine. [online]. Available at: https://www. sharesmagazine.co.uk/article/ranking-the-ftse-100-on-its-commitment-to- esg [Accessed 13 Apr. 2021].

www.spglobal.com. (n.d.). Exploring the G in ESG: Governance in Greater Detail – Part I. [online]. Available at: https://www.spglobal.com/en/research-insights/ articles/exploring-the-g-in-esg-governance-in-greater-detail-part-i.

University of Alberta. (2013). What Is Sustainability? [online]. Available at: https:// www.mcgill.ca/sustainability/files/sustainability/what-is-sustainability.pdf.

World Economic Forum. (2018). The Global Risks Report 2018. [online]. Available at: https://www.weforum.org/reports/the-global-risks-report-2018.

World Population Prospects 2019 Data Booklet. (2019). [online]. Available at: https://population.un.org/wpp/Publications/Files/WPP2019_ DataBooklet.pdf.

CHAPTER FIVE

Executive Directors on the Board

Chris Pearse, Monica Langa, and Lorraine Clinton

DOI: 10.4324/9781003142850-5

INTRODUCTION

There is considerable literature which focusses on the role of non-executive directors (NEDs), and the contribution they make to organisations in every sector, when it comes to executive directors, their role, as directors rather than as managers, is too often overlooked. When appointed to the Board, both executive non-executive company directors are considered, by the Companies Act (2006) to have equal legal and fiduciary responsibilities as well as potential penalties for not meeting legal or regulatory requirements. The challenges, however, for each are quite distinct – possibly more so for executives who temporarily have to relinquish their day-to-day divisional perspective for that of the longer-term benefit of the whole organisation.

Not all directors are company directors and most commercial organisations only appoint one or two to the board. Public sector boards can have far higher numbers, and consequent influence at board level, solving one problem but introducing others. Some charity/voluntary sector boards do not have any executive team members on the board at all. Each of these approaches brings their own unique set of challenges.

This chapter is dedicated to the role played by executive directors. It will explore the differences between the executive and non-executive director and some of the challenges that membership of the Board poses for executives. Approaches in different sectors will be considered.

EXECUTIVE DIRECTOR VERSUS NON-EXECUTIVE DIRECTOR

The contrast between these two types of director could not be clearer – one executes, the other does not. Yet, despite the clarity of the words, the roles are often misunderstood and even more frequently misapplied.

Most types of board members are directors or trustees and, unless otherwise specified, will be *company* directors, assuming that the organisation is incorporated as a company. Company directors are those whose details are registered at Companies House and have statutory duties which, if not observed, may result in being fined, prosecuted or disqualified. For the majority of organisations in the UK which are organised as registered companies, these officially registered directors may be referred to as de jure directors.

Many so-called directors are not registered at Companies House and are directors in name only. But it is important to note that the Companies Act 2006 states that a director is any person who occupies the position of director, by whatever name called. Thus, avoiding the title may not avoid the responsibilities in law.

According to the UK company law (GOV.UK, n.d.), a company director is compelled by law to:

- Follow the company's rules, shown in its articles of association (governing documents).
- Keep company records and report changes.
- File accounts and Company Tax Return.
- Tell other shareholders if they might personally benefit from a transaction the company makes.
- Pay Corporation Tax.

Anyone therefore assuming the title director, whether registered at Companies House or not, would be well-minded to be provided with, or to personally undertake, a legal briefing in what their formal directors' duties, are all too often one sees the upside; the prestige, the salary, the bonus plans and perhaps even a higher car allowance, but frequently the same individual fails to note the responsibilities and personal risks that sit alongside.

Significantly, there is no legal distinction between an executive and a non-executive director. The differences in responsibility, role and scope are therefore wholly determined by the board, in alignment with the understanding of the word *executive.*

Execute has long meant "to carry into effect" but derives from the Latin *exequi*, meaning "to follow". So, put crudely, the executive director follows the lead of the non-executive director. And this, largely, is how governance works best, with the senior, governing board charging the executive with carrying out the strategy and overseeing progress on an ongoing basis.

Commonly, the corporate strategy is created by the executive team prior to approval by the board. One might be forgiven for thinking that the strategy would emanate from the senior team (the board) but this arrangement would be hamstrung for two reasons. First, as the executive team is responsible for implementing the strategy, it needs to "own" it and be fully bought-in to the process of rolling it out – hard to achieve when someone with less operational knowledge than you, tells you what to do. Second, the executive, in general, will be far more cognisant of the strategic detail than the board. Should a board take on the task of developing a strategy, it would risk rejection by the executive both overtly and covertly.

Imagine a health service board where the non-executive directors, however well-intentioned, seek to prescribe a strategy where they cease a particular existing patient service. This decision may make complete sense in terms of its own financial and operational efficiency metrics, but are these non-medical NEDs capable of understanding the impact on/or reliance on these services from neighbouring departments – if one is shut? Will it serve to merely knock the inefficiencies down the line and equally, can this lay group really understand the various impact on related medical procedures which require the hitherto provided vital background ancillary services and support? In every type of organisation, the executive directors/senior management team/senior leadership team plays a key role in the organisation's success and sustainability so let us start by exploring the role and challenges faced.

In the vast majority of UK organisations, it would be highly unlikely to find the role of CEO and chair combined; however, it does occur in a small number of privately owned companies where the CEO may also be the majority shareholder. It is important to highlight that governance best practice, and governance codes recommend that the roles are separated and there are clear differences in the duties and responsibilities between the CEO and the board chair. In simple terms, the CEO is the top senior executive over management while the board chairperson is the head of the board of directors. Apart from the governance considerations, it is also important to note that for an organisation's long-term success a CEO who is dedicated to the responsibilities on a full-time basis is required at the same time, leading a board of directors is also a highly time-consuming role. Both positions are of such importance that when one person serves in both roles, it could be argued that it is just about impossible, to serve both positions well.

There are, of course, proponents of a combined CEO-chair role and they would argue that this approach can provide significant benefits, especially in a family-owned company where there is a clear majority ownership structure. Benefits are seen as a very clear line of command as well as continuity of leadership of the board and company, decisions can be reached very quickly and efficiently together with a much-enhanced knowledge of the company's operations being brought to board discussions and decision-making. A streamlined authority to act with speed to put board decisions into action is also cited as a benefit to this combined role approach. It is perhaps the reason why this model of governance persists in the United States. The 2015–2016 NACD Public Company Governance Survey (www.nacdonline. org, n.d.) found that 56% large-cap and 54% of mid-cap companies had a combined CEO-chair, although these organisations also had an independent board member acting in the role of "lead director" equivalent to the role of senior independent director in UK publicly listed companies.

FUNCTIONS OF THE MOST COMMON EXECUTIVE DIRECTORS ON THE BOARD

On top of their full-time executive position, executive directors may be appointed to the board, typically by the Nomination Committee, which is a committee made up of some of the NEDs or the entire Board of Directors.

THE CHIEF EXECUTIVE OFFICER (CEO)

The chief executive officer (CEO) or the managing director (MD) – is normally seen as the highest-ranking executive team member in an organisation, whose primary responsibilities include making major decisions, subject to the delegated authority from the board, managing the overall operations and resources of the organisation, acting as the main point of communication between the board of directors (the board) and corporate body operations and being the public face of the organisation. A CEO is appointed by the board and its shareholders/ stakeholders.

If one contrasts CEOs across the private, public, and charity/third sectors, an interesting view emerges. Previous studies suggest that in the private sector, CEOs have a big impact on the performance of their organisations and have a "style" that can be moved to and applied in different firms (Janke, Propper and Sadun, 2020). CEOs of large public sector organisations have a much less significant impact on performance. This might suggest that the role is less portable between the public and private sectors. The argument is made that the "turnaround CEO" approach to management is far less effective in the public sector than the private sector. In the charity/voluntary sector, CEOs face similar challenges to those of CEOs in the private and public sectors, whether it be recruiting and retaining the right staff, funding and delivering services, or raising profile and campaigning. It can be a lonely role, stuck between staff, board members/trustees, and other stakeholders.

THE FINANCE DIRECTOR (FD)

The chief financial officer (CFO) or finance director (FD) is a member of a senior executive team with responsibility for their organisation's financial health. The role combines operational and strategic roles, managing accounting and financial control functions, and establishing (subject to board approval) a financial strategy for the sustainable/ profitable long-term growth of the organisation.

The above executive director roles, are most commonly members of the board. This may extend to other executive roles, for example in a banking institution, the chief compliance officer and/or chief risk officer may also be board members, in a healthcare organisation, the chief medical officer and chief nursing officer, and so on. It should be stressed that there is no legal requirement for any executive to be appointed to the board of directors. Governance codes are also silent on the subject; however, many organisations appoint the CEO to the board in recognition of their key role as the conduit between the board and the executive team. Invariably, publicly listed companies appoint their CEOs to the board of directors.

The FD/CFO is also found on the board of publicly listed companies in reflection of the critical nature of the company's financial performance and its resultant impact on share price. In privately owned companies, should the FD not be on the board, it is likely that they will be called to attend board meetings as a matter of course, to report on the latest management accounts, and to be held to account.

OTHER EXECUTIVE DIRECTORS

Other senior executive directors are appointed to the board as a reflection of the significance of their role to the company. For instance,

SSE plc – the Energy Utility – has an Energy Director on the board to lead on SSE's wholesale businesses; the supply of energy and related services to industrial and commercial customers.

The pharmaceutical group GSK has its chief scientific officer appointed to the board in recognition of the critical role that pharmaceutical science plays in the success of the company. In a public sector bodies, it is also usual to find a number of executive directors appointed to the board.

Whether or not specialist executives are appointed to the board, they can still attend board meetings in order to report back and clarify progress within their realm of responsibility, at the behest of the chair. It is often seen as good practise for executive colleagues, who are not board members, to attend board meetings on rotation, as this approach can alleviate any feelings of inferiority or exclusion, should one be in regular attendance and another not.

Membership of a board can be seen by some as the epitome of career success. Yet once there, they may actually find themselves wishing that they were not, finding that many of the agenda items focus on the seemingly "stale" areas of policy, governance, strategy, and oversight when in actual fact the real "action" is on the operating board or management committee beneath. It is akin to saving for a Michelin star celebration and yet once there, longing for the familiar food and comfortable ambiance of your favourite local restaurant.

While it is common practice, though not mandatory, to give both the chief executive and the finance director a seat on the board. Less common is the appointment of the executive with subject matter expertise germane to the company's core activities.

With the growing emphasis on the need to comply with regulatory frameworks, many boards invite compliance officers to attend board meetings, as a matter of course. In the event of a board's failure to manage and oversee certain risks, the ramifications extend beyond the organisation, making directors personally liable.

The potential exposure to legal action and financial liabilities – corporate and personal – arising from non-compliance, or the failure to manage and oversee risk, has elevated the need for specialist executive officers. Risk and compliance expertise is often sector-specific – the need to comply with Financial Conduct Authority (FCA) or Prudential Regulation Authority (PRA) regulations will sit at the top of a bank's priorities in the same way that an educational academy may rank safeguarding of students as an overriding concern.

Another critical activity common to many larger organisations in all sectors is that of Human Resources (HR). In recent years the role of the HR Director (sometimes known at people director or chief people officer) has become central to both the strategic and day-to-day operational activities of a great many organisations. This is in marked contrast to the somewhat disenfranchised status that many HR managers and directors have laboured under in the past. Employment law and the clear causal link between employee engagement, culture, and profitability have driven this change. This has led to more and more HR professionals being promoted to the executive board as directors. In an increasing number of organisations, they are appointed as formal main board (de jure) directors.

Transitioned from the former "personnel directors" to today's "people directors" these professionals are often delegated leadership, from the board, of key company strategies – the environmental, social, and corporate governance (ESG) agenda and the equality, diversity, and inclusion strategy (ED&I) being two common examples. The task of weaving in and maintaining evidenced participation in, and assurance of the organisation's values through all processes and practises such as a reward, remuneration, and progressions is an additional emerging role and indeed as is cited by Netflix (Sepah, 2018): "The actual company values, as opposed to the nice-sounding values, are shown by who gets rewarded, promoted, or let go".

It is salutary to remember at this point that, regardless of title or executive responsibilities, if any person is deemed to be acting as a director by a court of law, they will be subject to the same legal duties, responsibilities, and potential liabilities as a de jure director. Perhaps the exception to this position, as covered in greater detail in Chapter 11 (Governance in the Charity/Voluntary Sector) is the position of charity CEOs where, in 2021, the high court rejected the Official Receiver's position that the CEO of a charity who was not a board member/trustee should be considered a de facto director. There was also criticism of the Official Receiver for holding the governance and operations of a charity to the standards expected of a commercial organisation, which suggests that the Courts take into account the type of organisation and the level of "sophistication" of all directors, in cases where the organisation fails.

There are advantages and disadvantages to having Multiple Executive Directors appointed to a Board, as highlighted by the global executive search firm Odgers Berndtson (The Curious Role of the Executive Director, n.d.) and can be seen in Table 5.1.

Table 5.1 *Advantages and disadvantages of multiple executive directors on a board*

Advantages	Disadvantages
Provides the board additional insight into the operation and performance of the organisation, especially when the organisation is complex	CEO succession planning may, in fact, not be aided by adding multiple executive directors to the board, in some cases identifying the lead internal candidate to be the CEO's successor may not always be clear-cut
A large executive team, on the board helps to ensure the "CEO is honest" – less danger of telling one thing to the NEDs and another to the executive management team	And what of those senior managers who are not promoted to the board? Selecting some individuals for a board seat while not affording the same preferment to colleagues
	with roughly equal responsibilities can be divisive. To avoid being forced to choose favourites, many organisations have opted to restrict executive board seats to the chief executive and finance director

Advantages	Disadvantages
Widening the pool of executive directors can be valuable professional development and supports succession planning and the retention	Appointing a large group of executive directors can also prompt an "us versus them" culture, with executives and non-executives lined up on either side of the boardroom table. An executive team that thinks and speaks "en bloc" is hardly conducive to good debate.
A board seat is also valuable from the perspective of the individual executive. It confers prestige and prominence and enhances the possibility of an external NED appointment, which makes for a more "rounded" executive director	Executive directors who join the board may also find it is difficult to be critical of other colleagues and their divisions. A reluctance to "stick your nose in to the day job of your executive colleagues"
A broader range of executive directors on the board can allow the NEDs an insight to behaviours and body language to reveal any tensions within the management team	A reluctance for NEDs to robustly challenge the CEO in front of other executive colleagues for fear of undermining them
Whether joining for board dinners, presenting regularly to the board, or merely observing board or committee meetings, senior managers can gain plentiful executive development and "board readiness" without necessarily having a formal seat at the table.	Although larger executive teams can provide the board with greater coverage of different divisions within the organisation, there comes a point when larger boards can suffer from coordination and communication problems and board effectiveness may decline.

For those organisations that prefer to keep the number of executive directors at board meetings to a minimum, an essential counterbalance is to ensure the chair and non-executive directors are in regular contact with those senior managers who do not serve on the board or attend board meetings.

It is very important to not overlook training for executive board directors, some organisations choose to do this "in-house" albeit external training where executive directors can learn away from the rest of the board and instead surrounded by other directors from a variety of organisations and sectors.

EMPLOYEE DIRECTORS

There has been debate, including at UK Government level, around how organisations might give greater representation to the "employee voice" in board decisions. This debate has centred around private sector companies, in particular those which are publicly listed. One way to aim for employee interests to be represented to and properly considered by boards is the addition of "employee directors" sometimes referred to as "worker directors". Employee or worker directors are either selected by the management of the organisations or elected by the workforce (possibly all those employed in an organisation or all those in a trades union). Some publicly listed companies such as FirstGroup plc have appointed an employee director as have many NHS boards as well as university courts, and it is a requirement of any employee-owned company too. In some private sector organisations these appointments may be considered to be executive board roles, while in some public sector organisations they are considered to be non-executive directors. Part of the rationale for such appointments is the potential for employee directors to help provide a fresh perspective on decision making as well as providing a better link between the board and the workforce; however, they are under the same legal duties as all other directors.

The law firm Pinsent Masons (What to consider if appointing employees to boards in the UK, Aug. 2020) points to issues around conflicts of interest and issues of confidentiality may prove more complex in the worker director context.

One has to be vigilant for any assumptions by the employee director themselves, or the rest of the board, that the employee director is in place to only represent, company law would not agree. The employee director holds the same legal, fiduciary, and moral responsibilities to act in the interests of all stakeholders (and shareholders, if applicable) as any other board director would be expected to do. Pinsent Masons suggest that "This level of responsibility, despite the seemingly focussed nature of the role, is one of the most often suggested difficulties of appointing a worker director".

Appropriate training and ensuring individuals understand the serious obligations to the organisation as a whole, not just to the employees, are vital factors in a successful appointment of an employee or worker director. Of course, once a prospective employee director understands the potential personal liabilities they are exposed to, they may be reluctant to join the board. In the case of an organisation running into difficulties, it is worth noting that section 1157 of the Companies Act 2006, provides the courts power to excuse a director from all or part of any liability for any breach of duty if they have acted honestly and reasonably, and having regard to all the circumstances of the case they ought fairly to be excused. However, this is not a straightforward issue and would require an individual being able to demonstrate to the court that such relief was appropriate, that they had acted honestly and reasonably, and that may not be easy to do if a serious situation has arisen. Being appointed to a board, even with the best intentions of providing representation for employees can bring about unforeseen potential liabilities, which may prove very off-putting to the individual employee director.

There are also some practical considerations that a board should consider, once it has decided to appoint an employee director, Pinsent Masons (What to consider if appointing employees to boards in the UK, Aug. 2020) suggest the following are important decisions to be made:

- Selection and eligibility criteria – what qualifications and/ or experience for the role, if any, must the candidate have? Will they be appointed or elected, and by whom? How many worker directors will be appointed? In large organisations, how will the board identify candidates that represent all workers, including those overseas, or a sufficiently wide cross-section? If unionised, what role will the union and its representatives play?
- Preparedness and support – how will a worker, particularly if inexperienced, be prepared for a board role? There should be the offer of training, but boards will need to consider additional assistance – the use of mentors, perhaps, or external support. What role should the company secretary play?
- Right to time-off for board duties – a board position is a serious and often time-consuming role. How long should worker directors be required to commit to the role? How long should they have to prepare for and attend each board meeting outside of their "day" job?
- Compensation – if appropriate, should the employee director receive remuneration for the role? If so, what would be appropriate?
- Consulting with colleagues – how will this take place? Are there pre-existing forums and bodies that a worker director can engage with? Are terms of reference required? How will the board assure themselves that the worker director remains "of the workers" rather than "of management", such that their input remains valuable?

CHALLENGES FACED BY EXECUTIVE BOARD DIRECTORS

Without doubt, the vast majority of boards have the best interests of the organisation at heart in their deliberations and decisions.

Regrettably, that alone fails to ensure good governance. Human factors and frailties inevitably impinge on the dynamics of the board, impeding its ability to act for the good of the organisation at all times.

A board can have an impassioned CEO and sales director who are both absolutely convinced that their new product is truly exceptional the "new sliced bread". Totally driven and utterly wedded to the notion that their sales are set to rocket, they demand marketing budgets and promotional activities be increased and increased again in the face of disappointing sales figures, and the board want to support their colleagues, sharing their optimism and not wanting to question nor doubt their efforts. Over time, however, this can lead to unsustainable pressures on working capital, rendering insolvent trading a harsh reality. The board, while trying to be supportive and entrepreneurial has failed, as sadly, has the company.

One such dynamic is *Groupthink* in which like-minded individuals all carry the same cognitive biases, blithely unaware of its impact on the team's working. The propensity for teams to suffer from this is exactly why the selection of independent and diverse non-executives is critical to high-functioning boards. But groupthink also can affect the executive management team's decision-making process. With commercial pressures, deadlines, and budgets driving the executive team's decisions on a daily or hourly basis, the ability of someone to step back and see the bigger picture, including risk, compliance, reputation, and long-term impact, is critical to the organisation's success. Typically, this falls to those free of executive responsibility.

LEARNING POINT

A new executive director was appointed to the UK Management Board of a major international technology company. Bonuses for senior employees, who were not board members, were discussed. The new member of this board noted that a senior sales executive was to be awarded a large bonus; however, this individual was

---

highly rated due to being very adept at political navigation within the organisation, rather than actually producing good results, he was also highly disruptive and did not promote positive working relationships with colleagues. As the rest of the Board did not raise any issues, the new executive board member felt himself to be a lone voice and said nothing. The following year, the same executive bonus scheme was discussed, and the same disruptive individual was in line for another large bonus. This time the executive board member felt morally compelled to raise his concerns, as soon as he did so, other executive board members commented that they had the same concerns and a useful discussion ensued with a better decision made.

Speaking up and voicing concerns takes courage, especially when a board member suspects that they are a lone voice, or there is a concern around raising an unpopular issue. This, of course, is a duty, once you join a board and it is often the case that others have similar concerns to you, it is a matter of sometimes being the first to bring up the "elephant in the room".

Another common director behaviour that can easily undermine good governance is the failure to observe the boundaries between executive and non-executive responsibilities. Typically, this manifests as undue interest by the board in *how* a strategic objective will be implemented. The words of Second World War General Patton (.com, n.d.) ring true here:

Don't tell people how to do things, tell them what to do and let them surprise you with their results.

Not only is this good governance, but it is also good leadership and good management. The executive *owns* the task in hand; the board owns the objective. In this respect, the board is now the driver of our afore-mentioned car and inputs the destination into the Satnav. The Satnav, like the executive, determines the best path to take and can adapt to local conditions.

As clear as this may be on paper, it can prove intensely difficult for enthusiastic directors with subject matter expertise and experience to eschew the how, and stick to the what. The chair needs to be particularly vigilant in her defence of this boundary.

LEARNING POINT

The CEO was also the founder and majority shareholder of a technical components company, which he grew to a £20m turnover business. He appointed a number of executive and non-executive directors to the Board but dominated every meeting and promptly removed (as was his right as a shareholder) any directors who asked too many questions or suggested ideas that were not his. Executive directors, in particular learned quickly to be quiet, and the best ones became rapidly disengaged and left the Company.

It takes a very insightful founder (and majority shareholder) to appoint a board, and then accept the constructive challenge that makes for good governance.

Common challenges faced by the executive board team as highlighted by the HR Consultancy People Space (The People Space, 2017) can be summarised as shown in Table 5.2.

It is too easy to see the problems of the board in terms of the lack of ability or simply pathology of the individual members. There are many examples in all sectors of very talented and dedicated executive directors, albeit there are cases of directors who make it to board level with remarkably mediocre ability. Others have exploited their particular personal pathology such as narcissism or paranoia to rise in the organisation. But it is to be hoped they remain in the minority, though in some organisations, this is far from clear.

Table 5.2 Summary of challenges faced by executive board members and possible solutions

Challenge	Description	Solution
Bloated Membership	Too many executive team members wanting to be "in the top team". It is seen as a "sexy, well-paid and a job with power".	The board needs to be clear about who is on the board and why. Setting an optimal number and a clear policy will help.
Blind Ambition	Yearn for the top job; "head honcho". They see their career clocks ticking and feel the urge for the money, power, and prestige of the CEO.	Clear succession planning and an open, explicit and apparently fair selection process.
Conspiracy of Silence	Coping with difficult or emotive issues by not mentioning or ignoring them.	One way to stop groups conspiring to be silent is to help them put the issues on the table. It is an issue of EQ not IQ and an area that talented NEDs can add huge value to the board.
Resisting Centrifugal Forces	Board members heading off in different directions. Their values and priorities can soon lead to the executive team losing its cohesiveness and focus. This is most frequently the problem where individuals have difficulty delegating.	Effective delegation should liberate board members to concentrate on strategy and the vision. Encouraging uniformity of approach and focus in the executive team and regularly looking at board alignment helps.
Ambiguity of Roles	This is not unique to top teams but can be very destructive. Executive team members are answerable to many different constituencies, which presents challenges.	The board as a whole need to specify very clearly how the group is to make decisions and what those decisions are about. What is, and is not, in the executive board member remit. And once clarified, stick to it.

Challenge	Description	Solution
"Hobby Horses"	The boardroom is an ideal place, some believe, to promote personal causes; to ride hobby horses. An opportunity to have important and powerful people pay attention to their personal issues is too attractive in opportunity to miss for some directors. There is a danger of agendas which can highjack board meetings for hours!	Having a clear agenda and sticking to it. Boards need to be told on a regular basis what they are there for, and what is not relevant.

The People Space. (2017). Six problems of executive teams and how to deal with them. [online] Available at: https://www.thepeoplespace.com/ideas/articles/six-problems-executive-teams-and-how-deal-them

It is the role of the chair as well as the entire board to get the best out of the entire board through optimum membership; appropriate control and openness; ensuring all members are focussed; with clarity of role and a joint agenda. Sounds easier said than done, and requires a high level of emotional intelligence (EQ) with a distinct lack of self-importance, the essential ingredients to ensure successful board functioning.

EXECUTIVE BOARD DIRECTORS IN DIFFERENT SECTORS (PRIVATE, PUBLIC, AND CHARITY/VOLUNTARY) – SOME PRACTICALITIES

While many of the practical implications, for executive board directors, may be similar in nature between types, size, and

CHRIS PEARSE ET AL.

sector of the organisation they work for and serve on the boards of, there are also some nuanced differences between the private, public, and charity/voluntary sectors.

The sheer range of types of organisations that the private sector comprises of, mean that there are some differences in practical implications for executive directors, depending on the type of organisation. While large publicly listed companies have a formal approach to the appointment of executive board directors, a different approach might be taken in privately owned organisations. In private sector organisations, the shareholders (or members in companies limited by guarantee) have the right to appoint and remove executive board directors; in some privately owned organisations, all or some of the executive management team are also the shareholders. While considered not to be good practice in many organisations, the situation does arise in private companies and in partnerships that one of more of the executive directors decide on the selection and appointment of the entire board of directors; this includes all executive board directors and even the non-executive board members. This proves an interesting conundrum. Yes, it is an opportunity to plug a gap of knowledge, skills, and context around the board table and yes, it is a further opportunity either to replicate some prior success in candidate choice or, indeed, avoid hitherto pitfalls. However, do you really want the future colleague who is so much more knowledgeable than you in a particular area, or someone who is an acknowledged board disruptor in terms of thought chain or who has a ferocious reputation for holding boards to account?

Alternatively, you could choose the seemingly much easier option in the form of another candidate who still has the market knowledge and governance experience, but seems much more gentle, easy going, and acquiescing in nature. The correct choice much depends on the particular board fit and culture, but just as many of the successful football managers can be described as robust characters, taking the easy option is not necessarily the best option in terms of what will stretch the executive team, board, and subsequent organisation.

LEARNING POINT

During a period of difficult trading, the finance director of a global advertising and marketing group of companies – promoted and appointed to the board the previous year – was asked to estimate the number of redundancies required to achieve a cost-saving to bring the group back into profit. She performed this task with ease but when asked to take on her share of the cuts, she fought tooth and nail to protect her department from sacrifices she saw as being wholly the responsibility of the fee-earning side of the business. The rest of the board had decided, unanimously, that every department was to share the redundancies, regardless of their perceived culpability in the diminishing fortunes of the business. During conversations with the CEO and chair, it became apparent that the FD had developed very close personal relationships with staff that she knew would be in the firing line. Eventually, the FD acquiesced, realising that her stance had become untenable and a career-limiting liability. Executives promoted to the Board need to understand that the new role carries a legal, moral, and fiduciary duty to put the interests of the organisation first, before those of the executive's division or department.

The transition to executive director requires a shift in responsibility that even the most competent executive can find challenging. Boards should not take this for granted and provide appropriate training and support.

Measuring the performance of executive directors in the private sector varies between types of organisations in the sector. Executive directors in publicly listed companies and some larger non-listed companies are measured, and rewarded based on earnings per share (EPS) and total shareholder return (TSR). The High Pay Centre (MinuteWorks, 2015) published a report in 2015 suggesting that there is "evident mis-alignment over the long-term between pay based on these measures and actual corporate performance". The report highlights a number of issues, first that companies apparently see no issue with the use of the same financial metrics to measure both short and long-term performance, and second, the preference for relative measures (e.g. a % growth in EPS relative to competitors) rather than absolute measures, which the report argues "puts further strain on the already tenuous link between an individual's contribution to corporate performance and the proportion of shareholder funds which are used to reward that individual".

The role fulfilled by executive board directors, especially in publicly listed companies, is challenging; they are expected to execute their core duties while, as the Harvard Law School Forum on Corporate Governance (Couvelier, Rossman and Pitcher, 2019) highlighted,

> juggling a cacophony of often competing voices: activist investors; increasingly vocal shareholders owners; index and pension funds wielding the power of their vote; shareholders demanding action on environmental, social and governance issues; employees and unions; local and national political leaders; social media; and of course management itself.

Executive board directors also face the issue to having a legal responsibility of the long-term sustainability of the organisation, while also being under pressure to produce quarterly or half yearly results for shareholders. This often-competing pressure between focussing on short-term as opposed to longer-term success is one of the reasons that some executive board directors prefer roles in other organisations in the private sector. Privately owned, family-owned, and mutual organisations tend to use different measure of performance, success and with some exceptions tend to take a much longer-term strategic view than their public-listed counterparts. For example, mutually owned organisations, such as building societies and friendly insurance societies, may not remunerate the executive management team at the same levels of publicly listed companies; however, the opportunity to lead organisations where stakeholder interests are especially well aligned (members, management, employees) where success is measured over many years, is very attractive to many executive directors.

In a similar vein to many plc and private sector boards, public sector organisations, such as the NHS, also include a number of executive directors as full board members and often invite executive directors, who are not board members to attend board meetings. This shift in the balance of power vis-à-vis charity/voluntary sector and company boards resolves the challenge of underrepresentation but brings others in its train.

Executive board directors in the public sector are generally measured against a set of outcomes These outcome-based initiatives encourage executive board members, and the wider board, to think things through and connect their actions to specific results. Equally, in the public sector, there appears to be a greater emphasis on innovation and creativity, although this requires an appetite for risk and it could be argued that public sector, is generally known for being extremely risk-averse in approach. The challenge for executive board directors and the wider executive management team (EMT) is based around risk-taking in an environment that is perceived as being less tolerant of mistakes. Public services are, quite understandably open to public scrutiny, often via the media and are often highly regulated. At the same time, it is understandable that any executive board member would not wish to be the "face" of an initiative that did not go well and find themselves under detailed media or ministerial scrutiny. On the other hand, being considered to lack initiative is not career enhancing either so knowing how to achieve the right balance, when operating to a high degree of public scrutiny takes time and a degree of resilience. Building resilience is an important factor for leaders in the public sector, especially when striving to meet the expectations of politicians and the public while overseeing often large teams of employees and not "burning out" themselves. Developing relationships and keeping the lines of communication open with all the various stakeholders while not having the same levers at their disposal the colleagues in other sectors have (e.g. no compulsory redundancy policies) can produce a level of stress that is unique to public sector executive directors.

It is also worth noting that, while other sectors might be influenced by the policy of the government of the time, for executive directors in the public sector, it can be argued this has the greatest influence. It impacts on the strategy of the organisation, standards and key performance indicators (KPIs) that the organisation, and executive management team, is measured and monitored against. This means that the strategic direction that the executive board directors can decide on, is subject to the policy and strategic objectives of the government of the time. Often this limitation is accompanied by high levels of regulatory oversight, and differences in areas such as legal structure and a non-profit-making focus. It is also important to note that the levels of remuneration/reward/bonus, for executive board directors, can be different in the public sector in contrast to both the private and charity/voluntary sectors, and this may also go some way to explain why cross-sector moves by senior executive directors into or out of the public sector are not particularly common. One criticism that is levied at executive directors in the public sector there is a lack of cross fertilisation of knowledge between leaders in the public sector and those in other sectors. There is a tendency for executive directors to seek out others in similar positions in other public bodies as a first step when seeking to learn from others, albeit there are initiatives which seek to build closer mentoring relationships between leaders in the public sector and those in the charity/voluntary sector.

In the Charity/voluntary sector, it could be suggested that executive directors/the executive management team (EMT) operates in a more complex and challenging environment than those of private and public sector organisations, especially as it is common for executive directors not to be appointed to the board. In a commercial organisation, the focus – rightly or wrongly – can be brought back to financial matters to restore common purpose, while a public body may be guided by government/ministerial policy. With a charity/voluntary sector organisation, the executive management team may find themselves working with a board whose motivations and aspirations may be incompatibly diverse, and not always financially motivated. This presents an interesting path for the EMT/leadership team to navigate. In many charity organisations, only the non-executives or trustees are appointed to the governing board, with the CEO or MD attending meetings as a matter of course, but without a vote and potentially, with minimal influence. This can easily disempower and disenfranchise not just the CEO but the entire EMT, unless the chair is adept at including the CEO at every relevant juncture. While this position is partly historical, in that charity organisations were traditionally set up as charitable trusts in the 18th, 19th, and 20th centuries and required independent (non-staff) trustees for all decision-making, it is worth noting that Regulatory bodies such as the Charity Commission have been concerned about the potential conflicts of interest that can arise from executive team members of a charity holding a position on the board. One example cited is in the event of a charity board considering a merger, those board members who are employees, such as the CEO, might not act in the best interest of the charity if their job was at risk. There is, however, an argument (Wilkinson, 2016) the CEO and even the whole senior management team should be board members too. The inclusion of executive directors has the potential benefit of bringing the added viewpoints of those working in the organisation and add to the boardroom debate.

There is an increasing viewpoint that the result of making senior management/executive director members of the board, the result could be a stronger, better governed sector that is more focussed on strategy and risk which, in turn, leads to more efficient, accountable, and resilient organisations. Where executive team members are not members of the board, shared ownership of the strategy needs to be recognised as a key to executive team engagement and performance and with no formal board representation, it becomes especially important to maintain a healthy relationship between board/trustees and the executive team, by the governing board regularly reminding itself of the need for mutual consideration and respect.

Attracting and retaining executive directors, especially in the CEO role, can be particularly challenging in the charity/voluntary sector. With competition from both the private and public sectors, it can be difficult for organisations in the sector to stand out. At the same time, remuneration packages paid to the executive management team in sector continue to be under intense scrutiny, perhaps more so than in the private and public sectors. Writing for the Guardian newspaper in 2017 Toby Porter (Porter, 2017) touches on a number of issues in the sector namely, some erosion of public trust, especially is some of the largest charities and those with international operations. He points to the continued argument used by the largest in the sector that "the complexity of the role, [...] compels them to offer salaries that attract the kind of CEO candidates that their organisations and missions demand"; however, he suggests that this appears not to be going down well with much of the public, whose support it vital for these organisations to retain. Porter recommends that boards and the executive management team think very carefully about setting remunerations levels and think carefully about the balance between attracting suitable talent and how the reputation of the organisation and the credibility of mission and aims be impacted.

LEARNING POINT

In January 2017 Oxfam published a pre-Davos report on global inequality, which considered high levels of global remuneration in the private sector. There was an immediate social media backlash when it was pointed out that one of the organisation's US executive directors had been awarded a remuneration package of $500,000 – unsurprisingly the word "hypocrites" was levelled against the organisation.

There is no easy answer, as executive pay is under increased scrutiny in every sector; however, in the charity/voluntary sector the topic has to be approached with great sensitivity.

NEWLY APPOINTED EXECUTIVE BOARD DIRECTORS

Being appointed to or promoted to an executive board position, for the first time can present the appointee with a number of interesting issues that not all are initially equipped to deal with. The shift in perspective required, together with the need to discriminate clinically between managing and governing the organisation, does not come easily to every executive director.

In this respect, NEDs have an advantage: they are simply not required to involve themselves in operational matters. Executive board directors, on the other hand, need to be able to dip in and out of their divisional or departmental responsibilities maintaining the split personality of governor and manager.

First and foremost, every executive board director needs to be crystal clear on the boundaries between governance and operational management, which equate to those between setting strategic objectives, and the execution of plans to achieve them.

Many new executive board directors may have decades of operational experience which, quite suddenly, has to be put to one side in favour of the much broader, collective remit of the board. Abandoning ownership of a prior role can prove tough for those who identify with their previous successes.

LEARNING POINT

The newly appointed engineering director to the board of a food and drink manufacturer had been instrumental in adopting highly innovative technology for the bottling plant that he was responsible for. Under no illusion that this success had helped him onto the board, he proceeded to find every opportunity to demonstrate how his wins were transferable to some of the food lines, which he

---

deemed outdated and inefficient. Eventually he was approached by the chair and asked to keep his valuable insights on operational efficiencies for meetings with the executive team, not the board of directors. The chair also took the opportunity to educate him on his new remit and where the boundaries lay. The director took the instruction well and is now a valued member of the board.

The ability to shift perspective – literally change your point of view – should never be underestimated. For some directors it comes naturally, for others it has be learnt and for the unfortunate minority it is never mastered.

THE BOARD AND EXECUTIVE DIRECTOR TEAM DYNAMICS

Relationships between board members are frequently given little consideration and their impact underestimated. When they work, they are taken for granted and remain barely visible. When they become dysfunctional, they can bring the effectiveness of the board, to a grinding halt.

The single most influential of all these relationships is that between the chair and the CEO. The chair has more influence over the shape of the board and its strategy than any other individual. The CEO has more influence over the execution of that strategy than anyone else. The nature of their rapport is therefore critical to the success of the enterprise.

When chairs and CEOs fail to maintain mutual respect, the relationship between board and executive can easily become adversarial – two silos competing for power. The solution frequently appears binary: either chair or CEO has to go – maybe both. Often, the chair has the upper hand in the struggle but not always, as both are appointed or removed, by shareholders. In a public sector body, there may be a single shareholder, namely, a government minister and just as such board appointments are known as ministerial appointments, ministers have been known to remove an entire board and replace it with another where the behaviour has been deemed to go against government policy of a code of governance.

A third option for resolving chair-CEO conflict can and does work. Conflict resolution (or management), when properly applied, can train either or both parties to understand the dynamics of conflict and how to transcend the antagonism regardless of the details of the dispute. Depersonalising conflict is the only sure-fire way of resolving it. However, it is important to note that not everyone is either willing or capable of undergoing the necessary shifts in understanding and perspective to benefit from this kind of personal development. In this case, the binary options are best implemented before the fallout manifests beyond the boardroom.

The optimal balance between chair and CEO therefore is one of mutual, healthy respect, a bit like a marriage or civil partnership, that is, one where challenge can prevail without either party feeling "insulted" that their view has been questioned or refuted yet simultaneously free to share vulnerabilities and concerns without fear of rebuke.

Many boards content themselves with the notion that a close, friendly relationship between chair and CEO is the desirable alternative to that described above. But close relationships can also be just as damaging to the organisation as antagonistic ones, and sometimes more so due to their invisibility. With the chair setting the agenda for the board, and the CEO responsible for its enactment, this axis of power can effectively subjugate or at least bend the collective, democratic will of the board to its own. And there need not be any nefarious intent either, simply a "we know best for the good of the organisation" attitude between them.

It is not uncommon for the executive directors on the board to feel restrained by the deliberations of the non-execs. Rather like the relationship between upper and lower houses in a democratic legislature, executive directors can perceive their non-executive colleagues as being somewhat reactionary and regressive. Differences in age can play into this: executive directors are not necessarily, but likely to be younger than their non-executive counterparts. This age factor is difficult to avoid when NEDs are often required to have already gained senior executive experience.

The value-adding NED appreciates that they have one mouth and two ears as a ratio for good reason and often with more NED's than executives around a board table, the NED must learn to ration their input. That said, woe betide the executive who "rocks" up to a board meeting, thinking they can "wing it" without having given due preparation beforehand. Board packs can be large and full of financial detail and the "driven" executive may feel that their strengths and benefit of focus lie elsewhere. However, sticking with our sporting analogy, the winning team is those who are credible, supporting, thinking, linking, encouraging, and anticipating every pass and opponent on and off the ball.

The caution and due diligence displayed by NEDs may prove frustrating to CEOs and FDs but is in reality a healthy reflection of the fact that they are just as accountable as any executive director, while lacking the direct command and control that only the executive team can wield. Imagine the CEO at the wheel of a powerful vehicle with the FD sat next her, navigating. They are going off-road as fast as they feel safe to do so. The rest of the board are sitting on the back seat. Some of them are nervous as they have driven this way before and believe they know the road, they warn of accident hot-spots ahead and recommend either slowing down a little or even an alternative route, but ultimately it is the CEO who has their foot on the accelerator.

It is also important to be mindful that executive board members have a working relationship with each other outside of the boardroom and that with the CEO present, those executive board members who have a reporting line to him/her may feel constrained in what they say at board meetings.

Differing team dynamics between members of the executive team themselves, is another area that the whole board should be sensitive to, especially if some members are on the main board and others are not.

For any organisation to function well, in addition to effective board dynamics, a cohesive executive management (EMT) team is also vital. Having a well "knitted together" EMT who work positively as a team can be disrupted by the fact that some members are also members of the board and others are not. We have touched on the idea that non-board members might attend board meetings, if could be unwieldy to accommodate the entire EMT, a solution could be to invite attendance on a rotational basis; however, there are likely to be certain sensitive discussions that only actual board members should be party to.

Equally, board members, especially the NEDs, and chair should be sensitive to occasional divisive behaviour whereby an executive board member uses boardroom discussions as an opportunity to "settle scores" with non-board member colleagues. Navigating this sensitively and with a good dose of emotional intelligence is the key to rewarding and positive boardroom relationships where each executive and non-executive director "plays their part" effectively.

KEY MESSAGES

- Formal executive board director status brings statutory responsibility regardless of title.
- Knowing when to talk and when to listen can help you find your voice and to influence, especially if newly appointed to the board.
- Board relationships are critical with the whole board but especially that of chair and CEO.

- Many executive board directors and CEOs are promoted from within the organisation, so mentoring and preparing your successors is also an important part of your role.
- Serving on a board with an organisation-wide mindset and avoiding "hobby horses" makes executive directors a valuable asset to any board, as they bring insight into the operation and performance of the organisation, especially when the organisation is complex.

FURTHER READING

https://www.boardeffect.com/blog/role-executive-director-board-management
https://insights.diligent.com/executive-director-non-executive-
    director#:~:text=An%20executive%20director%20is%20a, executive%20
    or%20a%20board%20member.

REFERENCES

Couvelier, C., Rossman, J. and Pitcher, Q. (2019). Under pressure: Directors in an era of shareholder primacy. [online] The Harvard Law School Forum on Corporate Governance. Available at: https://corpgov.law.harvard. edu/2019/07/23/under-pressure-directors-in-an-era-of-shareholder-primacy/ [Accessed 3 May 2021].

GOV.UK. (n.d.). Being a company director. [online] Available at: https://www. gov.uk/guidance/being-a-company-director.

Janke, K., Propper, C. and Sadun, R. (2020). The impact of CEOs in the public sector: Evidence from the English NHS. [online] VoxEU.org. Available at: https://voxeu.org/article/impact-ceos-public-sector [Accessed 8 Apr. 2021].

MinuteWorks. (2015). The metrics re-loaded: Examining executive remuneration performance measures High Pay Centre. [online] High Pay Centre. Available at: http://highpaycentre.org/pubs/the-metrics-re-loaded-examining-executive-remuneration-performance-measures [Accessed 3 May 2021].

Porter, T. (2017). When it comes to salaries, charity CEOs still want to have their cake and eat it. [online] The Guardian. Available at: https://www.theguardian.com/voluntary-sector-network/2017/jan/20/salaries-charity-ceos-criticism-marketing-supporters [Accessed 3 May 2021].

Sepah, D.C. (2018). Your company culture is who you hire, fire, and promote. [online] Medium. Available at: https://medium.com/s/company-culture/your-companys-culture-is-who-you-hire-fire-and-promote-c69f84902983#:~:text=The%20actual%20company%20values%2C%20as [Accessed 23 Mar. 2021].

The Curious Role of the Executive Director. (n.d.). [online]. Available at: https://www.odgersberndtson.com/media/2264/the_curious_role_of_the_executive_director_board_paper_revised_sept2013.pdf [Accessed 28 Apr. 2021].

The People Space. (2017). Six problems of executive teams and how to deal with them. [online] Available at: https://www.thepeoplespace.com/ideas/articles/six-problems-executive-teams-and-how-deal-them [Accessed 2 Apr. 2021].

What to Consider if Appointing Employees to Boards in the UK. (Aug. 2020). Pinsent Masons. [online] Available at: https://www.pinsentmasons.com/out-law/analysis/what-to-consider-appointing-employees-boards-in-the-uk [Accessed 28 Apr. 2021].

Wilkinson, H. (2016). Charity chief executives should be on the board of trustees. [online] The Guardian. Available at: https://www.theguardian.com/voluntary-sector-network/2016/apr/19/charity-chief-executives-board-trustees [Accessed 25 Apr. 2021].

www.goodreads.com. (n.d.). A quote by George S. Patton Jr. [online] Available at: https://www.goodreads.com/quotes/15381-don-t-tell-people-how-to-do-things-tell-them-what. [Accessed 20 Jan. 2021].

www.nacdonline.org. (n.d.). 2015–2016 NACD Public Company Governance Survey. [online] Available at: https://www.nacdonline.org/insights/publications.cfm?ItemNumber=19733 [Accessed 21 Apr. 2021].

CHAPTER SIX

Role of the Company Secretary

Sheelagh Duffield and Gayle Watson

DOI: 10.4324/9781003142850-6

INTRODUCTION

It can be argued that in larger organisations, the person in the board room who should know most about the organisation's governance is the company secretary. In some organisations this role is referred to as the board secretary, the clerk to the board, or charity secretary. In this chapter we will use company secretary but these other terms are inter-changeable. Whether dealing with internal processes and procedures or external legal or regulatory requirements, the company secretary fulfils an important role as the governance expert in the board room. It is widely recognised in every chapter of this book that the importance of good governance and the requirements for organisations to demonstrate good governance has increased greatly over the years. As the profile of good governance has grown, so too has the responsibility of the company secretary to advise the board on a wide range of governance matters. Some of this role is about knowledge sharing and guidance around regulatory matters but, performed well, the role can, in many varied ways, make a large contribution to the board's effectiveness. The approach to appointing a company secretary differs between sizes and types of organisation and there can be a level of misunderstanding of the role. This chapter will explore the various aspects of the role in different types of organisations and highlight why the company secretary has the potential to be the board's respected "governance adviser" and an important asset to the board.

COMPANY SECRETARY – MAIN DUTIES

The task list of the company secretary is a long one. Some tasks appear quite administrative where others are highly complex. In certain types of organisations, it is undoubtedly a demanding and responsible role.

In the private sector, only publicly listed companies need be concerned with UK Listing Authority Requirements and companies with no share capital (e.g. companies limited by guarantee) will have no share and capital requirements, although communication with members is the same as shareholder communication. It is worth remembering that many charity/voluntary sector organisations and some public sector bodies are set up as companies limited by guarantee and therefore communications with members is an important role fulfilled by the board/company secretary. Depending on the size and nature of the organisation, Report and Accounts requirements will differ but the following task list may be recognised by many across a wide range of organisations.

The Institute of Chartered Secretaries and Administrators (ICSA) Guidance Note: The Duties and Reporting Lines of the Company Secretary (www.icsa.org.uk, 2013)

- Board meetings.
- General meetings.
- Articles of Association.
- UK Listing Authority requirements.
- Statutory registers.
- Statutory returns.
- Directors' duties and transactions.
- Corporate governance advice.
- Report and accounts.
- Share registration and shareholder monitoring.
- Share and capital issues and restructuring (including mergers, acquisitions, and disposals).
- Maintenance of share capital and distributions.
- Compliance with corporate governance codes and other financial and legal regulations.
- Management of stakeholder administration and communication.

In the public sector, even though there are no share capital matters and the governance documents are called standing orders, the role of the board secretary or clerk is not dissimilar to the list provided above, the responsibilities of the clerk of the governing body include:

- convene meetings of the governing body;
- attend meetings of the governing body and ensure minutes of the proceedings are produced;
- maintain a register of members of the governing body and report any vacancies to the governing body;
- maintain a register of governors' attendance at meetings and report on non-attendance of meetings;
- give and receive notices in accordance with:
  - notification of vacancies and appointments;
  - resignation;
  - removal of board member; and
  - notification of disqualification.
- report to the governing body as required on the discharge of his or her functions; and
- perform such other functions as may be determined by the governing body from time to time.

Charity/voluntary organisation Company Secretaries also play a key role in providing support for trustees. Karl Wilding, director of public policy and volunteering at the National Council for Voluntary Organisations (NCVO), notes: *"Charity trustees are more aware than ever that good organisations need good governance."* The NCVO Know-how report (Davis, n.d.) suggests that the key figure in a UK charity or non-profit is the Charity Secretary. Trustees might depend on the Charity Secretary to assure compliance. The person occupying the role of Charity Secretary is expected to have a good understanding of both charity and company law, along with a solid grounding in other relevant legislation, such as employment law, health and safety law, among others.

THE NEED FOR QUALIFICATIONS FOR THE COMPANY SECRETARY

There is a requirement in the Companies Act 2006 for a public company to have a company secretary but no such requirement exists for private companies and many other bodies. Some public sector organisations specify a requirement for a board secretary; clerk to the board or governance officer, which are often found in further education college institutions.

Governance codes, directed at publicly listed companies that offer securities to the public, refer to the responsibilities of the company secretary, but many other governance codes tend not to mention the role, although governance codes for the college sector do. It is common for companies across all sectors to place importance on the role of the secretary and an organisation's governing documents may state the need for a secretary of the organisation.

In the private sector, the directors of a public company must take all reasonable steps to ensure that the company secretary has the requisite knowledge and experience to discharge the functions and is appropriately qualified. Qualifications listed in the Companies Act include barristers, advocates or solicitors admitted in any part of the UK; chartered accountants and chartered secretaries and a wider discretion to consider a person who, by virtue of another qualification or position, has demonstrated that he or she is capable of the role.

The Companies Act also imposes obligations on companies regarding the conduct of their affairs. Responsibility for ensuring compliance with these matters ultimately rests with the directors. However, the company secretary is an officer of the company and if directors appoint a company secretary, they rely on that person for these functions. Most of these requirements are backed up by criminal sanctions so that, in the event of a breach, the company and every officer of it who is in default is liable to a fine and, in some cases, imprisonment. In addition, the company secretary, as an officer and agent of the company, owes fiduciary duties to the company. The company secretary therefore has similar duties to directors as fiduciary duties include the need to act in good faith in the interests of the organisation; to avoid conflicts of interest; and not to make secret profits from dealings for or on behalf of the organisation.

The need for a company secretary may be dictated in different ways – legally with particular qualifications for publicly listed companies; recommended in governance codes for private companies and some public sector organisations and written into Articles of Association for others. It is undoubtedly a responsible position and many company secretaries seek to ensure that they are qualified or trained to perform the role.

The Chartered Secretary qualification is overseen by the Institute of Chartered Secretaries and Administrators (ICSA): now known as The Chartered Governance Institute and can take up to four years of study to complete, it is equivalent to a post graduate degree. For company secretaries in other organisations, where there is no legal qualification requirement, shorter courses exist, also provided by ICSA as well as by the Institute of Directors (IoD) which is a one-day course. The short courses provided by ICSA are based on study time of between 6 and 24 months and are sector-specific qualifications in financial compliance, corporate law, education, sports, and health service governance. Graduates are eligible to become Affiliated members of ICSA and courses available in the following areas:

- Certificate in Corporate Governance
- Advanced Certificate in Corporate Governance
- Certificate in Employee Share Plans
- Certificate in Company Secretarial Practice and Share Registration Practice
- Certificate in Charity Law and Governance (England and Wales)
- Diploma in Charity Management
- Certificate in Academy Governance

- Certificate in Clerking of School and Governing Boards
- Certificate in Sports Governance
- Health Service Governance (England)

The Chartered Institute of Management Accountants also offer training for Company Secretaries and accountants who have company secretarial duties. The Chartered Institute for Public Finance and Accountancy (CIPFA) also offer short courses for company secretaries exploring the core duties and critical role played by the company secretary to ensure legal and governance compliance.

This level of qualification and training may surprise those who have misunderstood the role as administrative or as "the note taker" – "the coffee maker". These terms belie the importance of a carefully nuanced minute and a comfortable, well organised board meeting and these examples are only two of a broad spectrum of tasks. Some directors who have served on boards where the company secretarial role is viewed and undertaken at an administrative level, are often very surprised when they move to a larger, more regulated organisation and are confronted by a highly qualified individual who is not only a senior executive but also the governance expert in the room.

Those taking on the company secretary role, and their colleagues, should understand that the common thread through all the different types of organisations described above is the need for good governance. It is correct that reliance is placed on the individual or team of people within the corporate secretarial function to support the organisation, and its directors, to comply with legal and regulatory requirements and to work as an effective and efficient board.

THE GOVERNANCE FRAMEWORK

Understanding the functions, roles, and responsibilities of each part of the governance framework is an essential part of good governance. The role of shareholders or members is distinct from the

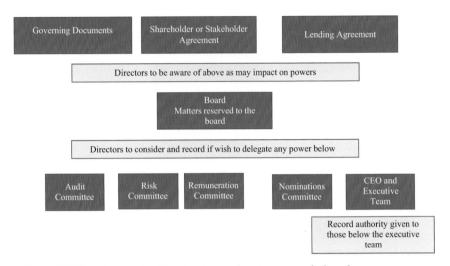

Figure 6.1 Typical example of the structure and main powers of a board.

role of the directors and the job of executive directors and management is different from the function of non-executive directors. Important checks and balances have to be in place to achieve the correct level of accountability but at the same time empowering directors and management to operate the organisation effectively. A typical governance framework showing these roles and responsibilities is given in Figure 6.1.

THE ROLE OF MEMBERS/SHAREHOLDERS

The Company Secretary in each sector plays an important role ensuring that each part of the governance framework is understood. What are the responsibilities of the members and how does the company or organisation report to them? There are formal legal requirements for Annual General Meetings (AGMs) and General Meetings when decisions will be made by members. These apply to public and trading private companies and charities. Public bodies do not hold AGMs as such but will be subject to reviews by key funders who will look at areas such as accountability, performance, and governance arrangements.

In some cases, public bodies have one shareholder in the form of the government (UK or devolved) so will be subject to an annual review by the relevant government minister's office. Mutual organisations such as building societies and co-operative organisations such as credit unions are member-owned and exist for the benefit of members, making AGMs and wider member engagement a very important aspect of their operating models.

There is also a need for directors to have an awareness of views and expectations of members and this will be done in different ways depending on the number and variety of members – more formality with publicly listed companies and less with some private companies. Indeed, the regulation required for publicly listed companies helps to keep the roles of the members and the board distinct, whereas with private companies, where it is more common to find shareholder appointed directors, the formality can often slip requiring the company secretary to diplomatically remind decision makers what is a shareholder matter and what is a board matter and, when it is both, the important order of taking each decision.

LEARNING POINT

Private companies often attract investment at different times, in different ways and at different levels. This can result in complex share capital structures with different classes of shares each with different entitlements. In addition, companies frequently require debt funding and the funder can request control over areas of the business. On a daily basis a company secretary can be referring to articles of association – shareholder agreements and lending agreements – to determine who needs to authorise what and against a back-drop of these matters requiring board approval first. Some shareholders will have nominated directors and some funders may require a director or observer role. This results in multiple relationships and often multiple different views. It is essential for

---

good governance that each role is performed and, for example board decisions, should not be by-passed because a controlling shareholder has final approval. Consider the process for approval of an annual budget that requires approval of a funder and a shareholder:

1. Drafted by management and presented to the board;
2. Considered by the board (including nominee shareholder director and funder appointed observer) with perhaps amendments proposed. All of this captured in board minutes;
3. Considered and approved by funder and shareholder (not as directors but in this different capacity). Negotiations may be required. Final approval should be recorded in some formal way.

It is easy to see how roles can become blurred and the governance framework becomes less effective if each check and consideration of the budget is eroded in the chain of approval. Equally it is easy to see how multiple players in the approval chain could become frustrated if the process is not efficient and well conducted.

THE ROLE OF DIRECTORS

Members or shareholders must not over-step their mark and prevent the board of directors from performing their role. Directors are appointed by members and once appointed have a job to do, albeit that they can also be removed by members if they are unhappy with the director's performance. Equally, directors must respect the requirements of members whether that is a legal, regulatory or contractual requirement.

With the exception of charities, most boards are made up of a mix of executive and non-executive directors. Other chapters in this book cover the important differences between the roles of non-executive and executive directors which is also an important governance balance.

While the chair and other directors have a collective responsibility for defining corporate governance arrangements, they are supported by the company secretary who is the guardian of the governance framework, constantly thinking about the bespoke requirements for the organisation and ensuring that each role is performed effectively and efficiently because every check and balance within the framework delivers another part of good governance. The company secretary should be involved in the induction of all directors and senior management (see more regarding this below) where the description and practical operation of the governance framework should be explained and discussed. From this initial induction colleagues should begin to understand the role of the secretary as "governance adviser" gaining respect for the role and seeing it as facilitating the easy working of the governance framework.

THE GOVERNANCE FACILITATOR

REPORTING LINES AND HAND OFFS

There is a need for the board/company secretary to operate in relation to board matters with independence and always to act in the best interests of the organisation and this is common across all sectors. Directors rely on the secretary to give impartial advice and all directors should have access to that advice. It is therefore important that no director or group of directors has undue influence over the board/company secretary. It is likely to be for this reason that the UK Corporate Governance Code (UKCGC) requires that both the appointment and removal of the company secretary should be a matter for the whole board and this is frequently reflected in the Articles of Association of Public Limited Companies (PLCs) and private companies. While such provisions are less likely to appear in the public sector or charity/voluntary sector organisations, it is important that the board protects the integrity of the board/company secretary to enable the individual to act independently and impartially. If this integrity is not protected, one of the important in-built internal controls available to the company is likely to be seriously undermined.

In practical terms this is not always easy because the secretary cannot report to all the directors but establishing workable reporting lines is a crucial factor for maintaining integrity around this role. It is good governance for the secretary to report to the chair on board matters (www.icsa.org.uk, 2013) but it is likely that the individual will also report to the CEO as a member of senior management team. The remuneration of the company secretary should be a matter for the board or remuneration committee and ensuring that the Chair is involved in performance reviews in some way will help to alleviate risks of the CEO or other executive directors having undue influence over the individual.

In reality, the effective working of all of these different relationships comes down to the behaviour of the company secretary. It is a challenging area demanding good emotional intelligence and the ability to demonstrate a balanced and unbiased approach. There will be times when the chair and CEO do not agree and the board/company secretary "taking sides" with either of them is unlikely to assist. The role as a governance facilitator is brought sharply into focus as the board/company secretary dispassionately sets out the arguments on both sides and draws on other board relationships to reach agreement. The UKCGC requires that a senior independent director (SID) be appointed to the Board and this role is often fulfilled by the vice/deputy chair in public and charity/voluntary sector boards. A strong relationship with the SID or vice/deputy chair is very helpful, as is support from other executive colleagues who "have the ear" of the CEO.

The secretary has both a technical and a relationship management role to play with directors, in the private sector, who have been nominated by shareholders (nominee directors) or observers. In the public and charity/voluntary sectors, observers may include key funders and even members of the public. It is often very helpful to the Chair to receive technical advice which may help to prevent observers acting as directors and thereby assuming director duties and responsibilities. Equally having a clear understanding of the difference between the nominee director's role as "director" and "shareholder" and designing efficient ways to secure shareholder approval when a topic has also been considered at length in the board room.

In the public sector and in some charity/voluntary sector organisations, board meetings may include observers too, in the form of a government representative or representatives of key funders. Many public sector boards are even encouraged to hold board meetings in public unless there is a good reason for them not too. One could argue that a government minister's representative observing a board meeting is less likely to contribute views and therefore less likely to become a de facto director than an observer in an early-stage private sector company.

As a member of the senior management team, within a large or medium-sized organisation, the company secretary is likely to work closely with or have shared responsibilities with many colleagues across the organisation such as corporate affairs, finance, risk, legal, and HR. A strong working relationship with each of these areas is important to facilitate good operation of the governance framework and effective board management.

GUIDING THE BOARD ON DELEGATED AUTHORITY

In every sector, the matters reserved for the board to approve should be clearly set out in the governing documents and, for efficient management and to make best use of the experience of individual directors, board work can be delegated to committees or to the executive team. This delegation needs to be carefully recorded by the board/company secretary either in formal committee terms of reference that have been agreed by the board or in specific board minutes, the extent of the delegated authority requires to be respected with appropriate reporting back to the board.

Board colleagues who are not involved in committees need to trust their colleagues to do the work and report only enough to keep the board sufficiently informed for decision making. Repeating the work of the committee at full board meetings defeats the time saving and value adding purpose of delegation. The company secretary has a key role in the management of these processes, and in providing support and guidance to the board, which are important to ensure directors act within any authority delegated to them. The work of the remuneration and nominations committees can often be sensitive where topics for discussion include performance, remuneration and succession planning of directors and senior management. It is not unusual for the secretary to be the only executive team member in the room for certain parts of these discussions. This requires a high level of professionalism and confidentiality. There is a need to act dispassionately, record conversations appropriately in minutes finding the balance between confidentiality and sharing sufficient information to demonstrate that directors thoroughly considered the correct matters.

LEARNING POINT

It is helpful for organisations to be transparent about procedures and processes around their board work. There should be no reason not to publish this externally on a website (and certain companies are required to) but certainly internally for employees to understand. Formal board and committee terms of reference can often be lengthy documents and it is helpful to publish a summary internally that shows either in a diagram or bullet point list which matters require board approval; which require executive team or CEO approval; the dates of meetings and the timescales for submitting information. Explaining to the roles of formal committees is useful too.

Other board matters will require confidentiality. Executive colleagues know the privileged position of the company secretary, but they may probe and ask questions nonetheless, expecting information to be shared. Particularly with remuneration and nomination committee work, the secretary should take care about what is communicated and agree this with the CEO and chair as necessary.

In these areas it is best that the secretary never shares or passes comment on discussions that they are privy to even privately with other executives who were in the room. If the trust of the chair and other directors is lost, it may be very difficult to regain.

BOARD INDUCTION

Non-executive directors are not normally required to have a qualification, with possible the exception of audit committee chairs, where holding a chartered accountant qualification is not mandatory but often deemed appropriate in the appointment process. Generally, board and former career experience is usually all that is assessed in determining the suitability of individuals for the role. It is extremely important to recognise the importance of developing and equipping directors to perform the role that is expected of them. This induction and ongoing development should fall to the company secretary to organise, contribute to, and guide the Chair to consider ongoing development opportunities for directors.

As mentioned above, the secretary will be responsible for explaining the company's governance framework and the detailed workings of the board, ensuring that directors have access to a governance manual that contains all the documentation they require (including a high-level summary for easy digestion!) A generic list of likely content is provided below but the list needs to be designed for each organisation and "regulatory briefing" will depend on the nature of the organisation – from charities to large listed financial organisations the requirements will be different.

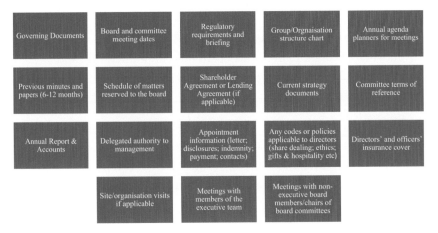

Figure 6.2 *Suggested induction documents/activities for new board members.*

A generic governance manual, for presenting new board members with as part of the induction process is suggested in ICSA Guidance Note on Induction of Directors (www.icsa.org.uk, 2015) may include the following documents and activities (Figure 6.2).

The company secretary should engage with all new directors and senior management to ascertain their individual training requirements – some will have a greater understanding of governance best practice than others; some will have a better knowledge of the sector and organisation; and some may be used to a regulated environment (if this is applicable). Induction should be tailored to the requirements of each person. Organisations have a tendency to overload directors with information in the early days of joining a board and the company secretary should consider if there is benefit in planning activities over a wider time frame – many directors admit that "induction" would have had more impact for them after a few months of engaging with the company. The company secretary has a role in introducing a new director to the key people and procedures within the organisation and this is often a good opportunity for site visits and meeting employees. Meetings with key stakeholders; customers; suppliers and the regulator may be sensible depending on the organisation. When new senior managers join the company, it is a good idea to consider giving them the opportunity to have a similar induction ensuring that they meet the board if they are likely to work closely with them.

BOARD MEETINGS

Board meetings are arguably the most important part of board member calendars, it is where decisions are made – the core of what the board does. In order to ensure that board meetings are effective, it is vital that the company secretary plans accordingly. It is up to the Chair, closely supported by the secretary to make sure that materials needed for board meetings are suitable, and to ensure that the programme of meetings allows for directors' discussion – both formal and informal. Advance preparation is a key aspect to ensure that, during the meeting itself, board members can concentrate on making decisions. This important planning work starts with the board agenda.

AGENDA PLANNING

Much of the work of the board/company secretary, in every sector, will be done to assist the chair. It is a key responsibility of the chair to ensure that there is effective running of board meetings. The list of responsibilities for directors continues to grow and the number of topics appearing on the agenda mirrors this. It is a challenge for many boards to cover all of this and to ensure that time is spent wisely – not delving into too much operational detail; knowing enough about operations to hold management to account; leaving sufficient time to look forward at strategy and how to build a better organisation. This requires careful balance and planning the board's time together is essential. The company secretary plays an integral role here, guiding the chair, supporting the CEO and sharing ideas from executive and non-executive directors regarding how meetings can be shaped to cover what is required. An annual agenda planner, in line with the organisation's financial year end, is important as it highlights when key matters need to be approved by the board and allows for the identification of "space" to deal with other matters. This also allows the company secretary to plan and share with colleagues what lead time is required for preparation. It is an important project planning exercise but, of course, also needs to be flexible to cater for the unpredictable operational issues that will inevitably arise. Therefore, meeting to discuss agendas with the chair becomes a regular feature in the life of the secretary. Board agenda planning often involves the CEO while the audit committee will include the CFO/FD; the remuneration and nominations committees perhaps the HR Director. Having one person overseeing this planning is efficient as there are hand offs between committees that are important to pick up.

Agenda planning should also ensure that directors have the opportunity throughout the year to discharge their wider duties and increase their awareness which will assist board work. A number of governance codes require boards to consider values and culture. Gaining knowledge of stakeholder views, particularly employees, is an important part of good governance and ensuring that board members directors believe they are appropriately monitoring the culture within the organisation needs to be built into board and other meetings with the organisation. All of this requires careful planning and coordination and undoubtedly should be led by the governance facilitator.

BOARD PAPERS

Board packs (and the size and quality of them) is a favourite topic of directors and is one of the most challenging areas of board efficiency. The board/company secretary is in the front line hearing all comments (good and bad) and must listen carefully to the feedback and work with colleagues, particularly the chair and the CEO, to ensure that quality information is provided to directors.

The very common phrase, "I have only made this letter longer because I have not had the time to make it shorter" has been attributed to Blaise Pascal, mathematician and physicist as well as Cicero, Mark Twain, and others.

Authors of board papers should be mindful of this much used phrase. It is worth taking the time and developing the skill of distilling complex detailed information into key issues that succinctly capture what is required. Equally non-executive directors should take care that they do not ask for detailed information that is unnecessary for the strategic decisions they require to make. Good team work is essential to develop the best board pack and while the Chair is undoubtedly the team manager in this regard, the company secretary has a role as referee.

To assist colleagues drafting board papers it is advisable to develop a template for their use which will provide a structure to each paper and help directors gain a familiarity with the format. The template should also ask authors to address certain areas enabling directors to cover information that is required for them to appropriately discharge their legal duties. For example, asking authors to consider the appropriate requirements in the Companies Act 2006 or any regulatory matters and to meaningfully note how these have been included, will add structure to the content.

LEARNING POINT

The governance facilitator will encourage executive colleagues not to play the "non-executive game" of challenging non-executive colleagues to find the difficult questions to ask. Too often executives leave the board room saying "I was surprised they didn't ask me …" or "I was glad they didn't ask me …" when the correct team approach is to lay out for the non-executive directors the key areas that need to be considered and debated.

> Rather than testing the non-executive's analytical skills, it is more important to use their valuable experience in addressing the issues that the executives already know are the most challenging. This will lead to a much better board room debate.

BOARD MINUTES

Just as there is an art in writing a good board paper, there is an art in crafting a good board minute. It is a task that is frequently dreaded by company secretaries, but it should not be seen as an administrative duty because a well written board minute can protect the company and its directors. Like board papers, minutes should be concise but still contain sufficient information to allow the reader to follow the point and be absolutely clear regarding how it was decided. Many board papers will contain a recommendation as to what directors are being asked to approve. It is good to think about the exact wording that will be used in the minute and include this in the paper. Then directors will be in no doubt about what will appear in the minute and they will have the ability to frame it exactly as they mean the approval to be stated. A brief summary of the paper should be recorded and a paper can be incorporated by reference into the minute.

The challenge comes in capturing the debate and how a decision was arrived at. For large organisations, thought also needs to be given to demonstrating how directors have fulfilled Companies Act or other relevant Standing Orders or Regulatory considerations. In capturing the debate company secretaries will be guided by the style preference of the Chair. Some Chairs will want detail noted with comments being attributed to individuals where others will be content with a summary of the discussion and the final agreed decision. Some topics may be sensitive and require to be captured in a different way, some directors will demand that their view is recorded – whatever the board requirement it is essential that the secretary is aware of sensitivities, personalities and steers a professional and impartial course through the drafting. Minutes are approved by the board in its subsequent meeting, but in many organisations, the secretary may draft a minute to be shared with the CEO before its approval by the chair and it is that final draft that is shared with other directors.

In the public sector, minutes are usually published on the organisation's website. This allows for public transparency and accountability. With many regulated entities minutes are shared with the regulator who may dictate the format requiring evidence of certain matters, such as board challenge. This adds complexity for the writer who not only has to take into account the style preferences of the chair but must also meet the requirements of the regulator or ensure that minutes withstand public scrutiny.

In summary, board minutes should:

- Be a record of decisions (including rationale for decisions) rather than a record of discussion (unless a director asks for this for example when disagreeing with a position).
- Be a record of actions agreed, persons responsible, and a date to be actioned.
- Be clear enough that an absent director would later understand why a decision was made by the board on reading the minutes.
- Not include ambiguous terms such as "perhaps", "might", or "should" and instead use clear terms such as "is hereby agreed" and "will".
- Include a date in relation to when every decision takes effect.

LEARNING POINT

The board/company secretary should mark out their diary for the board meeting and the day after to allow proper time for writing board minutes. Unless this type of discipline is adopted it is hard to find time for the job as it always seems that something more

---

important or urgent than minute writing arises. Most articles of association or board procedures will have a requirement for minutes to be shared with directors within a timescale (i.e. 7–14 days) and it is easier to write a minute "fresh" than it is to leave it until the deadline looms. Time needs to be allowed for the Chair to review also.

Do not underestimate the importance of the good minute – this is not an administrative task to be rushed through. It requires crafting with a careful choice of words and sensitivity to the related issues.

As well as crafting an excellent minute, the board/company secretary can assist the chair by being a good reader of the room. Carefully listening to director's contributions and watching how they receive information and behave as a result is important in assisting the chair in good board management. A debrief with the chair after a board meeting can be valuable as the secretary can provide their impartial commentary of the meeting and discuss how things could be improved taking notes back to other executives and adopting a continuous learning approach.

THE RESPECTED "GOVERNANCE ADVISER"

Through this chapter we have developed a profile of a senior executive with key board level relationships that plays an integral part in the facilitation of the governance framework within any organisation. Much of this relies upon the secretary developing the trust and respect of directors and other colleagues. The route to becoming the respected "governance adviser" may take time but it is likely to add value to the organisation once it is achieved. Being an effective listener for the company, a voice of reason, the provider of impartial, factual information to seek resolution to a debate is a role that will be appreciated by all directors.

The governance adviser will:

- develop a relationship with the chair where they can be relied upon as the chair's right-hand woman or man;
- "have the backs" of all the directors by designing good induction programmes; equipping them with good board materials and minutes demonstrating how they are discharging their directors' duties and provide refresher training on relevant legislation or regulatory developments;
- proactively advise directors of new governance developments and trends and suggest appropriate procedures to accommodate changes; and
- act with integrity as the "corporate conscience" and not be afraid to call out poor behaviour.

IMPORTANT ASPECTS OF THE ROLE IN THE PRIVATE SECTOR

The private sector is comprised by many types of organisation and these will be considered starting with the publicly listed company. A suitably qualified company secretary is a legal requirement for boards of publicly listed companies. In addition, compliance with the UK CGC must be supported by a company secretary to ensure that the board has the policies, processes, information, time, and resources it needs in order to function effectively and efficiently. The role of the company secretary in supporting the board's effectiveness is further detailed in the FRC Guidance on Board Effectiveness (Guidance on Board

Effectiveness, 2018) which highlights the *responsibility* of the company secretary to ensure compliance with board procedures and advise the board on all governance matters and to support the efficient running of the board and committees. The UKCGC goes further by stating that all directors should have access to the advice of the company secretary, who is responsible for advising the board on all governance matters. The QCA Corporate Governance Code similarly describes the role of the company secretary as a trusted adviser to the chair of the board and playing a vital role in relation to legal and regulatory compliance and a proactive and central role in ensuring good governance.

While there is no legal requirement for a private company to appoint a company secretary it is common for medium to large companies to follow what is seen as best practice governance and appoint qualified company secretaries. The Wates Corporate Governance Principles for Large Private Companies ("the Wates Principles") states, "the chair and the company secretary should periodically review the governance processes to confirm that they remain fit for purpose and consider any initiatives which would strengthen the governance of the company". A footnote then acknowledges that "private companies are not required by law to have a company secretary, although it is good practice for a company to do so; therefore, some companies may have alternative arrangements".

It is also understandable that secretaries to the company have been appointed by many private companies because the share and capital complexities; reporting requirements and governance issues are often no less challenging than those found in publicly listed companies. Indeed, it could be argued that private companies wishing to demonstrate good governance had a more challenging job than publicly listed companies because, until the Wates Principles were published at the end of 2018, there was no specific governance code for large private companies and most reported against the UKCGC which was not entirely fit for private company purpose. Private companies often have complex share capital structures and many varied shareholders. It is more common to find shareholder appointed directors on the board of a private company than it is on publicly listed company boards and that can lead to interesting challenges within the governance framework. All of these elements mean that the company secretary role in a private company should not be underestimated.

IMPORTANT ASPECTS OF THE ROLE IN THE PUBLIC SECTOR

The public sector is made up of a variety of organisations ranging from non-departmental public bodies, specially constituted trusts, registered companies, and organisations that are registered as charities. There is no single approach to the structure of role in the public sector and there are a few different job titles used such as board secretary or clerk to the board. One example is in the college sector, the Code of Good Governance for English Colleges specifies that

> the board must appoint a person to act as the clerk to the corporation. In dealing with board business, the clerk should be solely responsible to the board and have a direct reporting line to its chair. The board must protect the clerk's ability to carry out his/her responsibilities, including appropriate training and development and ensuring adequate time and resources to undertake the role effectively.

The Scottish equivalent has similar wording as does the Welsh version, albeit the latter goes further to call the role as the clerk/governance officer. It also goes on to state,

> The clerk must inform the governing body if s/he believes that any proposed action would exceed its powers or involve regulatory risk or (where the clerk has other management responsibilities at the college) if there is a potential conflict of interest between his/her clerking and management roles.

The equivalent Northern Ireland Guidance for Governance goes as far as to say that while the Board Secretary is an employee of the college and works directly for the governing body, the individual "should not hold any other position in the College".

In reality, the board secretary position in the public sector is often under-valued, possibly as there is no legal requirement for it or definitive guidance as to what is required, unlike in publicly listed companies. The time commitment required to assign to the post can often be grossly under-estimated and be only a part-time post. In such cases, the board secretary may be working almost full time in a part-time position which poses its own difficulties.

A common mistake is also viewing the role as largely administrative and there are instances where these roles have been assigned to administrative roles within the organisation. The importance of the role cannot be underestimated and although board minutes are seen by many directors as administrative, they are in fact key in documenting extremely important matters for the board.

While not a legal obligation, the board secretary role should only be undertaken by those appropriately qualified or at an appropriate level to understand the importance of the role.

IMPORTANT ASPECTS OF THE ROLE IN THE CHARITY/ VOLUNTARY SECTOR

As with privately owned companies, charities and other voluntary sector bodies are not legally required to appoint board/ company secretaries and relevant governance codes are silent on the subject. However, organisations in the sector understandably wish to demonstrate high levels of good governance and it is likely that if there is not a full-time board/company secretary within a charity the responsibilities will have been assigned to an individual as part of their role – often the finance director, sometimes the chief executive or managing director. Trustee directors of charities not only have to be mindful of their duties and liabilities under the Companies Act, if the organisation is registered as a company, but have to be aware of their responsibilities and liabilities under the relevant charity acts, reporting requirements and regulatory requirements. Once again, we see the importance of the board/company secretary supporting trustee directors performing roles under the watchful eye of a regulator and often under a spotlight of public interest and comment.

The Good Governance Code for larger charities in England and Wales (Charity Governance Code, 2020) states that the board working as a team includes,

> The board collectively receives specialist in-house or external governance advice and support. The board can access independent professional advice, such as legal or financial advice, at the charity's expense if needed for the board to discharge its duties.

It should be noted that even in larger charities, in-house advice is rarely from a full-time board/company secretary, and various responsibilities are typically assigned to the Finance Director, sometimes the Chief Executive or Managing Director. External governance advice and support is usually sought from charity sector network bodies, specialist lawyers or consultants, whether on a paid or pro bono basis.

All charity trustees (regardless of underlying legal structure) have to be aware of their responsibilities under relevant legislation, together with reporting requirements and regulatory requirements from the Charity Commission of England and Wales, or OSCR in Scotland. In addition, trustee directors of charities have extra responsibilities in line with their duties under the Companies Act, reflecting that the charitable organisation is also registered as a company; this is where the guidance of a board/company secretary could be of great value.

Where a charity is large enough to employ staff in senior roles, such as a finance director or chief executive, the potential for conflict of interest should be noted in relation to certain governance functions. It can often be difficult in a combined role to remain independent particularly if the individual is directly affected by the decision, and should resources permit, the role of board/company secretary should ideally be a separate role to avoid such conflicts. If this is not possible it is important for the board to recognise conflicts of interest that a board/company secretary may have as a consequence of their dual role and take this into account.

KEY MESSAGES

- While not a requirement in every organisation, the board/company secretary or clerk/governance officer should play an important role in supporting good governance and best practice on a board.
- The role in support of the board is diverse and includes a mix of advisory/guidance-related and technical/administrative tasks, some of which are very complex.
- The secretary to the board should have an influence on board papers and minutes, which can have a profound effect on the quality and effectiveness of board and board committee meetings.
- The board/company secretary or clerk is a resource for the whole board, not just the chair; the company secretary should also build a good working relationship with the whole board.

FURTHER READING

https://www.frc.org.uk/directors/corporate-governance-and-stewardship/
    uk-corporate-governance-code
https://www.iod.com/training/open-courses/role-of-the-company-secretary
https://www.icsa.org.uk/professional-development/short-course-qualifications

REFERENCES

Charity Governance Code. (2020). Charity Governance Code. [online] Available at: https://www.charitygovernancecode.org/en/front-page. [Accessed 15 Mar. 2021].

Davis, A. (n.d.). Roles on the board — NCVO Knowhow. [online] knowhow. ncvo.org.uk. Available at: https://knowhow.ncvo.org.uk/governance/ governance-structure-and-roles/roles-on-the-board [Accessed 27 Mar. 2021].

Guidance on Board Effectiveness. (2018). [online]. Available at: https://www. frc.org.uk/getattachment/61232f60-a338-471b-ba5a-bfed25219147/2018-Guidance-on-Board-Effectiveness-FINAL.PDF. [Accessed 3 Mar. 2021].

www.icsa.org.uk. (2013). ICSA The duties and reporting lines of the company secretary. [online] Available at: https://www.icsa.org.uk/knowledge/ resources/duties-reporting-lines-of-company-secretary [Accessed 24 Feb. 2021].

www.icsa.org.uk. (2015). Induction of directors. [online] Available at: https:// www.icsa.org.uk/knowledge/resources/induction-of-directors [Accessed 24 Feb. 2021].

CHAPTER SEVEN

Recruiting and Maintaining an Effective Board

Monica Langa and Arturo Langa

DOI: 10.4324/9781003142850-7

INTRODUCTION

In order to recruit and maintain an effective board, it is important to "start from first principles" in terms of absolute clarity on the role that the board fulfils as well as the parts of governance codes, and other regulatory codes, that have a bearing on board recruitment and evaluation. There was a time that it was very common for board appointments to result from being "tapped on the shoulder" with candidates chosen from a narrow pool of individuals. Such appointments are becoming increasingly rare due to a combination of government, regulatory, shareholder, and other stakeholder pressures, which has encouraged not only the professionalisation of board recruitment but has gone a long way to broadening the talent pool under consideration for such roles. This chapter will touch, on key areas that should be considered, both before, and during the process of seeking and appointing directors to the board, and practical steps for maintaining an effective, collegiate, and positive board of directors.

While this chapter touches on executive board recruitment, the main focus is on the approaches to recruitment of non-executive board directors and the structure of a board as well as common themes and common recruitment mistakes. It is also important to note the recruitment of executive directors is one of the key responsibilities of non-executive directors (NEDs) so the nuances of how boards operate with both executive and non-executive directors will be explored. This chapter also highlights good practice in recruitment approaches taken in different sectors together with the topics of diversity, board chemistry, and board behaviours. The importance of board evaluation will also be considered and practical tools such as board skills matrices and evaluation checklists will feature towards the end of the chapter.

In order for the above themes to be put in context, an important starting point is understanding the role a board should fulfil. Understanding the board's role is worth reiterating as this informs best practice in recruiting and evaluating the performance of board members. The vital role that a board fulfils is covered in detail in Chapter 1 (Governance and the Role of the Board) so we will focus initially on understanding the structure of what a board is made up of.

WHAT IS A BOARD MADE UP OF?

As covered in Chapter 1, the role fulfilled by the board of directors, which may also be called trustees or governors and in some organisations, it is called a board of management, is vital to the success and long-term sustainability of an organisation. In order to establish, recruit and maintain an effective board, it is important to understand the role of the board. First, it may be helpful to highlight what the board is made up of – this may vary from organisation to organisation but it is not unusual to find a mixture of board and non-board members in attendance at board meetings. It is also important to note that while a private company is required, by law, to have at least one director, publicly listed companies must have at least two. Thereafter the various members of the board may have different roles within the board and within the organisation. What constitutes the board varies from organisation to organisation, most boards are made up from a combination of executive and non-executive directors and there may be others with the courtesy title of director or functional director/ head of division or department that may attend all or parts of board meetings but such roles have no standing in law. It is worth noting that in some organisations in both the private and charity/voluntary or not-for-profit sectors, the entire board comprises only non-executive directors. Non-executive directors (NEDs) are also known by different names in different types of organisations and are sometimes called lay board members, trustees, governors, independent directors, and some organisations appoint a senior independent director (SID). One of the NEDs fulfils the role of chair of the board, sometimes the title used is convenor. Figure 7.1 highlights an example of a board structure where not all participants are members of the board.

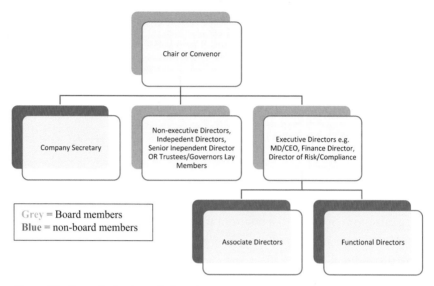

Figure 7.1 *Example structure of a board.*

Formal members of the board hold the legal role of registered directors of the company/organisation with the authority to act as specified in the governing documents of the organisation, they can vote on board matters.

Those in attendance may attend for part or for the entirety of board meetings but are not legal directors, as defined by the Companies Act (2006). In the case of a corporate body which is not a company, the governing documents define which roles are formal members of the board and the parties in attendance who are not, this includes the board/company secretary who may advise on matters of board process and governance but has no part in board decision-making.

According to UK law (Companies Act 2006) there is no distinction between the executive and non-executive directors (NEDs) on a board, the entire board is collectively responsible for the long-term success of the organisation and is required to fulfil its legal responsibilities by ensuring effective stewardship and governance oversight. Appropriate board structures and the balance between executive and non-executive board members will be considered in detail in the sections below; however, in the most general sense, the role of the board is to set the strategy/direction of travel, set the risk appetite and to make the important, collective decisions acting in the best interests of the organisation, protecting the interests of shareholders/stakeholders.

While the Companies Acts do not differentiate between executive and non-executive directors, the UK Corporate Governance Code 2018 (the Code) does.

As discussed in Chapter 2, Governance Codes, while the UK Corporate Governance Code does not apply to public sector or charity/voluntary sector organisations, it is considered a "gold standard" in governance terms and therefore worthwhile for board members of any organisation not only to be aware of but to strive towards meeting any of the standards that may be applicable to their respective organisations. It is therefore worth highlighting the aspects of the Code that are relevant to the recruitment, refreshment, and maintenance of an effective board of directors. The Code states that board recruitment must be part of "a continuous and proactive process of planning and assessment, taking into account the company's strategic priorities and the main trends and factors affecting the long-term success and future viability of the company".

The Code further states that

> Appointing directors who are able to make a positive contribution is one of the key elements of board effectiveness. Directors will be more likely to make good decisions and maximise the opportunities for the company's success if the right skillsets and a breadth of perspectives are present in the boardroom. Non-executive directors should possess a range of critical skills of value to the board and relevant to the challenges and opportunities facing the company.

Importantly, the Code specifically mentions the role of NEDs, it highlights the importance of holding the executive directors/executive management team to account. The role of a non-executive director is *NOT* operational – this is crucial, it requires a specific mindset. Overall, both those recruiting to the board and those wishing to join should understand that the NED role is to provide collective wisdom and experience; create clarity, direction and a culture of strong decision-making; to aid in preventing the emergence of "emperor's new clothes" syndrome and its variant – "group think"; to participate in robust decision-making; to help the organisation avoid mistakes and to air concerns. It is most important that if there is fight to be had, it should ideally be aired and resolved in the board room rather than in the public domain. The role of the NED is not to dictate how agreed strategy should be implemented, rather to check that the management team has developed a thought-out plan that stands up to scrutiny and to hold the management to account in ensuring it is delivered. It is also important to note that the role of the Board is to be the top team in the organisation, which sets the culture and tone not only for how that organisation is governed but how it is led, and it sets the tone for how every other team below it operates.

In order to consider how to strengthen the appointment and effectiveness of directors, it is worth highlighting the nuanced similarities and differences between executive and non-executive members of the board.

EXECUTIVE AND NON-EXECUTIVE BOARD MEMBERS

From a legal viewpoint, there is no distinction between an executive and non-executive director. They share exactly the same individual and collective duties and responsibilities (IoD 2018). At the same time, the role of the NED is crucial, bringing constructive challenge and providing an independent balance to executive directors, helping to ensure that the whole board functions effectively (Bain and Barker 2010).

The balance in the roles between executive directors and NEDs is based, as Bain and Barker comment, on the executive director's,

> intimate knowledge of the company, [whilst] the NED may be
> expected to have a wider perspective of the world at large. Where
> the executive director may be better equipped to provide an

entrepreneurial spur to the company, the NED may have more to say about ensuring prudent control.

Recognising that all directors with board-level roles retain a fiduciary duty, the Code suggests that at least 50% of board members are non-executive or independent. The ideal balance of non-executive directors to executive directors may vary depending on the type of organisation and its governing documents. In some charities, for example, the entire board is made up or non-executive directors – or trustees and members of executive management may attend board meetings but have no board decision-making role. Where executive directors hold a position on the board of directors, the main difference is that they have "executive responsibility" for running the company's business. Executive directors are company employees, in addition to being board members, this is explored in more detail in Chapter Executive Directors on the Board.

A key aspect of the role of NEDs is not only to appoint executive directors but to oversee the level of rewards paid and to hold the executive management of the organisation to account. NEDs also fulfil responsibilities on board sub-committees. The existence and number of sub-committees depends on the size and needs of each specific board; however, typical committees include audit committee, risk committee, nomination committee, and remuneration committee. Sometimes these are combined (e.g. audit and risk assurance committee or remuneration and nominations committee). Nominations committees take on responsibility for board recruitment, although it is not uncommon for this process to be led by the chair of the board. A remuneration committee, if one exists, would be responsible for proposing the remuneration levels for executive directors as well as any remuneration paid to NEDs, for approval by the board.

Unlike executive directors, who are employees of the organisation and receive a salary and other benefits and, in some cases bonuses, share options or other long-term incentive plans (LTIPs), NEDs receive a director's fee; they are not employees, but are appointed on the basis of a contract for services, often in the form of an appointment letter which specifies a term in office and the terms of any period of renewal as well as a maximum term. It is important to note that although set terms in office are good practice and indeed a requirement set by many regulatory bodies and often in an organisation's governing documents, some private companies do not set a maximum term. Listed company non-executive directors are expected to step down after nine years, if not this must be explained in the annual report. In practice it is not common to see non-executive board members stay beyond the nine-year term, unless there is a good reason or exceptional circumstances. Similarly, public bodies set a maximum number of terms in office, as do most voluntary sector organisations.

It is also worth noting, that non-executive director remuneration varies considerably between types and size of organisation and also between sectors. Voluntary sector not-for-profit organisations typically do not remunerate non-executive directors (trustees), albeit there are some exceptions involving specifically constituted trusts. Some public sector organisations remunerate NEDs (e.g. NHS Trust Boards) and typically the remuneration is lower than that in equivalent-sized private sector companies.

Board appointments for executive directors are in the "gift of the board" with decisions being made on promotion of internal employees or external executive search and advertising by the board as a whole or the directors on the nominations committee. The following sections will consider board recruitment mainly with regard to appointing NEDs. The first step is to consider the structure and size of the board.

STRUCTURING A BOARD

A key matter to consider when deciding on, or reviewing the size and structure of a board of directors is that "one size does not fit all". The way in which directors are appointed will be prescribed by an organisation's governing documents. These will also often set a minimum and maximum number of directors. Such documents. such as articles, can, of course, be changed as long as appropriate processes are followed. We have already noted that while the requirements of the UK Corporate Governance Code only formally apply to listed companies. It is however important to emphasize that it is generally regarded as best practice for all companies whether they are large or small, public or private. Turning to what the Code mentions on this subject, it does not specify a number of directors, instead suggesting,

> The board should be of sufficient size that the requirements of the business can be met and that changes to the board's composition and that of its committees can be managed without undue disruption, and should not be so large as to be unwieldy.

ICSA The Chartered Governance Institute, states in its 2019 report – The Future Board – Getting in Shape for Tomorrow's Challenges (ICSA 2019):

> When contemplating possible future models for the structure and role of the board, there are perhaps four overlapping considerations to be borne in mind:

- Capacity – how much time does the board need to carry out its responsibilities, and how can it be used most effectively? If the board does not have sufficient time to do all the work that is expected of it, is the answer to increase the time commitment or reduce the workload?
- Capability – what skills and information does the board need, and where does it get them from? Do you need all the relevant expertise and all the different perspectives around the board table or can they be obtained more efficiently in a different way?
- Control – what visibility does the board have over the organisation it leads, and what levers can it pull to influence behaviour and performance? Are they sufficient?
- Closeness to the issue concerned – is the view from the top necessarily the best view? Is the boardroom the best place in the organisation to deal with all the issues currently on the board's agenda?

The vital characteristic of a successful and productive board is a balance of skills and experience. There should ideally be a mixture of executive directors and independent non-executive directors.

There is a view that the ability of the board and/or any form of
committee to make decisions and exercise proper scrutiny becomes
increasingly difficult at sizes in excess of 10–12 members. Equally,
directors may also be very aware of the need to provide value to
stakeholders and therefore the size and total remuneration of the
board should be in line with what is appropriate for the size and
turnover/budget of the organisation. A smaller board size may
improve the quality of communication and with more focussed
discussions, albeit this can create an issue if one board member is
suddenly indisposed. The smaller the board, the easier to organise
meetings albeit, it is vital to check the governing documents regarding
what constitutes a quorum – if three directors are required for a
decision or resolution to be quorate and the board is made up of only
four directors, there is a greater risk of having less than three directors
attending a board meeting than if the board size was six or more
directors. Equally, the smaller the board, the fewer the diverse skills
and experience and the fewer individuals to take up separate board
committee roles.

Having touched on the Corporate Governance Code, it is worth
mentioning the Corporate Governance Guidance and Principles that
exist for other types of organisations such as unlisted organisations
including privately owned companies and those in the public and third
sectors. Unlisted Companies in the UK are not subject to a mandatory
code; however, the IoD in association with ecoDa and sponsored by
Deloitte in 2010, produced a guidance, which states that

> Once a company reaches a certain size and level of complexity,
> an independent board, i.e. a board containing independent non-
> executive directors and not entirely composed of company or
> family insiders, becomes essential to the long-term success and
> survival of the company.

> A key stage in opening up the company to external scrutiny
> is taken by the appointment of independent (non-executive)
> directors. This signals a firm's willingness to become more open

and accountable in respect of its decision-making and performance assessment. The replacing of the owner-manager or founding entrepreneur by external managers can also be perceived as an important step in this direction.

Once the appropriate size and structure is decided, the next step is agreeing the composition of the board.

DECIDING THE BOARD COMPOSITION

There is no single correct approach to deciding on board composition, each board should be the result of a bespoke design that suits the operating environment, size, and governance arrangements for the individual organisation. It is also important to remember that just as the operating environment for any organisation may change, so too should the size and structure of its board to suit the circumstances at a given time. To support the endeavours of suitable board composition, a helpful set of questions is provided by (Bain and Barker, 2010) who recommend asking the following.

- What will be the ratio of executive to non-executive directors?
- What are the likely future needs of the business and what knowledge and skills are current and prospective directors likely to need?
- Is there a proper process for appointing directors?
- What are the succession plans for the members of the board and senior executives?
- What are the procedures for appointing the chairman and the chief executive?
- What are the terms of reference for the nomination committee? Do they ensure that the range of potential candidates is wide enough? Is the selection process rigorous enough?

- Is the contribution of each director assessed in an annual review? Can individual development programmes be arranged where necessary?
- Is a comprehensive induction program available for new members of the board?

No matter what board composition is decided on, the most important aspect of any board is the quality of board debate and input and having individuals with appropriate skills and mindsets is the key to board effectiveness. It is succinctly put by the Financial Reporting Council (FRC) in its report titled Guidance on Board Effectiveness (July 2018), which recommends,

> The boardroom should be a place for robust debate where challenge, support, diversity of thought and teamwork are essential features. Diversity of skills, background and personal strengths is an important driver of a board's effectiveness, creating different perspectives among directors, and breaking down a tendency towards 'group think'.

While few would argue with the statement above, there are many examples in all sectors where boards struggle to achieve a healthy balance between robust debate, diversity of thought and genuine teamwork. All too often, the root cause of board ineffectiveness is due to mistakes made in board recruitment.

COMMON MISTAKES IN BOARD RECRUITMENT

Having highlighted the importance of effective directors in a board context, the serious legal and fiduciary responsibilities they face and some of the worrying criticism presented in the FRC's review of boards, highlighted in Chapter 1, it is worth exploring some of the common themes and mistakes in recruitment to the board that lead to ineffective or dysfunctional boards. The FRC points to issues around the deficiency of a significant number in the important tasks of defining purpose and culture – arguably two of the most important tasks of directors. Inappropriate culture, lack of understanding of the role and unconscious bias can, in combination lead to ineffective boards of directors.

In the private sector, it was not unusual, even towards the end of the 20th century for some public listed company board appointments to be based on a relatively small network of individuals who knew each other well to be "tapped on the shoulder" to join each other's respective boards. Increasing regulation, shareholder pressure and demands for greater transparency have created an environment where listed companies are required to show in their annual accounts, how they have gone about refreshing their boards. This has led to an uptake of using executive search firms in order to identify suitable candidates from a broader pool. Similarly, public sector and many charity board appointments are advertised. There are, however, still many private companies and some other organisations where personal networks are used to identify and appoint non-executive directors without a competitive selection process and/or a weak appointment approach.

Frequent mistakes include:

Creating the role around a liked individual rather than ascertaining the need. The result can lead to a lack of value being brought to the board and a vital skills/experience gap not being filled. The potential is for missed opportunities, lack of appropriate challenge or board discussions not focussing on key strategic issues that could have major implications for the organisation.

Appointing a "big name" – without objectively understanding the skills and experience the individual brings (or lack of) and importantly, the motivation of the new appointee and the understanding to their role as a NED. A 'big name' who does not understand the legal and fiduciary duties or the non-executive nature of the role, or who is not motivated to be an active contributor to the business of the board, can in time become a hindrance rather than an asset to the board.

Someone like me/unconscious bias – it can be somewhat counter intuitive to choose NEDs who look and sound very different to the Chair and current board members. Different skills and life experience as well as career experience, different outlook, education, and different priorities. A common mistake is recruiting NEDs in one's own image under the guise of "cultural fit" or "board chemistry" the result can be a dangerous group think leading to less robust decision-making.

Narrow sector or technical focus – replicating the same sector experience as the executive team has, in the NEDs. This can exacerbate a lack of broad perspectives that can be so valuable in having NEDs on the Board.

Not understanding the role/not checking the candidate understands the role – recruiting a NED where the person making the appointment decision lacks an understanding of the role of a NED can lead to obvious problems associated with seeking out skills/aptitudes/experience that are not relevant to role. Equally, not checking that the appointee understands the role he or she is being appointed to can lead to the wrong person being appointed to the wrong role, not engaging in the work of the board in an appropriate manner or even being disruptive to the board and wider organisation.

Experience over mindset – focussing entirely on a director's experience while ignoring mindset and attitude, can be highly detrimental to the workings of a board. There are times, when attitude is more important than either experience or skills. Murphy (2012) points to his study of people who fail in their roles (by being dismissed, receiving poor performance reviews or written warnings) within 18 months of starting. This study of "bad hires" found that in 89% of cases the reason was attitudinal. A director could have all the qualifications, skills, and experience to appear an excellent member of the board, on paper; however, if the individual does not engage appropriately, listen, and contribute in a board context, he/she is, at best, of little value and, at worst, a destabilising influence on the board and the wider organisation.

LEARNING POINT

A new voluntary sector, grant-making organisation was created to oversee a considerable sum of money to be allocated as grant funding to other organisations. The large board of directors was established with the best of intentions, and directors chosen from among the "great and the good" of the public sector, including directors of social work and senior civil servants. The problem was that the new organisation was effectively a start-up company facing the challenges of establishing rigorous and agile funding protocols from scratch. None of the board had any experience in the challenges faced by early stage companies nor of creating financial management processes. It took a refreshment of the Board in order for the organisation to move forward in an appropriate manner.

When establishing a board, the importance of giving deep thought to the strategic aims and anticipated challenges the organisation is likely to face, cannot be underestimated. The skills and experience of the board must be a match for what the organisation is trying to achieve and to the circumstances involved.

BOARD DIVERSITY

Hesketh, Sellwood-Taylor, and Mullen (2020) comment that
Corporate boards are under increasing pressure to diversify
their ranks – adding more women and minorities, as well as
executives with different cultural and functional backgrounds – to
better represent the people their organisations employ and serve.
At the same time, the bar for "board readiness" has never been
higher: directors are scrutinised for their ability to understand
more complex businesses, demonstrate technical know-how,
deliver effective governance, and generate sustainable long-term
performance.

They point to the term "boardroom capital" and suggest that the very
skills required to be a successful senior executive in an organisation,
are not the same as those needed for the boardroom, specifically in a
non-executive capacity, because "the levers of operating power" are no
longer in the gift of the NED.

Charlotte Valeur, former chair of the Institute of Directors, comments,
"We need to help new participants from under-represented groups to
develop the confidence of working on boards and to come to know
that", further adding, "this is not rocket science".

Diversity in its broadest sense can be seen as a form of anti-fragility,
Taleb (2012) comments that being anti-fragile (the opposite of
fragile) is the property that is "behind everything that has changed
with time: evolution, culture, ideas, revolutions, political systems,
technological innovation, cultural and economic success, corporate
survival". Dealing with risk and potential "black swan" events is at the
core of what is expected of directors in the board environment and
"group think" is a well-recognised as a core aspect of numerous well-
documented scandals and failures in every sector. Boardroom diversity
is seen as an effective method of dispelling group think; yet it presents
its own challenges.

One of the challenges presented by achieving boards with greater diversity is time taken to reach decisions. It can be argued that a diverse board tends to take longer to reach decisions, with more perspectives and input from a wider variety of board members, debate, and discussion invariably takes longer. The flip side of this is that it is highly likely that after a longer and more thorough debate, decisions agreed by the board are more robust and lead to better longer-term outcomes for the organisation and its stakeholders. A more diverse board requires excellent leadership from a skilled chair to ensure positive engagement by all members of the board and a positive board culture. From a board recruitment viewpoint, it is often commented on by boards that they struggle to find candidates from a more diverse pool that possess the skill sets required. The validity of this comment rests very much on the selection parameters set by the board.

In the private sector there has been much debate on the topic of board diversity, in March 2018, the Independent newspaper published an article with the headline "More people called David and Steve lead FTSE 100 companies than women and ethnic minorities". If a board wishes to appoint more diverse candidates but stipulates that candidates will only be considered if they have been the CEO of a FTSE 100 company, one can see how finding a diverse pool of candidates would be tricky.

While in early 2020, data suggested that the government's Hampton-Alexander review was successful in one of its two key gender diversity targets with women filling 33% of board seats in the top 350 UK listed companies. However, this figure has been reached to a large degree by appointing a greater number of women to non-executive roles, the picture is not quite the same when it comes to women in leadership teams of firms listed in the London Stock Exchange's FTSE 100 and FTSE 250 indices. A lack of women on top leadership teams – often called executive committees, which are one level below the board – has long been considered one of the main barriers to increasing gender balance in the boardroom, as they are seen as providing the pipeline of future directors. It is argued that in order to the Hampton-Alexander review's second goal, half of all available FTSE 350 leadership roles would have needed to go to women in 2020.

In 2016, Sir John Parker, who was part of the Davies Review of Women on Boards, published a report (the Parker review 2016) into the ethnic diversity of UK boards. As with many of these reports, the findings focus on UK PLCs; however, it could be argued that it is likely to be a proxy for other sectors and types of UK company.

The report found that UK PLCs did not reflect the ethnic diversity of the UK, or of their stakeholders, on their boards. With 14% of the UK population being a person of colour, only 1.5% of FTSE 100 board positions were held by this demographic. 53 FTSE 100 companies did not have any directors of colour and only nine people of colour held the role of Chair or CEO in the FTSE 100.

A summary of some of the recommendations includes:

- Every FTSE 100 board should have at least one director of colour by 2021 and each FTSE 250 company board should have one by at least 2024.
- Nomination committees should source qualified people of colour to be considered for board appointments when vacancies occur.
- The principles of the voluntary code of conduct for executive search firms regarding gender should be extended to the recruitment of ethnic minority candidates of FTSE 350 companies.
- The description of the company's diversity policy in the annual report should include commentary on a company's efforts to increase ethnic diversity within its organisation, including at board level.

In the public sector, the UK Government declared an ambition that, by 2022 half of all new appointees should be women and 14% of appointments should be made to those from ethnic minorities. While in 2017, the Scottish Government introduced the Gender Representation on Public Boards (Scotland) Bill with the aim to improve the representation of women in non-executive positions on public sector boards to 50% by 2020. However, diversity goes beyond gender and ethnicity; it is about promoting the NED career to competent professionals from the widest range of backgrounds. It is also important to note that in order to have a choice suitably experienced and diverse candidates for future board appointments, it is necessary to encourage diversity throughout organisations in order to encourage the next generation of diverse business leaders.

Interestingly, it appears that the charity/voluntary sector in the UK has somewhat lagged behind both the private and public sectors with respect to board diversity. In fact, at The Civil Society Charity Finance Group's annual conference in 2019, the lack of any diversity targets were heavily criticised. Cordelia Osewa-Ediae, senior consultant at Green Park, commented that some initiatives set up by organisations such as the Institute of Fundraising were a positive step but said that the charity sector was still behind the private sector in some respects.

She said,

> What we don't do and what makes all of this fall apart time and time again is we don't hold ourselves to account. In the private sector, you have the Hampton-Alexander review that has set a target of a third female representation in boards in FTSE 350 companies and similarly you have the Parker review, which has recommended that you should have at least one ethnic minority board member at FTSE 100 companies by 2020. We don't have any of these in the charity sector so we keep on going round in circles while we are waiting for leaders and for organisations to take the lead and actually set targets.

LEARNING POINT

A successful, private sector engineering company made two board recruitment mistakes in short order. First, when looking for a new managing director an individual, who was very successful at a competitor firm, was approached an appointed. No thought was given to the very different circumstances that the appointee had built a strong reputation in, which were very different to the relatively small engineering company; no independent process was used to assess strengths and capabilities. The appointment was not a good fit and the Board wondered why the new MD spent time on things he was good at and enjoyed, but were not required in this company? The Company's turnover and profitability suffered throughout the length of the appointment and for six months after the departure of the MD. The Company then went on to make a first NED appointment. The Board comprised six executive directors, all mechanical engineers and it insisted on only considering NED candidates who were also mechanical engineers, who had spent careers in similar engineering companies. Both recruitment exercises failed to deliver the benefits the Company had hoped for.

Diversity of thought and of composition has been shown to be very important to the successful operation of board and some questions for the Board to guide a Board discussion on diversity include:

Where are we missing key perspectives and insight which would add value to our decisions?

Where are there obvious gaps in our diversity which need to be addressed through recruitment?

Being aware of gaps in skills, experience and background can help board members to consider when they need assistance on key decisions and plans with wider groups who may be able to offer more insight. This also allows the board to take a systematic, targeted approach to recruitment of new members where they feel these gaps are significant. It's all about ensuring the effectiveness of the board's decision-making.

APPROACHES TO BOARD RECRUITMENT

There are many common themes in the approaches to board recruitment across all sectors; however, there are some nuanced and interesting differences, which are worth highlighting. Taking the main private, public, and charity/voluntary sectors, in turn, albeit due to the less cohesive approaches and vast differences in the private sector – we have further subdivided the private sector into a number of categories:

PRIVATE SECTOR

LISTED COMPANIES

There was a time that Britain's largest PLCs predominantly advertised board positions in newspapers, this has been replaced, to some extent, by the use of executive search firms, many of whom have signed up to the Voluntary Code of Conduct for executive search firms. Search firms use a variety of methods for identifying candidates from desk research and analysis of companies in the chosen market; advertising; searching social media, their internal databases; and seeking recommendations. It is not unusual for current board members to suggest individuals for the search firm to also consider along with candidates "unearthed" through the search process. An important factor in the search process is independence and avoidance of conflicts. PLC board members are closely scrutinised by shareholders, activists, analysts, rating agencies, and in certain sectors, by regulatory bodies as well. This means finding suitable board members involves a "jigsaw" puzzle of considerations in terms of skills, experience, culture fit, diversity, independence, and lack of perceived conflicts of interest. A new board member cannot be appointed to board A if she/he also sits on another board with one of the current board members of board A, listed company NEDs are normally required to retire after nine years, and each board member is scrutinised over how many other board appointments he/she has.

While many approaches to board recruitment, taken by Britain's largest firms are similar to other types of organisation, there are nuanced differences between organisations in different sectors but also in types and size of organisation. It is worth considering the strengths and challenges of the practical approaches these varied non-listed organisations use when recruiting to the board.

UNLISTED COMPANIES

Private sector companies, which are unlisted include family-owned companies, partnerships, employee-owned companies, start-ups, and early-stage companies, which may be angel investment, venture capital, or private equity-backed.

Similar challenges apply when recruiting board members for family-owned companies, private equity/venture capital-backed companies and in start-up companies. It is worth considering some of the nuanced differences that often apply in practice as follows:

FAMILY-OWNED COMPANIES

A family-owned business may be defined as any business in which two or more family members are involved and the majority of ownership or control lies within a family. Family-owned businesses may be the oldest form of business organisation.

If one considers that multigenerational family-owned companies by their nature have developed, often over many centuries and built success by populating their boards with family members, it is not uncommon to find a lack of any "outsiders". Even when non-family members are considered for non-executive roles on the board, often trusted advisers are turned to for recommendations or even appointed. Advisers, or their recommended appointees, may of course have the skills and experience to make excellent board members; however, one should be asking if they bring the fresh, independent viewpoint that is so valuable in non-executive directors? At the same time an understanding of, and empathy with, the dynamics and values of a family-owned company is vital. Numerous second, third, fourth, and fifth generation family-owned companies are driven by a strong sense of corporate social responsibility, perhaps the business is the main employer in a remote setting. The measures of success are typically much longer term than a listed company with external shareholders would experience and ultimate control and decision-making may involve complex family relationships.

A family business could be described as an interaction between two separate, while at the same time, connected systems – the business and the family – with uncertain boundaries and different rules. Numerous private equity funds have found to their cost that the management team, that they conducted so much due diligence on, prior to investment, may not be the real decision-makers in the company, the true decision-making may, in fact, happen over Sunday lunch in the family matriarch's house. It is perhaps not surprising that adding a non-executive board member who has only been exposed to "big city" firms can lead to a significant lack of "fit" with the organisation and frustration for the individual.

MUTUAL AND EMPLOYEE-OWNED COMPANIES

A mutual is a private organisation that is owned by its customers, policy holders, or employees. They take several forms, including friendly societies, building societies, co-operatives, asset managers, credit unions, and housing associations. As many of these types of organisations operate in the financial services sector and other highly regulated sectors, there are often regulatory requirements governing the recruitment of board members. In addition, governing documents for the organisations may also specify how non-executive directors are appointed, for example, many mutual organisations appoint from their members. Increased regulation, especially in the financial services sector, have resulted in the net being cast wider than membership for Non-executive director candidates as increased specialisms in areas such as financial risk management are increasingly required. As a result, recruitment of board members via executive search services has increased considerably albeit cultural fit and an empathy with the values and approach taken by mutual organisations is a vital component.

Employee-owned organisations are owned by their employees either via a significant or total ownership of shares. In the UK this is most commonly achieved through an employee ownership trust, which includes employee representatives sitting on the Board and, depending on size or organisation, one or more independent non-executive directors – normally individuals with leadership and/or board experience in a non-competing employee-owned company.

PRIVATE EQUITY/VENTURE CAPITAL-OWNED COMPANIES

Companies that have external investors but are not listed on a stock exchange are most likely to have taken investment from private equity (PE) or venture capital (VC) funds. While there may be other shareholders, such as the founders, typically the PE or VC investors may hold a majority stake and may hold the key decision-making role as to who makes up the board of directors.

It is not unusual for PE or VC funds to have a network of trusted individuals who could be shareholders of the fund, experienced entrepreneurs who have successfully built and sold a business, and other advisers, who are asked to join the board as a NED or Chair. In the authors' experience this can be very effective, at the same time it could be seen as a rather narrow approach that does not always produce the desired result. One might ask how many potentially more talented and skilled potential board members were never even considered because the majority shareholders "fished in a narrow pool" of candidates?

START-UP COMPANIES

Start-up companies may also fall into the category above; however, a start-up may be at the stage that it has not yet received external investment and may be considering how to arrange its board or the founders may not yet be aware of what a board is for. Equally, founders often turn to contacts or recommendations of contacts for many or all of their senior appointments and non-executive directors.

The IoD's guide (IoD Factsheet: Setting up a Board 2018) highlights key issues that apply to all of the sections highlighted above from family-owned to start-up companies:

> During the early years of the company's existence, owner-managers may be uncomfortable about inviting outsiders onto the board. They may not yet be ready to share sensitive company information and decision-making powers with external persons. Hence the board often consists of an owner-manager's colleagues, family members, or close friends.

> However, this may result in the board lacking expertise in a number of key strategic areas, e.g. relating to strategy analysis, marketing, finance, human resources management, or international trade. As a result, it may make sense to create an additional advisory board, which can fill the expertise gaps in these areas.

> An advisory board should only be regarded as an interim step. Over time, non-executives should be added to the main board. Providers of external finance are also likely to insist on non-executive directors joining the board.

As the company grows, more focus will be placed on the board, which is the key decision-making body of the company. As the success of the company will depend more and more on the board, it is in the owner-manager's interest to get the best possible people onto the board.

In an owner-managed company, it is likely that a single person will initially fulfil the roles of both chairman and chief executive (or managing director). A separate independent chairman may not be commercially justifiable. However, the person holding both roles should remember that the responsibilities of chairman and CEO are distinct, and should be viewed separately.

Boards should comprise people with different perspectives, backgrounds, and experience. Board renewal is important to ensure a flow of new ideas.

PUBLIC SECTOR

Public Sector board appointments are often called Public Appointments and these vary from government oversight bodies to government-funded organisations such as NHS Trust boards. Some appointments are remunerated and some are not. The roles are advertised on government websites including HM Government Appointments (England and Wales), Appointed for Scotland, and NIDirect (Northern Ireland). The most common approach used is that applications require candidates to use a competency-based method for demonstrating skills and ability, interviews follow a similar path, albeit may also include exercises such as a short presentation, role play and analysis of a board paper. Providing a list of one's previous roles is just not enough for public sector board appointments processes. The anecdote of a former CEO of a major utility company not being shortlisted for interview for the board position of a utilities regulator, still circulates, the candidate had not demonstrated sufficient knowledge and understanding of the utilities sector was the reason given! Being familiar with the competency-based approach to answering questions is very important if one wishes to pursue public appointments, it is not necessarily an approach that many from the private sector are familiar with. This approach is discussed in detail in Chapter 8 - Gaining Your First Non-Executive Board Appointment.

Public Appointments are overseen by a panel, normally including the chair of the organisation and an independent person, the appointments panel select a recommended candidate; however, the final decision is not made by the panel but by the government minister responsible for the area in which the organisation sits. This can involve a long process that may not appear as transparent to those used to operating in other sectors. Some candidates express frustration with the process, while public sector officials express some frustration at the lack of a broader diversity of candidates, especially those from the private sector. Public bodies and government departments aim to recruit non-executive directors from a wide range of backgrounds. Professionals with private sector experience are in demand especially as NEDs with a commercial background may provide a useful dynamic to the boards of public bodies and advisory committees, play a strong role in the key issues of governance, bring complementary skills and knowledge and have an impact on the quality of management information. A report published by the Ethical Standards in Public Life Commissioner (UK Report on A Survey on Time Commitment, Remuneration and Other Aspects of The Role of Public Appointees 2020 (Summary Version), 2021) highlighted issues for board members regarding a significant time commitment being required to adequately discharge the role, well above the advertised, and a dissatisfaction with the level of remuneration paid to board members. This may also affect how attractive such appointments are to candidates not already strongly committed to the public sector.

CHARITY/VOLUNTARY SECTOR

The Charity/Voluntary sector's approaches and challenges in effective board (trustee) appointments are as varied as the sector itself as seen in Chapter 11 - Governance in the Charity/Voluntary Sector. Much depends on the size and constitution (governing documents) of the organisation. As with very few exceptions, third sector organisations do not pay trustees/non-executive board members, some struggle to find suitable board candidates.

Recruitment processes vary but there is a move towards advertising board vacancies and going through a competitive recruitment process, with some larger charities using search firms. There are also a large number of charities who still recruit from their contacts, user groups and local communities. Some will have requirements stated in their governing documents about the need to appoint some board members from particular groups that they may support or with particular skills or characteristics. Many also carry out skills audits to ensure a mix of skills on the board. Some even take board dynamics into account and consider whether they are looking for a negotiator, challenger, etc.

Charity/voluntary sector organisations often advertise their vacancies in many ways. It can be word of mouth, formal advert in an appropriate journal or through local volunteering structures. Those that advertise often use a sector specific website or sector infrastructure organisations such as volunteer centres. Some business support organisations such as the Institute of Directors (IoD) will also advertise on behalf of their charity members. There are a lot of local third sector interfaces or volunteer centres across the UK. A simple web search should take you to your local sources for finding opportunities.

In recruiting new Trustees, a board should consider the following:

- The role, what is involved, time commitment, and skills and experience required.

- The method of recruitment – advertisement, word-of-mouth, recruitment company.
- The application and selection process.

Some boards will interview and select the right "fit" for their purposes. However, an overly formal process can be a deterrent for some people. Care must be taken to ensure that any process is fair, attracts the interest of a wide range of people and is accessible to all. Alternative forms of application are required to ensure people can access the process and apply in a manner that suits their abilities for example, applications can be made in writing or in audio form.

Some boards allow prospective members attend and observe board meetings. This gives both parties an opportunity to test the waters and see if there is a good fit between the board and the candidate. Following the recruitment and selection process, the members still approve all board appointments. New Trustees can join a board mid-year on a co-opted basis, but the appointment will not be ratified until the subsequent AGM when members vote to confirm the position.

As many organisations in this sector work in a collegiate, co-operative manner, it is not unusual to find a board member or senior executive from another charity sitting on a selection panel in order to bring extra independence to the process.

HOW TO RECRUIT THE RIGHT BOARD MEMBERS

The different types of organisations described in the previous section highlight some nuanced differences; however, there is a common theme in making excellent board appointments. At the heart of best practice board recruitment is the delicate balance between achieving positive board chemistry, to facilitate good working relationships between individual board members, while ensuring a suitable diversity of thought, experience, skill, and outlook. It is a balance that is not easy to strike, as human beings we are "hard wired" to feel most at ease with those we identify being as like us and can lead us to be drawn to candidates who we like. This unconscious bias was touched on in the earlier section on common recruitment mistakes; however, it is important to note that it can be very difficult to be objective about recruiting to the board. After all, these are a group of people who carry great individual and collective responsibility (legal and moral) with different views and perspectives who have to come together in consensus in an often challenging and every changing operating environment. Using a structured process and tools to identify a list of the skills and attributes required can help considerably, as can using external specialists such as a search firm.

The principles here are based on conducting a skills and competency gap analysis; these are especially valuable if you have one or more vacancies on an established board. This means that when a vacancy arises, it is important to take stock of what skills, experience, and competencies/behaviours are present on the board and what is missing as well as where the organisation is heading. It may be that a technical specialism becomes evident as missing, but it's equally important to consider if you need a diplomatic skill set, or an analytical style in order to balance what you already have on the board. Equally, if the organisation is about to rapidly grow, reduce, acquire another entity, and so on. it is useful to recruit someone with that experience.

Conducting personality tests on the entire board, as you might do with any team, to find out if you have a good balance of styles and to help identify what you might want in a new recruit to that board, is a very good idea. Boards work most effectively when creativity, analysis, strong negotiation skills, vision, curiosity, ability to challenge, structure, and fluidity are all represented.

The very act of refreshing board members at suitable points in time, is valuable as you may start off with a very diverse skill set on a board but over time as people work together "group think" is a danger.

Equally important is recruiting for the future rather than the present and not being afraid to say goodbye. By this we mean that board members should be recruited for skills and abilities that match where the organisation wants to go rather than where it is now, but once that objective is achieved, don't be afraid to replace that board member with a new one who has the skills and aptitude for the next again step.

In considering a possible competency framework that can be used to undertake a gap analysis, the Institute of Directors produced a framework in 2016. Unlike other frameworks that are specific to particular professions or sectors this framework was designed to be relevant to every member of any board, in any sector, industry, geography, and size of organisation.

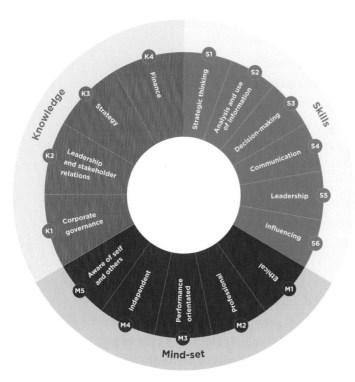

Figure 7.2 *IoD Director Competency Framework – Institute of Directors (2016).*

The competencies above can be further developed to make up a board matrix by adding in technical skills or experience required, and used to identify what is already available on the board and what gaps become apparent.

DIRECTOR SELECTION

More and more boards are engaging in independent, structured, and professional processes for director selection. Smaller boards may undertake the whole process together as a group, while for some boards a nominations committee will lead on director appointments. Such processes will generally take into account:

- Alignment of skills with strategic direction.
- Value added to the current board composition.
- Cultural fit with the board.
- Time it will take to be an effective contributor.
- Capacity and avoidance of conflicts.
- Succession planning.

Building the right board requires an understanding of director competencies, which involves consideration of the director's experience, skills, attributes, and capabilities. Director competencies encompass two distinct areas: technical competencies and behavioural competencies. Technical competencies are a director's technical skills and experience ("what you need to know and are able to do") such as accounting or legal skills, industry knowledge, experience in strategic planning and corporate governance. Behavioural competencies are a director's capabilities and personal attributes ("how you apply what you know and your personal and interpersonal skills") and include, for example, an ability to positively influence people and situations; an ability to assimilate and process complex information; time availability; personal integrity; and high ethical standards. Sometimes too little attention is paid to personal traits and capabilities that may not be evident in a CV. It is very important to consider whether the board needs a mix of directors who are able to:

- Quickly understand and process complex information.
- Develop and articulate a cogent argument.
- Be innovative and be able to imagine beyond the current possible, and
- Understand issues at the "big-picture" and detailed levels.

All board members directors need to have the ability to articulate points succinctly and effectively at board meetings and be able to strike a careful balance between being silent and trying to dominate all discussions.

Prior to reappointing, nominating or appointing individuals as directors, the board should consider:

- The strategic aims of the organisation, including the anticipated challenges and opportunities ahead.
- What competencies and skills the board, as a whole, should possess to meet the challenges/opportunities ahead.
- Assess what competencies and skills each incumbent director possesses and highlight any gaps.
- Are there any gaps once every director's contribution is added to the whole picture?

It is also important to take other factors into consideration such as dates that each board member is due to rotate off the board, the specific experience and skills that are present as well as missing, skills that support a positive board dynamic and to factor in diversity aspects such as age, gender, and ethnicity. Some boards go further in considering other diversity factors such as geographic, educational level, and economic status.

In addition to making new appointments to the board, it is important for fair and transparent processes to be in place or appointing board members to board committees and indeed as chairs of board committees and chair of the board. A board matrix to assess current board members can be most useful in this respect. It essentially helps to identify the current skills, knowledge, experience, and competencies of the board and can be used as an internal tool to integrate board evaluation and succession planning as it supports an impartial analysis of any gaps in skills or competencies that could be addressed in future director appointments.

To be of benefit to the organisation and the board, the board skills matrix should be created with the unique circumstances of the particular organisation in mind as well as the key qualifications and experience essential for the organisation's strategy and expected future needs.

BOARD MATRICES

Board composition is a broad term that encompasses issues such as who is on the board and the skills mix of the board. It involves both structural and cultural issues and board effectiveness depends on obtaining the right mix of skills and experience. Board composition varies significantly between organisations and is influenced by:

- Legal requirements including the organisation's constitution and purpose.
- Board size.
- The balance of executive and non-executive directors.
- Director competencies.
- Terms of office for directors, and
- The structure of the shareholding or membership.

Stable boards with long-serving, committed members will have the advantage of a thorough knowledge of the organisation and its mission. However, it is important that the board represents and reflects the interests of its owners/members by injecting some "new blood" occasionally. Selecting new directors to build a board that is right for the organisation is not a simple task.

In summary, when creating a board skills matrix give thought to the following pillars underpinning the creation of a board matrix (Figure 7.3):

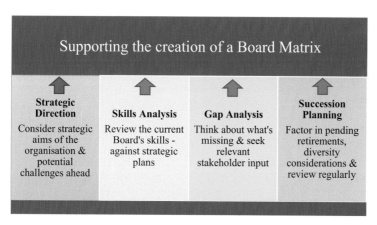

Figure 7.3 Pillars underpinning the creation of a board matrix.

Following the steps above will help in developing a suitable board matrix that can be employed to assess the board's capability requirements against the mix of current directors. There is no "one size fits all" when it comes to developing a competency matrix, and it should be tailored to the requirements and areas of importance for each organisation; however, the following is an example with a mix of sector, technical, and behavioural competencies that could be modified to suit the requirements of an organisation (Table 7.1).

Table 7.1 is designed to be a "catch-all" example for every sector and can be added to and headings changed to suit the style of and matters of most importance to the organisation it is being designed for. In addition, a matter not to be underestimated is to consider candidates' willingness to devote time and energy to the role.

Table 7.1 Example board matrix

Knowledge	Board Director A	Board Director B	Board Director C	Board Director D	Board Director E	Board Director F
Knowledge of sector						
• Regulatory knowledge						
• Financial/Audit/ Accounting						
• Legal						
• Human Resources						
• Risk Management						
• IT/cybersecurity						
• Marketing/PR/Social Media						
• International Markets						
• Mergers and Acquisitions/financial restructuring						
• **Experience**						
• Leadership						
• Specific industry experience						
• Commercial						
• Listed Company						
• Public sector						
• Voluntary/Not-for-profit						
• Investor/stakeholder relations						
• **Skills**						
• Strategic thinking						
• Analytical						
• Challenging constructively						
• Articulate						
• Active listening						
• Diplomatic						
• Politically astute						
• Financially literate						
• **Attributes**						
• Intellectually curious						
• Innovative						
• Emotional Intelligence						
• Collaborative mindset						
• Strategic in outlook						
• Integrity and honesty						
• "Big picture" and detail oriented						

LEARNING POINT

A transport organisation had not considered the requirement to include maximum terms on the tenure of its NEDs. After 28 years on the board, it became apparent that the knowledge and connections of the Chair and some of the other NEDs had become obsolete. Over the years, the environment in which the organisation operated had changed entirely and the lack of regular reviews of the Board was not perceived in a good light by stakeholders.

Reviewing the Board regularly is very important, one needs to ask, does the Board include expertise needed to meet the organisation's key strategic aims? Each director/trustee should review themselves and others on the board. Ask – what is missing?

Include stakeholder input as appropriate (this may be management team, key shareholders, beneficiaries, etc.). Pending retirements should be factored in as well as diversity considerations. Finally – don't forget to discuss it together as a board.

BOARD BEHAVIOURS

It is possible to have "best in class" governance in terms of structure and documentation, while having a highly dysfunctional board due to poor board behaviours. Strong behavioural governance can make all the difference. For example, when a CEO and Board Chair have a high level of trust and mutual confidence, they are more likely to share "clouds on the horizon" with each other sooner and more openly, and to work together to avoid performance lapses. When individual board members are able to speak out forthrightly and constructively, yet in a respectful challenging manner without fear of retribution or emotional reactions, better decisions are made in the long-term interests of the organisation.

Boardroom dynamics can be viewed as the relationship between three aspects of governance: governance structure, culture, and behaviours. Governance structure is concerned primarily with the process and task of the board – a good governance structure is a necessary foundation to excellence in the boardroom. A good governance structure is underpinned by fair and transparent processes and by building in good practice such as strategy days and opportunities for NEDs to have discussions without the presence of the executive board members or other attendees – for example, pre-meetings before the start of a board meeting.

Governance culture relates to the set of unspoken and unwritten norms – and this cultural context is vital. These norms may not be articulated but they exist none-the-less. For example, some boards are highly bureaucratic in the way they approach decision-making – driven by rules and policy. Others may be quite relaxed and casual and driven by relational dynamics between directors. Some boards have a strong leader who sets a hierarchical tone. Some may focus heavily on process, while others may primarily focus on results over process. Some may behave very much like a family while others could be highly business-like. Every director on the board knows what the cultural expectations of them are, and if they don't, they will soon learn. After just a meeting or two the new director will understand how to "fit in" with the culture.

It is in the cultural context that a board must take care not to fall into a pattern of "groupthink". As highlighted in earlier sections, the longer the directors work together on the same board, the more likely they are to engage in group think. This means they will be less likely to generate questions that could risk breaking the cohesiveness of the group. Cultural norms in a boardroom, are not in themselves problematic unless they discourage directors from exercising their direction and control responsibilities or if unhealthy cliques form. It can be relatively easy for cliques to form in a board environment. Board members working closely together, or who already knew each other prior to joining the board may become friends and enjoy each other's company. The danger in any clique lies in the risk of board members becoming too familiar, potentially reacting negatively to proposals or comments raised by other board members. Additionally, an "us vs them" mentality is at risk of developing, which in light of the moral, legal, and fiduciary duties that that board members are required to fulfil individually and jointly, could lead to disaster. The obvious danger is "group think". As individuals become comfortable hiding in the clique instead exercising independent thought and judgement.

Equally, board members who are not part of the clique can quickly feel discouraged from speaking, left out of the collective decision-making and unfairly treated. Eventually, board members in this position may become disillusioned and disengaged.

Behavioural or attitude-related skills, often described as "soft skills", are vital to effective board function and include a combination of a sense of personal responsibility and self-management, integrity and honesty, emotional intelligence, a collegiate attitude, demonstrating servant leadership and an ability to work positively with other genders and cultures.

These are demonstrated in positive board behaviours and include:

- Taking personal responsibility for actions and decisions.
- A sense of confidence mixed with humility.
- Interacting with others and make decisions with integrity and honesty.
- Being in control of emotions – responding appropriately rather than reacting.
- Productive and constructive attitude.
- Championing board decisions, whether originally in favour or not.
- Consistently demonstrating discretion, confidentiality, unity, and responsibility.
- Challenging management and other board colleagues in a constructive and respectful manner.
- Being prepared to trust – but verify.

Poor behaviour in the boardroom is just as easy to recognise as the good behaviour. Examples of dysfunctional behaviours are sometimes seen to include the development of board cliques which are not spotted or nothing is done to discourage them. Individual board members who regularly miss meetings or arrive late, are not prepared, step over the board/management line or act inappropriately, such as losing their temper or demonstrating misaligned agendas Personal agendas, wherein one or more board members are preoccupied with self, own compensation, own pet peeves and interests, own perspectives and become defensive if own position, point of view, or perspective is challenged in any way, are some further examples of poor behaviours.

Attempts to manipulate others in order to get one's own way are an equally dangerous behaviour and the authors have seen this issue develop in situations where there is a very strong CEO/MD who has a fixed agenda in mind and attempts to "deliver the board" to achieve a set outcome. This theme is very close to the idea of keeping score in order to create a "win" for self, rather than ensuring a "win" for the organisation and/or blaming others for their own failures. Other dysfunctional behaviour that is important to recognise is dealing poorly with conflict by behaving emotionally (anger, frustration, crying, threatening, accusing, blaming, slamming doors, etc.) or criticising anything that is not what they want. Behaving differently outside the boardroom than inside (e.g. speak against board or management decisions and strategies in the community), becoming easily stressed by the small things and be unable to see the bigger picture and demonstrating difficulty listening to others, preferring to hear own voice above all others, all have equally negative effects on the functioning of a board and on the important governance functions it fulfils.

Brown and Brown (2011) highlight numerous causes of dysfunction in the boardroom and point to the top five being:

- Boards are often comprised of senior leaders and entrepreneurs more used to leading the team than being an equal member of it.
- Lack of appropriate governance education.
- Serving on the board for the wrong reasons.
- A weak Chair.
- Emotional immaturity.

RECRUITING FOR THE OPTIMAL BEHAVIOUR MIX

It is better to get the right directors on the board at the outset to avoid having to take corrective action at a later date or when the board is trying to focus on dealing with matters of strategic importance or a crisis. If the board is of sufficient size, a committee should take responsibility for nominations, on smaller boards, one or two NEDs might take specific responsibility for appointing to the board or the Chair may take the lead. If a Nominations Committee exists, it is equally vital for the right people to be on that committee – ensure the individuals have the appropriate skills and understanding of board appointments. Educating those responsible for appointments to the board on what is expected of NED (including behavioural expectations) and on the needs and strategy of the organisation. Finally, be prepared to use appropriate tools to determine character and behaviour of prospective and existing NEDs (this could be through effective interviewing as well as personality tests or other tools).

Having highlighted the issue of a weak or not sufficiently skilled Chair as a potential cause of boardroom dysfunction, it is important to touch on the specific considerations that should be made when appointing the board chair. As Chair, the following attributes are vital:

- A healthy and productive relationship with the CEO/MD, which is not overfriendly.
- The competence to lead the board, including the emotional intelligence to engender a positive culture, where views are heard and positive behaviours are encouraged.
- The respect of the board and management.
- A personal sense of calling to, and understanding of, the role of Chair, and;
- An understanding of the importance of board chemistry, which is a vital ingredient in maintaining an effective board.

MAINTAINING AN EFFECTIVE BOARD

Within a company, the board of directors is the principal agent of risk taking and enterprise, in other words, the principal maker of commercial and other judgements. Discharging these responsibilities means thinking not only about particular tasks but also about ways of working as a board, and ensuring individual directors can be fully equipped to play their part. Once directors have been appointed to the board, the work of maintaining the effectiveness of the board begins, it is vital to consider; the board composition and organisation, clarifying board and management responsibilities, how board and board committee meetings are planned and managed, and the continuous development of the board to ensure its effectiveness. These activities are normally undertaken by the chair of the board, an important part of this role is to manage board business and act as its facilitator and guide.

NEDs play an important part in assisting the chair to fulfil their role by regularly and rigorously assessing the effectiveness of the board's processes and activities. Although NEDs bring an external perspective to a board, given that board evaluations involve honestly assessing one's own and fellow board colleagues' attributes and areas for improvement, employing an independent party to undertake such an evaluation, at least every three years is seen as best practice.

LEARNING POINT

A venture capital fund invested in a technology company, whose products provided a highly bespoke solution and selected a Chair, who had successfully built and sold a company involved with a similar underlying technology but aimed at a high-volume market. No one checked that the newly appointed

Chair understood the role of a NED or Chair and no training was provided, the individual also came with an "ego" and the relationship with the founders/executive management team deteriorated to the point the company was almost destroyed. The Chair stood down and a new appointments process commenced, this time through an independent search exercise, with consideration to behavioural skills, rather than sectoral experience, a number of candidates were considered, and a condition of the appointment included appropriate training.

The second appointment was a success and the organisation was able to move on to scaling the business.

Maintaining an effective board starts from the very first principles – recruit for character and train for competence. Many boards do this the other way around by seeking specific skills during the nominations process, and then attempt to influence behaviour after appointment. A director can be highly skilled in a particular competence yet poor in character and behaviour. It is not uncommon for the authors to remind board appointment committees that it is possible to bring a new director "up to speed" on the nuances of the sector and regulatory requirements for a board position – it is next to impossible to train for character once someone has already joined your board.

Ensure a governance structure encourages behaviour and character aspects to be considered in the recruitment process. Providing prospective candidates and appointments committees with clear expectations around boardroom behaviours as well as information about the roles and responsibilities of a director.

Behavioural and character aspects should form part of the annual evaluation process. Including questions on the topics of boardroom behaviour, relationships, and aspects of character will not only highlight any challenges in this area but may also provide a helpful mechanism for beginning a dialogue about how to resolve them.

Board training and development should include a focus on "soft skills" as well as structural and process matters.

Terms of reference for board members should include the behavioural expectations of directorship.

Decide on an optimal competency and behavioural mix for your board using tools to determine the character and behaviour of prospective and existing directors.

Finally, having an effective board evaluation system is a very helpful tool in measuring how effective the board is, periodic independent board evaluations can be especially enlightening.

INDEPENDENT BOARD EVALUATIONS

An efficient appraisal system is a key tool for underpinning and supporting improvements to board effectiveness. Creating an effective board is facilitated through a process of appraisal linked to continual development. This enables directors' performance to be monitored and improvements made.

There are many benefits to a company, and to its board, of a **regular review**. They help to clarify the individual and collective roles and responsibilities of directors; raise awareness of any current or future skills gaps with a view to filling them; improve working relations between the board and managers encouraging greater candour between directors' and senior managers (they also show that the board is leading by example), and finally they help keep the board focussed on improving its effectiveness.

The appraisal process involves:

- Defining board tasks and objectives.
- Measuring board resources and capabilities.

- Consultation with board members.
- Consolidation and review of the results.

Boards should also regularly monitor future performance against the appraisal findings. The UK Corporate Governance Code 2018 states that

> There should be a formal and rigorous annual evaluation of the performance of the board, its committees, the chair and individual directors. The chair should consider having a regular externally facilitated board evaluation.

Effective self-appraisal is not an easy process; it requires board members to make insightful and sometimes harsh judgements about themselves, each other and about issues that may affect all stakeholders in the organisation. It is important that the appraisal methodology is effective, very robust and focus on the contribution made by individual directors, the various processes of the board and its overall effectiveness. The appraisal exercise should be an annual process and be led by the chair or by the senior independent director (SID), if one has been appointed.

The Higgs Review annex also includes a section on "Performance evaluation guidance". It includes a series of questions to support boards in assessing how they are performing and to identify how certain elements of their performance areas might be improved. It further states that "Boards need to think deeply about the way in which they carry out their role. The behaviours that they display, individually as directors and collectively as the board, set the tone from the top".

Boards are also encouraged to consider arranging board evaluations to be conducted by an independent professional, the Code states that "The use of an external third party to conduct the evaluation will bring objectivity to the process".

The Guidance also points to the importance of Board evaluations in informing and influencing succession planning. Such evaluations should be both thorough and rigorous and they "should explore how effective the board is as a unit, as well as the quality of the contributions made by individual directors". The result is to provide an opportunity for boards to review skills, assess their composition and agree plans for filling skills gaps, and increasing diversity. They can help companies identify when new board appointments may be needed and the types of skills that are required to maximise board effectiveness.

The Charity Governance Code is authored by a steering group that includes ACEVO: Charity Leaders Network Association of Chairs; ICSA: The Chartered Governance Institute; NCVO: National Council for Voluntary Organisations; Small Charities Coalition; and WCVA: Wales Council for Voluntary Action, and is supported by the Charity Commission, which is an observer on the group. This code comments on board effectiveness and states,

> The board reviews its own performance and that of individual trustees, including the chair. This happens every year, with an external evaluation every three years. Such evaluation typically considers the board's balance of skills, experience and knowledge, its diversity in the widest sense, how the board works together and other factors relevant to its effectiveness.

A key factor that is alluded to above, in relation to how the board works together, is also known as board chemistry.

BOARD CHEMISTRY

Board chemistry is sometimes mistaken for the idea of how well the directors "get on". As with any team, it is, of course, important that a board of directors has a positive working relationship; however, the reason for giving careful consideration to this topic of chemistry is due to the implication of the character of directors and their fit with the current, or aspired to board culture. Some of the most vital attributes of effective directors include self-awareness, integrity, and high ethical standards. Boardroom dynamics will be impacted by the personalities and behavioural types present, so attention should also be paid to these qualities. Equally, chemistry should not be mistaken with who the chair, or other directors feel is most like them – as there is a danger of leading to "group think" and unfair discrimination. There is a fine line between selecting directors who will interact positively, be highly effective and provide constructive challenge and selecting directors who "fit in" because they are "just like us".

LEARNING POINT

A stock exchange listed company was established with an initial Board of four members, the Chair died suddenly, leaving the remaining Board of three members, one of whom stepped into the chair role with little board experience. Some concerns grew about the competence of one of the NEDs; however, the matter became complicated by some difficult and unpleasant behaviours directed at this particular NED by a key member of the executive management team. The addition of a 4th NED improved the board dynamics; however, the competence issues remained and board chemistry was not positive. A highly sensitive approach was required. An independent board evaluation was commissioned, this enabled the process to be dealt with in a transparent manner and the subsequent report facilitated a delicate and non-confrontational discussion resulting in the NED finishing his term early in an orderly and dignified departure.

Board evaluations an bring up sensitive issues requiring an independent perspective and therefore an independent, external board evaluation is advised at least every three years, this would typically involve:

- A self-assessment questionnaire (tailored to the specific circumstances of the board being evaluated) to be completed on an anonymous basis by each director including commentary on the effectiveness of each board committee and the chair.

- In in depth interview, conducted with each board member and relevant stakeholders.
- Observation of a board meeting.
- Production of a detailed report – highlighting strengths, areas for improvement and any skills gaps.

KEY MESSAGES

- Recruit for character, mindset, and attitude, train for competence.
- One size does NOT fit all" – structure the board to be "fit for purpose" in light of circumstances and environment and be prepared to change it (subject to governing documents).
- Get the brief right – otherwise even the best executive search will produce the wrong results.
- Embrace difference – diversity of thought is a powerful addition.
- Motivation, attitude, and behaviours are key – appraise and evaluate regularly and make use of independent evaluations; it's amazing what might come to light.

FURTHER READING

https://www.frc.org.uk/getattachment/61232f60-a338-471b-ba5a-bfed25219147/2018-Guidance-on-Board-Effectiveness-FINAL.PDF
https://www.frc.org.uk/getattachment/88bd8c45-50ea-4841-95b0-d2f4f48069a2/2018-UK-Corporate-Governance-Code-FINAL.pdf

REFERENCES

Bain, N. and Barker, R. (2010). *The Effective Board: Building Individual and Board Success*. London, UK: Institute of Directors United Kingdom.

Brown, D. and Brown, D. (n.d.). *Boardroom Behaviours and Governance*. [online]. Available at: https://www.governancesolutions.ca/governance-solutions/publications/pdfs/Behaviour%20and%20Governance.pdf. [Accessed 29 Sep. 2020].

Hesketh, A., Sellwood-Taylor, J. and Mullen, S. (Jan. 2020). Are You Ready to Serve on a Board? *Harvard Business Review*.

Iod.com. (2018). What Is the Role of the Board? | Institute of Directors | *IoD*. [online]. Available at: https://www.iod.com/services/information-and-advice/resources-and-factsheets/details/What-is-the-role-of-the-board. [Accessed 29 Sep. 2020].

Murphy, M. (2012). *Hiring for Attitude: A Revolutionary Approach to Recruiting Star Performers with Both Tremendous Skills and Superb Attitude*. New York: McGraw Hill.

Taleb, N. (2012). *Antifragile: Things That Gain from Disorder*. London: Penguin.

The Future Board Getting in Shape for Tomorrow's Challenges. (n.d.). [online]. Available at: https://www.icsa.org.uk/assets/files/free-guidance-notes/the-future-board-report.pdf [Accessed 29 Sep. 2020].

UK Report on A Survey on Time Commitment, Remuneration and Other Aspects of The Role of Public Appointees 2020 (Summary Version). (2021). [online]. Available at: https://www.ethicalstandards.org.uk/sites/default/files/publications/2021-02-05%20%28Summary%20Report%29%20-%20FINAL.pdf [Accessed 21 Mar. 2021].

www.abebooks.co.uk. (n.d.). 9780749437527: Standards for the Board: Improving the Effectiveness of Your Board (Good Practice for Directors) – AbeBooks – Institute of Directors: 0749437529. [online]. Available at: https://www.abebooks.co.uk/9780749437527/Standards-Board-Improving-Effectiveness-Good-0749437529/plp [Accessed 29 Sep. 2020].

www.civilsociety.co.uk. (n.d.). Charities Need to Set "Clear Targets" on Diversity. [online]. Available at: https://www.civilsociety.co.uk/news/

time-for-diversity-targets-charities-told.html#sthash.bztHN4XH.dpuf
[Accessed 4 Oct. 2020].

www.iod.com. (n.d.). Setting up a Board | Institute of Directors | *IoD*. [online].
Available at: https://www.iod.com/news/news/articles/Setting-up-a-Board.
[Accessed 29 Sep. 2020].

CHAPTER EIGHT

Gaining Your First Non-executive Board Appointment

Francesca Ecsery

DOI: 10.4324/9781003142850-8

INTRODUCTION

The landscape for gaining NED board appointments has changed considerably over the last two decades, many still remember a time when many such board roles were the preserve of a relatively narrow group of well-connected individuals. While board appointments are no longer the preserve of the few, gaining a first NED board appointment is often described as the most challenging aspect of the board journey. The ideas and tips shared in this chapter are designed to provide practical steps that an aspiring NED can follow in order to help in securing a NED appointment in the private, public, and charity/voluntary sectors. In this chapter a variety of practical learning points and ideas have been drawn together – indeed, all the things that the aspiring NED might wish to know as he/she starts on this path. The chapter includes advice on managing your personal and digital brand, networking, engaging with search professionals and conducting all important due diligence on any board opportunities you pursue, starting with the top tips for securing a first, and subsequent NED board appointments.

TOP TIPS

NED curriculum vitae (CV): the importance of having a great NED CV. You need to create one that is both different enough to stand out and one that highlights different skills from the executive CV you have. Create a personal brand, that is "Your You-est You". Be your own authentic person and stand your ground.

- T shape people: a "T-shaped" person is capable in many things and expert in, at least, one. Chairs look for expertise (functional or industry) but broad enough experience (such as managing director – MD/chief executive officer – CEO/vice president – VP) to be able to contribute in other discussions. Decide how to position your expertise.

- Chemistry: the boardroom is a "club" – you are in it for six to nine years. You need advocacy and to establish chemistry during your interview process will be key to securing a NED role.
- NED Pitch: be clear about what you can contribute, what makes you unique, great/relevant to the boardroom or committees and why you want to be on a board. You are selling yourself to a business so you need to "know the question you are an answer for".
- CV shelf life: head-hunters and recruiters may receive around 100 CVs a week so your CV might only have a three-week shelf life. Search professionals are the gatekeepers to most high-profile NED roles so your CV needs to "stand out in the crowd".

LinkedIn: make sure your profile is up to date and absolutely complete. Connect to everyone you know/have met. Connect with every relevant head-hunter and recruiter you have ever spoken to on LinkedIn so that they can get automatic updates that remind them of you (without stalking them). Remember that certain head-hunters have a sector-industry focus and therefore it is worth focusing on connecting with those who work on the NED searches in the area most of interest to you. Doing your research is important.

Networking – there is no substitute for Networking:

- You have to "get out there" – it keeps you fresh and you always learn something.
- NED head-hunters – make sure that the NED specialist in each head-hunting firm knows you are looking – they are different from your executive contacts, they are the "multipliers".
- Other NEDs – as experienced NEDs get most of the head-hunter calls – they can refer them on to you and positively reference you to them.
- Other networks – consider auditors, researchers, nominations committee chairs, new areas such as industry associations and private equity (PE) groups.

- Be upfront – tell people you want a NED. To be successful at networking, you must keep in mind that it really is not about you, it is about building relationships – not a one-way street.
- Add Value – make a list of the possible things you can do for people in your network such as connecting or, information sharing.

GENERAL TIPS

Resilience, patience, and determination are very important, it is a competitive market and you should be mentally be prepared to be rejected – several times!

- Use it as an opportunity to learn about a new business and prove that your skills are transferable.
- Board roles always take up far more time than you think! Plan for 20 to 30 days a year for each role, especially during the first year.
- If you have the time, especially if you are no longer in full-time employment, a balanced NED portfolio could involve four NED roles: perhaps one for good money, one for fun, one for a good network, one for giving back.

Interviews and applications: prepare for both and highlight the *evidence* in your experience (work and life) for each point in the role requirement:

- Follow-ups if appropriate. Get contact details of the people interviewing you and use the thank you email as opportunity to restate your interest in the role and to clarify important points – if the appointments panel is willing to share contact details.
- References – some NED recruiters like to secure references in advance of even proposing the candidate to their client so make sure you get them ready in advance. If you are in full-time employment please ensure that your existing company is happy with you taking on an external director role and find out if there are any area of exclusion due to competitive reasons. There is

nothing more frustrating for the appointment panel (and for you) than finding out part way through an appointment process, that you have to withdraw because your employer will not support you joining the board of a particular organisation.

Consider it to be a career pivot – this is not the same as an all-out career change. A career pivot involves taking the skills you have mastered over the years and applying them to another area such as board work.

Be open minded about opportunities – do not be too picky with your first NED role and use it as development opportunity. At the same time, remember a NED role comes with legal duties so make sure you spend time doing due diligence and bear in mind that you board experience will be heavily influences by how good the Chair is.

It is said that it is **never too early** to try to get your first NED/Trustee position, assuming you have built up some relevant experience. It is also worth starting the NED board journey before you finish your executive career entirely. Waiting until you retire is often seen as a sensible option, although it can take 2–3 years or more to secure a NED role and all of a sudden, your executive experience can be seen as rather dated or no longer current, especially if you are interested in NED roles in organisations where the pace of change and regulation is fast-moving.

LEARNING POINT

Resilience, Patience, and Determination

- NED roles are generally less well advertised publicly compared to executive ones and will feel like a more competitive process too, which is why having resilience, and a good network is key to finding NED roles and

---

opportunities as these will amplify your personal brand. It is competitive out there so be prepared to be rejected …..several times.

- Use it as an opportunity to learn about a new business and prove that your skills are transferable
- Board roles always take up far more time than you think! Plan for 20 to 30 days a year for each role, especially during the first year.

If you have the time, a balanced NED portfolio may involve four NED roles: perhaps one for good money, one for fun, one for a good network and one for giving back.

NED CV – YOUR PERSONAL BRAND

The main contribution a NED makes is through their ability to constructively challenge the thinking, decisions, strategy, and responses of the executive team. You bring intelligence and not just experience to a board. It is about being curious and able to think strategically rather than being about what you already know. The following suggestions will support you in developing your personal brand.

T shaped people: Chairs look for expertise (functional or industry) but broad enough experience (such as MD/CEO/VP) to be able to contribute in other discussions. Decide how to position your expertise. Need to create a strong and authentic CV which will get you noticed for the right reasons.

Create a NED CV that is different from the executive CV you have. Create a personal brand, that is the "Your You-est-You". Write your CV yourself and make it as personal and as memorable as possible.

Develop a personal profile, your elevator pitch, your professional statement and then experiment with by testing it with friends and people who know you well at first. If they frown or seem puzzled then you know that it has not landed well or it is unauthentic. Articulate clearly and authentically what makes you stand out as a compelling NED? What is your Unique Sales Proposition (USP)? Be clear about what you can contribute to a board and a business, what you bring to the role, what makes you unique, great/relevant to the boardroom or committees. You also need to be clear as to what type and why you want to be on a board "know the question you are an answer for". Ask yourself: what is my mission in this role, and can I add value and make a real difference?

KEY CV SECTIONS

- Personal (e-mail, contact number, address, two pages max; if sending to a head-hunter/executive search practice – send your CV in Word and do not put in any graphics as the CV will be changed into the search firm's own format and branding so make it easy for them, tailor it to different briefs, no need for CV title, no date of birth required.
- Professional impact statement; key landmarks (with evidence); major brands; financial highlights; stand out achievements (do mention if you have experience of audit, risk; remuneration, change management committees; shareholder/ stakeholder engagement; mergers and acquisitions (M&A); listing; delisting; fund raising; the City, business model pivots; digital).
- Start with board experience: list all Board experience including subsidiary and joint venture (JV) boards and sub-committee memberships. If you don't have any NED experience title the section "Board Experience" and list experience of dealing/working with boards.
- Executive experience: list recent executive experience with key company info such as turnover, number of employees, markets, market capitalisation, and ownership. Focus on key achievements

with key performance indicators (KPIs) and financials – The ten-year rule – beyond ten years just list companies and job titles – unless there is something highly pertinent to the NED role you are applying for, in which case expand.

- Academic and professional qualifications: no need for school-level results.
- Diversity of thought: anything that will evidence that you are different (languages, international experience) is prized so do mention if you can help boards in their endeavours. They are looking for gender diversity, ethnic diversity, geographic expansion experience, or any useful information that will make you stand out from the rest.

WORKING IT ON LINKEDIN WHEN LOOKING FOR A NED ROLE

LinkedIn is a highly authoritative platform, (The Muse Editor, 2015) a social media unlike any other and often considered to be *the* professional relationship database. It is an efficient way to stay in contact with people, to refresh contacts and find people. More importantly, it is unusual to meet a recruiter/head hunter who does not use LinkedIn and they will look at your profile when considering or building a long list of candidates. Many recruiters and job sites often use your LinkedIn profile to populate their own platform via API instead of keying the data manually. That is why it is so important that you make sure your profile is **up to date and complete**.

It is also important to list, as accurately as possible all the roles you hold or have held including any NED appointments and advisory committee roles as well as any professional qualifications. Head-hunters often express exasperation when checking LinkedIn profiles where individuals keep "secrets" such as stating they hold a number of listed board roles without mentioning which organisations or any dates. This is important as the head-hunter or researcher will be looking through a number of records and wants to ensure they are approaching potential candidates who have useful experience without obviously having a conflict of interest (such as being involved with a competing organisation). Another area that frustrates head-hunters is when a specific qualification is required, for example, when seeking an audit chair the appointment committee may require a qualified accountant, if you hold that qualification, state it expressly rather than just alluding to it!

LinkedIn has a very handy percentage rating on the side of the screen to signal to you how complete they think your profile is. It is well worth to endeavour to reach 100% as this will help the algorithm to feature your profile higher up on a search result listing.

LinkedIn is one of the best platforms to showcase your professional achievements. Turn on the privacy setting while you are actively building and amending your content or correcting spelling mistakes – but then turn it back on to public when it is good enough for people to see your activity (and, as with everything in life, "perfect is the enemy of good").

Working on your LinkedIn connections is recommended. It is helpful to have a high number of good 1st degree connections that will support your claim of expertise, personal interests and professional experience. A vast LinkedIn network is not necessarily effective but it is important that you connect to everyone you know or have met personally, and who you trust on a professional level. Once connected, look through their connections and connect to everyone you have met from their network too, especially if you want to diversify the industry that you most recently operated in. This will take time to build so make sure you make time for this activity.

Be active and regularly participate on the platform: publish, comment or share good thought pieces. This is important because it builds a digital footprint of your interest and expertise and it strengthen your authority on a topic. If you have your activity visibility set to "on" LinkedIn sends a helpful notice/reminder that you exist to your connections every time something happens to your LinkedIn profile (new connections, a "like" of a post or comment that you have added, a narrative you have shared, or even an original story you have posted). This allows you to be "top of mind" for your connections. You need to nurture your LinkedIn activity and make sure you do it regularly.

Connect with every relevant recruiter and head-hunter you have met or contacted through your job-hunting efforts, past and present. It is often said that for landing a NED role you need to be "at the right place at the right time"; however, it could be argued that you need to be everywhere at all times – which is impossible. Thanks to your activity on LinkedIn your contacts can get automatic updates that helpfully remind them that you exist (without stalking them!). Many head-hunters receive 50 to 100 CVs a week so, in this clutter, your CV may only have a three-week shelf life as well as requiring for them to have a live search assignment they can match you perfectly to, during that time window. Furthermore, recruiters and head-hunters can also move organisations themselves and it is quite a task to keep track of where they end up. LinkedIn can help you with all of that.

Another way to usefully leverage what LinkedIn can offer you is to join relevant LinkedIn Groups. You can join up to 50 groups. These could be in the areas you already have extensive expertise in or, if you want to be more strategic about how you do this join groups in areas you want to build expertise (NED, Risk, Environment, Social, and Governance – ESG, Digital, Big Data, artificial intelligence – AI, executive remuneration and other industry-specific ones). Once you have done all that, be active on those platforms with comments and posts. This activity can further enhance your credibility in, or knowledge around those topics.

Finally, you can also sign up for job alerts and get reminders for any NED roles published on LinkedIn. You never know, and you may not find your perfect NED role on that platform, if nothing else you can use it to practice or to understand what skills are required for the roles that you are interested in.

NETWORKING

Research often shows that most of us find networking unenjoyable and off-putting but it is none the less important to engage in, if you want to pivot your career towards NED work. The key is to look at this process as an open exchange of ideas, resources, information, contacts, and tips. A few tips on how to make this process more effective are as follows:

- Prepare: Before any event, research the attendees ahead of time by looking at the guest list or checking on the event social media page who is attending.
- Be clear and authentic: Explain what you really do and highlight one thing you want them to know about you? Being authentic is compelling, natural, it'll help you be relatable and it will build meaningful relationships.
- Use your elevator pitch: Focus on what makes you special, your USP, the question you are the answer for. Share a few sentences about your past, a few sentences about your present and a few sentences about your future. Don't be afraid to show your passion and what excites you about your work.
- Be engaging and connect. Instead of talking about job titles— what is your superpower? You want someone to say: "Tell me more!" You also need to be mindful that you don't let networking become a drain for the other person by taking too much time and attention for yourself. Take a genuine interest in them and seek nothing in return. Think relationships first, business second. Ask people about themselves, what keeps them up at night and what their biggest current challenge is.
- Ask Unusual Questions such as, "what are you excited about these days?" or "what would be the title of your autobiography?" or "what is your superpower?"

> **LEARNING POINT**
>
> Networking cannot be underestimated. Even in types of organisations that are required to show they used independent means (executive search or advertising) to find suitable candidates, board members can add their own suggestions into the mix for consideration alongside candidates found through search and/or advert.
>
> Equally, search consultants/head-hunters often ask board members from other organisations for recommendations of names so you never know who might recommend you for a NED role.

CREATING A DIGITAL BRAND

By creating a digital brand, you are taking control of your digital footprint and ensure that people see what you want them to when they look you up on the internet. There is a plethora of websites, publications, and "experts" on the subjects but here are some simple steps you may want to consider:

ONLINE REPUTATION CHECK

It is almost guaranteed that a head-hunter/recruiter will consult the internet about a candidate, "Google" yourself regularly to see what comes up. If you find negative content, try to mitigate this by creating positive content, photos, blogs, social media platforms and anything on line which Google favours; i.e. a website built using Google Sites or Word Press.

LINKED IN

- Many organisations use social media, such as LinkedIn for board recruitment.
- Make your profile 100% complete.

- Use the key words that employers might search for in your skills descriptors.
- Update it/improve it frequently – the tool communicates that there was a change to your contacts (not the specific change, just that a change happened) – keeping you top of mind with your network.
- Join Groups that build the picture of what you are interested/ expert in. You can also connect with people through the groups they belong to.

PHOTO

Get a great, high quality professional looking nice profile picture. Your Google ranking will be favoured if there are pictures/images on a web page, it makes reading more interesting and provides a resting area for the eyes when reading long Bios, and is helpful for recruiters to recognise you.

PERSONAL WEBSITE

- The best way to control what recruiters see about you – first.
- Make it into a virtual hub, curating all the relevant content of you.
- Flexible: make it really relevant for now but you need to keep it up to date and be easy to update.
- Purchase your own name URL.
- Many web-building tools available, some are free.

LEARNING POINT

During the COVID-19 pandemic many boards/appointment panels conducted interviews for NEDs online and some boards have chosen to continue doing so even when social distancing became no longer required. It is more difficult to read body language for both the appointment panel and candidate and as a

---

candidate you are faced with the faces of the whole appointment panel at once. A good tip is to try and look into the camera when speaking (this is the closest to eye contact for those you are addressing) and to vary your tone of voice, perhaps more than you normally would.

From your viewpoint as a candidate, one of the few benefits of online interviews is that you can have papers with facts, figures, and prompt points spread out around you, and not in screen shot, to support you.

OTHER SOCIAL MEDIA

Having mentioned digital brand, it is also important to be aware of your wider social media footprint, if you have one. There have been numerous examples in the press about individuals losing high-profile jobs due to a Twitter post or as a result of liking someone else's Twitter post, which were deemed inappropriate for the role the individual was in, or about to take up. Similarly, Facebook, Instagram, and other activities on social media can come in for scrutiny. Some employers conduct research on these matters prior to making a job offer and this is becoming more prominent in NED appointments too. For public sector body NED appointments, this information is looked at as a matter of course for all candidates shortlisted for interview. Being aware of this and how any social media posts may be perceived is important.

WHY DO BOARDS HIRE NEDs?

As covered in more detail in Chapter 5 (Executive Directors on the Board), being a NED on the board of an organisation is different from being an Executive Director. Good NEDs are not execs and have a more subtle, relationship-based and advisory approach than is the case for executive directors. They are there to ask questions, not to give answers. The best NEDs act as a "sounding board" and provide a check and balance at the same time, a complex balancing act! They also often add various attributes, which bring greater external, and wider strategic views deriving from broader experience and even a perspective on what might be "coming over the horizon". The most common skills/experience and attributes of NEDs can include:

- Broader business/sector experience.
- Provide checks and balances.
- Improve governance.
- Strategy, long-term vision, and planning.
- Valuable contacts with other organisations.
- General management and relevant industry expertise.
- Financial expertise, technology or digital leadership.
- Insights into new customers/distribution channels.
- Regulatory expertise.
- International markets experience.
- Diverse perspectives – gender, ethnicity, age but mainly diversity of thinking!

TO NED OR NOT TO NED?

Working as a NED on various boards can be rewarding and interesting but also can be quite challenging and is not for everyone. Some of the attractions and challenges of serving on boards as a NED are listed below:

Attractions	Challenges
Working "on" instead of "in" a business.	Not a lot of money – working as a NED is more about "giving back" and helping an organisation or a leadership team.
Proveing that your skills are transferable to other industries or size of business.	Takes more time than you think, especially in year 1 or when there is a crisis.

Stimulus of being "strategic" without the "grind" of running the operational side of a business.
Freedom to work in directions of interest.
Have more purpose in your work.

Flexibility, greater control over working hours (apart from meeting days) – lifestyle choice.
Build experience and knowledge.
Stimulation of learning new businesses, knowing new work practices.

Rewarding when you find the right one!
Variety, avoiding rut and repetition.

Regular income stream, albeit small or nil (in some cases).
Satisfaction of knowing that you are adding value despite the small number of contact points.
No politics – at least not much.
Helps to develop skills, profile and credibility in other lines of work or other industries.
No gender pay-gap (for once).
You can learn a lot.

Social – a NED is independent, and to remain so needs to keep a certain distance.

Can be frustrating – not in charge and can't make things happen.
You can't walk all over the flower beds – emotional intelligence at all times.

The role does carry liability: although not many cases in existence, NEDs can be sued if something goes wrong along with the executive directors. The biggest risk is to your *personal brand*. For the rest make sure you have "Director's Liability Insurance" and be clear what it covers. Undertake a thorough due diligence and induction process mitigates this risk. Whenever asking questions about Corporate Governance, get the answers in writing.
Missing the casual social interactions.

Missing managing people, finding, developing, and championing little stars.
Learning to question rather than tell.
Responsibility is not part time even if the work is.

DUE DILIGENCE PROCESS

Doing you own due diligence on an organisation is a crucial step in the recruitment process, especially for you as the potential NED, as it will provide insight and some reassurance that you are joining the board of an organisation that operates with integrity, adheres to its legal and regulatory obligations, and adheres to a robust set of governance policies (or seeks your support in developing these). The process also allows you to take proactive remedial actions if any deficiencies are identified and ensure that you would enjoy the role and feel you could add value too. A few areas to consider are:

Organisational Drivers and Strategy – stating the obvious but for you to do a good job it is important that you understand the business model, especially if the organisation is in a different industry from your executive experience. You need to understand its key operating drivers and some idea as to how the organisation plans to ensure its sustainability.

CEO and Chief Financial Officer (CFO) – they are often the most important executives in the boardroom and with potentially somewhere between four and ten meetings a year, board meetings will never be enough for you to know what is going on in the organisation. You need to feel you can trust their judgement.

Chair – the Chair is the most important person for you to like and trust and you need to feel some affinity with him/her. They set the tone of how the board operates and how productive the meetings are but also makes sure the CEO is focused on delivering the strategy. The Chair is also the hardest person to get rid of, if there is a concern.

Try to get a reading on some of the more important *board feedback loops* to understand the culture and effectiveness of the board dynamics:

- Chair and individual board members.
- Senior independent director (SID) and chair.
- CEO and chair.
- Board review/evaluation – especially if advisors are involved.

LEARNING POINT

It is important to remember that when being interviewed for a NED role, you as the candidate are also interviewing the appointment panel and, depending on the process, the whole board. It is vital to think carefully about the overt and more subtle signals you receive. While serving on a board together, potentially for nine years, is not about being good friends it is vital to ask yourself "can I work with this board?"

Another useful question to consider is "will this board value my contribution?" If the answer to either of those questions is no – walk away. Joining the wrong board and stepping off before the end of one's first term does not do your CV any favours and will require explanation in future appointment processes.

In the private sector related party transactions can be an issue, not just in smaller businesses or in a business where a board member has a large shareholding; this is often a key concern for many boards, and will be sure to keep you awake at night if the conflict of interest is not managed properly.

Management remuneration – important to understand its structure, its drivers and the amounts involved as early as possible in the due diligence process as otherwise executive remuneration can be a source of endless unwelcome distraction from a variety of stakeholders. Make sure you understand motivations of the senior leadership team in the organisation (e.g. is it growth vs pure exit)

Reports and Accounts – a lot can be gleaned by reading and analysing this document. You should look out for some basics:

Balance sheet – enough cash to survive a crisis (around two years). Operational matters/risk management/internal audit – these should be disclosed in the document and easily understood. Directors and Officers Liability Insurance (D&O) is this insurance at the right level (amount and structure of the company, especially important if you join a subsidiary board). Liabilities relating to the 3 C's (Cyber, Culture, Climate change) but also on pension reserves.

Risk and Control – culture of the organisation (how is success rewarded, how are stakeholders communicated with and what is the risk appetite)?

NO NED EXPERIENCE? LEVERAGE YOUR EXECUTIVE SKILLS!

You often hear that "you need to have NED experience" to apply and be appointed to NED roles. But you have to start somewhere so it is important to highlight the following in your background:

- Define what your primary skill set is (HR, marketing, finance) and communicate it clearly.
- Articulate why this skill set is valuable at board level (risk, strategy, governance, and growth or influence).
- Think about what the risks might be if someone with your skills was not on the board and make sure you share it with the recruiter.
- Define the organisation that will value and leverage your skills (what are you the answer for)?
- Define your interest for being on a board.

Having a couple of target organisations in mind when speaking to a recruiter means that you can answer the question, "What sort of board are you looking for?" Equally, it will help to provide you with a solid basis for developing the strategies and tactics required to gain that appointment.

SECURING A NED WHILE STILL IN FULL-TIME EMPLOYMENT

Some aspiring NEDs wonder how they could possibly find the time to work as a NED in another organisation when their existing full-time role is completely immersive. It could be argued that you are at your most attractive as a new NED when you are eye wateringly busy in your executive job so don't miss the opportunity to start gaining some NED experience if you have the chance! Women on Boards (Women on Boards, 2012) suggest the following:

- While your skills/knowledge are current, this might be considered "gold dust" and can be hugely helpful in a crisis, as long as you are able to dedicate the requisite time for the NED role.
- A directorship will be a point of difference on your CV when applying for a new executive role. It gives you the opportunity to build career and leadership skills that you may not be able to develop in your day job.
- You will grow your market and industry knowledge and networks through exposure to a diverse range of issues from the perspective of a director.
- Joining a board indicates to management and to your clients that you are interested and engaged in your community at a leadership level.
- Directorships improve career resilience and provide strategic understanding of workforce dynamics and the challenges of running an organisation.
- If you need to take a career break at any stage, a directorship can give you continuity on your CV.
- It will help you maintain professional contacts and could provide you with the confidence to re-enter the workforce more easily after a significant break.
- It gives you the chance to explore the idea of a post-executive board career. It gets you the "stripes" of having already served on boards in preparation for a portfolio career. If you chose to build a portfolio career you will not be considered a "first time NED".

- A NED role also provides important personal development which in turn can make you become a better executive director.
- It is never too early to start building your NED or trustee experience.

TRANSITIONING FROM EXECUTIVE TO NON-EXECUTIVE

Applying for a NED role is a highly competitive process as you will be competing against more experienced candidates. To that effect, preparation for the selection process is key, as is building resilience. Most new NEDs come from hands-on positions that require operational involvement at the helm of a company or division. A NED needs to be more of an advisor which means taking a step back and leaving the day-to-day running of the company to the executive directors. Your role as NED will be to provide guidance and to ensure that the executive teams are on the right course – a useful saying about the role of a NED is "nose in, hands out".

As you start your first NED appointment, you will not be able to indulge in management activities and your primary responsibility will be for the supervision and aiding of the executive directors. You will have to ensure that you learn the organisation and use your induction process to its maximum effect, even if the process that has been organised for you is not perfect. If you're joining a company that is in an industry outside your area of expertise, then before you start offering advice it will be important to listen to the experts, to those around you and to those who will help you build up your knowledge.

PRIVATE SECTOR APPOINTMENTS

As discussed in Chapter 9 (Governance in the Private Sector), not only is the private sector the largest of the three in the UK (by income, employees, and number of organisations), it is also the most diverse in terms of legal structures. It may be no surprise that there are very different approaches to board appointments in the private sector. Publicly listed companies are expected to use the services of a head-hunter and may advertise, while any organisation which is highly regulated, whether publicly listed or privately owned, especially a large one, is more likely to use similar methods. The advice on developing head-hunter relationships in the previous sections applies well to this type of NED appointment.

If you are interested in a NED appointment in medium or smaller organisations that are privately owned, professional partnerships, employee-owned, family-owned, or PE/Venture Capital (VC)-backed companies then networking with the professional advisers to those organisations is the best way in. If early-stage/start-up company boards are of interest, and you have funds to invest and are relaxed about not earning a fee in the early stages, then joining an Angel Investment Syndicate is a potential route to an appointment. Most early-stage or VC investors appoint an investor director to the board of a company they have invested in. The earlier stage the company, the greater the risk of company failure and the greater the amount of time you might have to give, it is not for the "faint-hearted" and the importance of conducting due diligence cannot be underestimated. Equally, the founders/executive team of an early-stage company may not have a depth of, or any, governance knowledge so you may find yourself in a teaching role – if you are new to being a NED – that might not be an ideal combination.

Family-owned companies do not always seek NEDs, especially those who are not in the family, when they do, often advice is sought from their professional advisers. Building relationships and being able to demonstrate an understanding/sympathy with the unique culture, approach as well as advantages/challenges presented by the family dynamic in organisational decision-making is vital. There are business organisations that support family-owned organisations, learning about these, and attending events and seminars are useful in gaining an insight. In a similar vein, there are organisations that provide support, guidance, and learning for employee-owned, mutually owned, and co-operative companies. If your passion lies in any of these areas, they are the places to network and build relationships.

With regard to publicly listed companies, it should also be noted that there is a stage before a company becomes a publicly listed entity – this is called the initial public offering (IPO) stage. The process of an IPO often involves the need to appoint independent NEDs.

JOINING A BOARD AS A NED DURING AN IPO PROCESS

An IPO (when a company initially lists on a stock exchange) is often a point in time where companies hire new NEDs and strengthen their board with complementary skills. Recruitment also tends to follow a more transparent due process than in some privately owned companies, and this presents an opportunity for NEDs looking for roles. It is, however, a very time-consuming process because you need to go through, in detail, circa 900 pages of formal documentation, prepared by the lawyers, the brokers, compliance services, and accountants all feeding into the public listing prospectus. Other thoughts are:

One the key benefits is that it is a uniquely "fast-track" induction process: all that reading will help you understand the business much better than through normal induction process as all information about the company is there, in one place and completely up to date. At no point in the company's life will you ever have all the key data in quite such an up-to-date manner.

Liabilities: joining a board at IPO stage means that, in addition to the usual board responsibilities, covered by normal D&O insurance, you do take on extra responsibilities linked to the listing event: The directors vouch for every single word, number, or claim in the submission document/placement brochure. This risk can be mitigated by getting public offering of securities insurance (POSI) but you will need to convince the company to pay for it.

As a director, you lend your reputation (as the hard work has been done by the executives) so make sure you get to know the leadership team and other members of the board well, as trust will be key to your comfort of taking on this liability. If such an opportunity is "on the cards", join as early as possible in the process as possible, to give you time to digest all the data. You will be joining a board that is new to publicly listed company board processes/timetables so need to be prepared to help them with and accept some teething problems. It will take time for the board to operate functionally.

PUBLIC SECTOR (MINISTERIAL) APPOINTMENTS

It is important to remember that public sector board appointments cover a wide variety of organisations from boards of NHS Trusts to oversight of parliamentary bodies and include organisations responsible for; waterways and canals, museums, national parks, regulatory bodies/ombudsman bodies, judicial appointments, further education colleges – the list goes on. It is useful to note that some roles are remunerated and some are not. Vacancies are advertised and web links to the relevant sites appear in the Further Reading section as the end of this chapter.

Public appointments processes involve completing a competency-based application form where candidates are asked to demonstrate how their experience demonstrates skill and understanding of the key criteria outlined in the application pack. There is something of an art form to these applications and basing answers on the STAR method – describing the S - situation, the T - task, A - action that YOU specifically took and the R - result as well as what you learned or may do differently next time is the key to answering these types of questions, they normally have a word limit and weaving in some of the language used in the question or job specification can be very helpful in order to get through the first sift. The interview process is normally competency-based and may be accompanied by a personality test and a practical exercise at interview. The practical exercise may involve making a short presentation and/or include an excerpt from a board paper asking you to identify key issues or questions you would like to ask if you were to be on that board. These are sent in advance so you can prepare, you are also normally provided a time limit so worth practising so ensure you answers/presentation does not exceed the time given.

These appointments tend to be very competitive and the appointment panel are required to provide a report to the relevant government minister of all candidates that could be appointed and a recommendation of the first choice. The minister together with relevant advisers makes the final decision. The key is not to be "put off" if rejected; it is very rare for someone to be appointed on the first application.

For appointments to UK-wide public bodies, the Commissioner for Public Appointments (Grimstone, 2016) states that "Ministers should be assisted in their decision-making by Advisory Assessment Panels, each of which must contain a strong, independent element composed of people capable of exercising the required judgments".

In Scotland, the Commissioner for Ethical Standards in Public Life oversees public body appointments. The commissioner has produced a Code of Practice for Ministerial Appointments to Public Bodies in Scotland. The Scottish Government is expected to follow the Code when making regulated public appointments. A selection of public appointments is overseen by assigning a public appointments adviser (PAA). PAAs are appointed by the commissioner and are answerable to him/her for their professional conduct and competence. In many cases, the PAAs provide oversight by participating as full selection panel members.

It is important to note that when applying for any public body board appointment, you are likely to be asked to demonstrate your appreciation of and alignment with the values that the organisation seeks to promote. There may be some differences in these between organisations; however, at the very least, a commitment the code of conduct for those in public life called the Seven Principles of Public Life, or the Nolan Principles, is likely to be asked for. These principles are explored in greater detail in Chapter 2 (Governance Codes);

however, in short, they include selflessness, integrity, objectivity, accountability, openness, honesty, and leadership.

While there are exceptions, most commonly applications for such appointments are based on an online form, and DO NOT involve the submission of a CV nor a list of previous roles held so it is important to find ways to demonstrate relevant roles and experience through the competency-based answers. There have been interesting examples such as a former high-profile CEO of a Utility Company not being shortlisted for a board appointment to a Utilities Regulatory Organisation because he had not demonstrated knowledge of the utility sector in the application, Similarly, a former Cabinet Secretary for Health was not shortlisted for an NHS board appointment due to her application not showing sufficient understanding of the health sector! Equally, it is very important to read any instructions given, both at the application stage and in advance of the interview stage, very carefully. The key processes involved and the role of ministers in each type of board appointment across the UK is summarised in Table 8.1.

Table 8.1 Comparison of public body board appointments within the UK

Administration	England and Wales and Non-devolved Appointments in Scotland and Northern Ireland	Appointments Devolved to the Scottish Government	Appointments Devolved to the Northern Ireland Executive
Role of Ministers	Ministers appoint candidates rated "above the line" they may ask for rankings on merit	Ministers appoint based on ratings of candidates made by the selection panel, combined with their own judgement against "fit and proper person" criteria	Ministers make appointment based on merit but also to ensure appointments are reflective of communities
Design of appointments process	Departments are responsible for a proportionate process with ministerial agreement and input	Ministers ensure appropriate processes for succession planning, keeping records, and informing the ethical standards commissioner	Departments ensure compliance with code; ministers involved in informing the process at beginning only

Appointments Panel	Overseen by panel which must include an independent member to add external perspective	Representative of the ethical standards commissioner on panel for high profile posts. For other panels, ministers encouraged to include an external member	Each panel includes a department official, rep from the public body and an independent assessor

Source: Commissioner for Public Appointments (Grimstone, 2016).

Feedback is normally offered to unsuccessful candidates following the interview/selection process. It is also worth noting that whereas, in the private sector, terms of office for NEDs tend to be for a maximum of nine years, in public sector board appointments, the most commonplace term of office is a three-year term with an appointment for a further three years making six years in total if performance has been satisfactory. For Chair roles, this is frequently extended to a 3rd term of office, making it nine years in total.

LEARNING POINT

A particular public appointment received almost 200 applications; instructions to applicants stated that the answers must not be longer than 3,000 words overall, although each individual answer must not be longer than 400 words. Some very strong applications were rejected due to the word count rules not being followed. While acknowledged by the appointments panel that the rules were complex, board members are expected to be able to analyse and assimilate complex information as part of the role and 80% of applicants did adhere to the requirements, which demonstrated that the instructions were not unduly complex.

This highlights the importance of reading the application pack fully and carefully and being cognisant of all instructions – they matter!

xx

OK

x

CHARITY/VOLUNTARY SECTOR APPOINTMENTS

There are still a variety of ways that third sector boards are recruited. There is very much a move towards advertising board vacancies and going through a recruitment process, with some larger charities using head-hunters. There are also a large number of charities who still recruit from their contacts, user groups, and local communities. Some will have requirements stated in their governing documents about the need to have some board members from particular groups that they may support or with particular skills or characteristics. Many also carry out skills audits to ensure a mix of skills on the board. Some even take board dynamics into account and consider whether they are looking for a negotiator, challenger, etc.

Those that advertise often use sector specific websites, which are listed in the Further Reading section at the end of this chapter. Additionally, sector infrastructure organisations (volunteer centres, interfaces, etc.) are a good place to start such as NCVO, NICVA, and, SCVO along with some business support organisations, such as the Institute of Directors, which also advertise charity board vacancies to their members. If you find a particular charity of interest, seeking out an opportunity to connect with one of more of the current Board Members/Trustees may be also be a good way to secure a board appointment.

It may also be worth considering what networks or events may help connect you into possible opportunities. Sector conferences, expos, and cross - sector business events (many legal and accounting firms have charity clients) may all be worth considering.

When considering a third sector appointment, you may want consider if there is a particular cause or part of the sector that you have a passion for, or are keen to be involved in – or whether you just want to add value and make a difference in a cause that is doing good more generally. It is worth looking at the relevant regulatory guidance on being a trustee and familiarising yourself with their governance code – Charity Commission (England and Wales), Office of the Scottish Charity Regulator (OSCR), and the Charity Commission for Northern Ireland. A well-developed board should have a full trustee "handbook" and provide a good induction to any new trustees.

Most third sector board positions are not remunerated and are held purely on a pro bono basis (although travel costs can often be met). It is worth checking what the time commitment will be (often more than you think), and whether there is an expectation to be on a sub-committee in addition to the board role.

Although mostly voluntary and unpaid, many voluntary/charity sector board members find the complexity of overseeing a charity is a huge learning experience as well as being hugely rewarding. It is also worth pointing out that, as long as you join the board of a well-governed charity, it could be an ideal opportunity to gain that first NED experience as charity recruitment processes are often less competitive than remunerated NED roles.

If you are considering becoming a charity trustee think about the following tips before embarking on, or during a search for an opportunity:

- Know yourself
  - What interests you?
  - How much time do you have?
  - Do you prefer a local community or large national organisation; a start-up or well-established, a specific specialist area or the sector in general?
  - What can you offer?
  - Why do you want to volunteer as a Trustee?
- Do your homework
  - Research potential organisations
  - Look at the website, read the governing document and annual accounts
- Understand
  - Individual and collective responsibilities
  - Expectations of you as a Trustee

Once you secure an appointment:

- Enjoy
  - Finding out more about the organisations, its services, and the team
  - Contributing and making a difference
- Share the message
  - Tell others about your experience
  - Enthuse and promote the role of Trustee

There are also many networking opportunities, cross sector business events and conferences that help connect the charity sector to people interested in Trustee opportunities. Many legal and financial firms provide opportunities for their employees to volunteer and Trusteeship is considered a worthwhile investment in developing their employees.

One of the first things you should do if considering becoming a charity trustee is to check out the guidance on the relevant nation's regulator's website. Also ask yourself:

- what are my interests/passions?
- what kind of charity would I like to be involved with – local community, national, big, small?
- what time can I commit?
- what skills can I offer?
- why do I want to become a Trustee?

If you find a charity that interests you, then look at the accounts, and research the organisation through its website, the charity regulator and Companies House (if incorporated) as well as looking at any available reports. This will allow you to make an informed decision.

APPOINTMENT BY ELECTION

It is also important to note that some organisations are required, by their governing documents, or in some cases by statute, to appoint some or all NED board members by election. This is most commonly found in the charity/voluntary sector, especially in membership-based organisations and some mutual organisations although it has been known to happen in public sector board appointments too.

The process may follow an application and interview process first with suitable candidates then going through a membership vote based on statements provided and possibly a personal address and/or question and answer (Q&A) session. In such cases it is important to note who the audience is and with whom your message may resonate with. As an example, prior to appointing a Chair to the Court (Board), some universities are required to put up at least two candidates for election, as the final stage of the recruitment process. The stakeholders with a vote include the rest of the court members staff and students. On the basis that students far outnumber all the other voting members, one could argue that they are the true final decision-makers. This holds true if the student body is engaged and interested enough to vote, so in practice it may be the staff vote that carries most weight.

No matter which type of organisation is involved, if you want to be appointed, ensuring that your message is tailored to the voters is a key factor.

THE IMPORTANCE OF A GOOD CHAIR

Many NEDs agree that serving under the leadership of a good chair is a key determining factor to how well the board functions, its impact on the business but also how enjoyable your time on the board will be. It is therefore important to find "a good one" and use the interview process to find answers to some of the following questions:

- How does the individual command respect/gain respect? How do they conduct themselves to gain respect?

- Understand their history, do they spend time talking to other executives or just the CEO?
- Time – how much bandwidth do they have? (to deal with potential activist investors, profit warnings, cyber-attacks, etc. – good chair keeps a little bit of head space to help during a crisis. That means ideally not more than three Chairmanships and perhaps one NED – not more).
- Does he/she have emotional intelligence (EQ)/empathy. They may not need to be very charismatic but having sufficient EQ to work people out, deal with people and be approachable is important.
- Is he/she known for having the ability to test assumptions in a collegiate way? A useful way to find more out is to seek out others who have served on boards with them for their experience, does everyone feel they can speak, that they are listened to and that they are informed?
- Is the Chair approachable? Is the Chair strategically sound?
- How do they stay current with the issues? (e.g. stakeholder sentiment, remuneration issues, key trends).
- Do they have the will to help other people be successful? (Succession Planning).

KEY MESSAGES

- Gaining your first board appointment is a career pivot. Pivoting is not the same as an all-out career change. A career pivot involves taking the skills you've mastered over years and applying them to another area such as board work.
- It is a responsible (legally and morally) role so you have to enjoy being strategic and happy to guide and mentor as opposed to "be in charge of it all" if so, then a NED career will be fulfilling and develop your knowledge in many new areas of interest.
- Resilience will be important and if you look at it as social experiment instead of taking potential rejections personally, the

recruitment process itself will be an empowering experience. It is highly recommended!

- A board appointment is a two-way process, you must want to join the board as much as the board members want you to join, being on a board carries legal, fiduciary, and moral duties, so the importance of doing due diligence cannot be stressed strongly enough.

FURTHER READING

https://goodmoves.org.uk/

https://www.acosvo.org.uk/trustee-voluntary-vacancies

https://reachvolunteering.org.uk/guide/recruiting-and-retaining-trustees

https://www.gettingonboard.org/

https://trustees-unlimited.co.uk/

https://www.volunteerscotland.net/for-volunteers/

https://www.charityjob.co.uk/volunteer-jobs/trustee

https://publicappointments.cabinetoffice.gov.uk/for public appointments in England (and some UK-wide bodies).

https://www.gov.scot/collections/public-appointments/for public appointments in Scotland.

https://www.nidirect.gov.uk/articles/public-appointment-vacancies for public appointments in Northern Ireland.

https://gov.wales/public-appointments for public appointments in Wales.

REFERENCES

Grimstone, G. (2016). *Better Public Appointments A Review of the Public Appointments Process*. [online]. Available at: https://assets.publishing. service.gov.uk/government/uploads/system/uploads/attachment_data/ file/507066/Better_Public_Appointments_March_2016.pdf [Accessed 29 Mar. 2021].

The Muse Editor. (2015). The 31 Best LinkedIn Profile Tips for Job Seekers. [online] *Themuse.com*. Available at: https://www.themuse.com/advice/the-31-best-linkedin-profile-tips-for-job-seekers. [Accessed 16 Feb. 2021].

Women on Boards. (2012). Women On Boards – We Support You To Get Non-Executive or Trustee Roles. We Have a Vacancy Board of Over 200 Live Vacancies. Organisations Gain Access to a Large and Diverse Pool of Board-Ready Candidates. [online] Available at: https://www. womenonboards.net/en-gb/reference-items/resource-centre-articles/7-reasons [Accessed 21 Feb. 2021].

CHAPTER NINE

Governance in the Private Sector

*Charlotte Valeur, Claire Fargeot,
and Patricia Barclay*

DOI: 10.4324/9781003142850-9

INTRODUCTION

The private sector plays an essential role in the economic and social development of the UK. Not only does the private sector contribute significantly to national income, it is also a principal provider of jobs. Private sector actors can have a huge influence on the development of urban areas with a sustainability and social impact bias, prioritising poverty reduction, employment, stability, and inclusion. The sector is both complex and dynamic, a key driver of employability, shareholder returns (funding pensions and other types of savings) with an increasing focus on wider stakeholders. The sector is made up of many different types of organisations, including those which distribute profits to shareholders and those which do not; the sector is often exposed to not only company law requirements but also governance codes and regulatory requirements that add complexity as well as increasing external scrutiny.

The authors of this chapter have a breadth of experience working in the private sector, as executive and non-executive directors and chairs with experience in IPOs, mergers and acquisitions and restructuring, gained with public listed, as well as entrepreneurial or private companies. This experience has been brought into the chapter through the learning points highlighted and through our views of the sector. We have tried to share our passion for the sector as well as our understanding and experience.

The UK has one of the oldest systems of corporate governance in the world, which started in the private sector. Company law in its current form dates from the mid-19th century; however, other forms of business association developed long before. As far back as the medieval period, traders acted through partnerships through common law whenever people acted together with a view to profit. Early guilds and livery companies were also often involved in the regulation of trade among themselves. Prior to the creation of the UK, England sought to build a mercantile Empire; corporations were established under a Royal Charter or an Act of Parliament with the grant of a monopoly over a specified territory. One of the best-known examples, as highlighted in Chapter 1, was the British East India Company, established in 1600. The precursor of the modern limited liability company emerged following the Joint Stock Companies Act of 1844. This Act created the Registrar of Joint Stock Companies and imposed requirements on companies to:

- issue a prospectus identifying promoters and their interest in the company;
- prepare basic, audited financial statements (that were made publicly available) and maintain financial information on a current basis;
- incorporate regulations for internal company affairs into the articles of association; and
- restrict insider trading.

In exchange for the above, business interests could form a corporate body with separate legal personality, including fully transferable shares and access to court. This was followed by the Joint Stock Companies Act of 1856, which is considered a forerunner of the Companies Act 2006.

DEFINING THE SECTOR

According to the Cambridge Dictionary (Cambridge Dictionary, 2019), the private sector is defined as "businesses and industries that are not owned or controlled by the government".

While Captial.com (capital.com, n.d.) describes the private sector as,

a significant segment of a country's economy, which is controlled, owned and managed by private individuals and businesses. With a major goal to earn money, the private sector usually employs more people than the public sector. Private sector companies are created by establishing a new enterprise or privatising a former public organisation. A large private sector corporation may be also publicly traded. Private sector businesses compete for consumers' money and drive down the prices for services and goods. In the developed countries, private sector businesses contribute a significant percentage towards the country's total gross domestic product (GDP).

The private sector constitutes the segment of the economy which is owned, managed and controlled by individuals and organisations seeking to generate profit, albeit not all of these companies distribute profit. While companies in the private sector are not under state ownership or control, however, at times the private sector collaborates with the public sector in a public-private partnership to collectively deliver a service or business venture to the population. A private sector company can come into existence through the privatisation of a public sector organisation or through a new enterprise by private individuals. Private sector companies, particularly large, stock exchange listed companies, have some of the most demanding corporate governance expectations, and corporate governance reporting requirements, imposed on them.

SCALE OF THE SECTOR

According to the study conducted by the Institut Européen d'Administration des Affaires (INSEAD) in 2015, (Commonalities, Differences, and Future Trends Board Chairs' Practices across Countries Contents, 2015) five million businesses in the UK employed around 25 million people. Privately held companies accounted for 99% of all private sector businesses while there were approximately 10,000 public listed companies. Data published by the Office of National Statistics in March 2018 (Ons.gov.uk, 2018), the private sector accounted for 75.99% of all UK employment and 92.12% of turnover (income) generated in the UK economy. The private sector remains a key driver of UK prosperity, jobs, and tax revenues.

Table 9.1 *Private sector definitions and terminology (GOV.UK, n.d.)*

Term	Description
Company	Companies can take a range of legal forms, including Public Limited Companies, Private Limited Companies, Limited Liability Partnerships
Large business	250 or more employees
Medium-sized business	50 to 249 employees
Ordinary partnership	Business run by two or more self-employed people
Small business	0 to 49 employees
Small and medium-sized enterprises (SMEs)	0 to 249 employees
Sole proprietorship	a business run by one self-employed person

According to UK Government data (GOV.UK, n.d.) small and medium-sized enterprises (SMEs), defined as organisations employing 250 people or less, accounted for 60% of employment and 52% of turnover at the start of 2019, while large businesses accounted for 40% of employment and 48% of turnover. Definitions and terminology are presented in Table 9.1 below:

ROLE OF THE PRIVATE SECTOR

The role of the private sector is integral to the continued development, growth, and health of our economy. It pays a vital role in a number of areas:

- *Significant stakeholders of the economy:* The private sector is an important player in the economy due to the input it makes to the national income. Particularly, it delivers vital goods and services, contributes to tax revenues, and ensures the efficient flow of capital.
- *Generating employment:* The private sector plays the pivotal role of generating employment opportunities within the country.

- *Innovation:* The private sector plays a key role in different types of new innovative developments. It enhances the process of community improvements through new innovative ways of operating and delivering services. It introduces new commodities, equipment, machinery, and technology and introduces innovative ideas that changes methods and means of production and leads to better overall sustainable development.
- *Provision of goods and services:* The private sector is the main provider of goods and services within the country and ensures it can satisfy market demand through innovation.
- *Promoting the diversification of business:* The private sector is full of companies conducting varied businesses. This sector provides new companies with the opportunity to develop no matter the type of business.

Historically the private sector has been mainly driven by an ability to generate unlimited profits (and therefore accumulate unlimited wealth), without having to worry so much about their reputation, stakeholder perceptions, and the overall potential negative social, environmental, and economic impact of their activities. However, since the UN launched its Social Development Goals in 2015 (United Nations, 2015), and the threat of climate change has become more apparent, there has been a real shift in focus towards a broader set of values. This change in focus has brought the public spotlight onto the impact, as well as the part, that the private sector plays. Following consumer and wider stakeholder and regulatory pressures, private companies are beginning their sustainability journeys with words and descriptions of their activities having positive impacts on the social and environmental aspects of their ecosystem.

HOW IS THE SECTOR GOVERNED?

Like the public and majority of charity/voluntary sector organisations, the private sector in the UK applies a single-tier governance system. A single tier system is also referred to as a unitary board of management where there is no clear separation of duties between executive and non-executive directors, who all sit on the same board. While in a two-tier board, two different boards are present, with one clearly responsible for undertaking management roles and the other for the purposes of check and balance and policy making. Also a one-tier board system is no mandatory structure, as such, for boards, albeit premium listed public limited companies (PLCs) are required by the UK Corporate Governance Code to have half of board roles filled by non-executive directors (NEDs). Other private sector boards tend to also apply a mix of executive and non-executive directors on boards. The board of directors being the highest governing body in most private sector organisations, with the board making key executive appointments and taking decisions about the remuneration of the most senior executives top-managers, strategy, major capital investments, risk management, and disclosure.

An exception to the single-tier governance system is often that of partnerships. You might imagine a law firm, set up as a partnership structure where they may be 30 or more equity partners (owners) and they might make up a management board, but for the purpose of making key strategic decisions, electing a supervisory board could make decision-making far more streamlined.

When it comes to governance influences on the private sector, much depends on the type and size of the organisations. In the context of the private sector, it could be argued that premium listed companies have the most onerous standards of corporate governance to comply with as well as the highest standards of directors' behaviours expected of them. The Boards of Premium listed companies are expected to "Comply or Explain" with the 18 principles and 41 provisions of the UK Corporate Governance Code, fully adhering to the Listing Rules and, where possible, role-modelling best practices, so setting the bar at a sufficiently high level that market integrity is maintained at all times. The Board is expected to be independent on balance and made up of a diverse set of appropriately skilled directors whose main efforts should be directed towards the long-term success of the company. The Board is expected to oversee the strategic development of the company and is responsible for ensuring that the company meets its statutory obligations.

Unlike companies listed on the London Stock Exchange (LSE), some public listed companies are listed on the Alternative Investment Market (AIM) and are not required to comply or explain with the UK Corporate Governance Code. Although many AIM companies choose to apply aspects of the UK Governance Code in a way that suits their size and stage of development. In the UK, the main difference between being listed on the LSE and AIM is that the Main Market (LSE) is usually reserved for more established businesses and has more stringent admission criteria and more demanding ongoing obligations. AIM companies are required to follow a recognised corporate governance code and to disclose on their website how the company complies with that code.

Regardless of which market a UK company is listed on, there is an expectation, on all PLCs that board members will do the "right things" this is scrutinised very closely once a year at the company's annual general meeting (AGM) where shareholders vote on resolutions, dividend proposals as well as the election and remuneration of directors. While PLCs are not the only organisations to hold AGMs, board members of PLCs can be faced with institutional shareholders, who themselves are expected to comply with the Stewardship Code and look carefully at matters of director re-election. Specific reasons why each director's contribution is, and continues to be, important to the company's long-term sustainable success is considered, the level of diversity on the board, the number of directors who are "over-boarded" (hold too many board appointments, for example, more than five PLC NEDs or more than two or three PLC Chair roles are considered as too much). Importantly, there is an increased focus on environmental, social, and governance (ESG) factors as well as greater scrutiny of remuneration policies proposed by boards.

Director remuneration continues to come under close scrutiny and proxy voting agencies (on behalf of institutional investors) are expected to vote against remuneration reports where there is substantial misalignment between executive director remuneration and: (i) performance; (ii) shareholder and employee experience; and (iii) where executive pay or total opportunity increases substantially outpace employee salary increases. Furthermore, packages should reflect a range of non-financial performance metrics (strategic, personal, and ESG) in their variable remuneration. Climate change is another topic of great institutional investor interest with premium listed companies being required to make disclosures consistent with the recommendations of the Taskforce on Climate-related Financial Disclosures ("TCFD") (Tcfdhub.org, 2019) or explain their non-compliance as well as explaining climate related considerations in their business models, governance, and reporting. All of these requirements and detailed scrutiny by shareholders means that PLC directors could be generally described as very much "held to account" and even though they are normally appointed for a term of nine years, this is subject to annual re-election at the AGM and NEDs do get voted down. It could be said that this tends to "focus the mind" and is an effective, if sometimes uncomfortable for the individuals standing for re-election, process for ensuring governance expectations are met.

The Companies Act also contains a reporting requirement for premium listed company directors (Legislation.gov.uk, 2010), where the annual report should detail how the directors have engaged with stakeholders (including employees) over the past 12 months and the effect that this has had on company decisions, strategies, and long-term success. Board discussions on assessing and monitoring culture, succession planning, and board evaluation are also expected to take place.

LEARNING POINT

In March 2021, the *Financial Times* (Flood. C. Mar. 2021) reported that BlackRock, one of the world's largest investment firms, outlined its intention "to push companies to step up their efforts to protect the environment from deforestation, biodiversity loss and pollution of the oceans and freshwater resources". It issued a statement saying it was ready to vote against the re-election of directors if companies had not effectively managed or disclosed risks related to the depletion of "natural capital", the world's stock of natural resources. It may also vote in favour of shareholder proposals that highlight natural capital risks. BlackRock has taken a similarly tough stance on executive remuneration with concerns about executive pay at Ocado, the UK online grocery supplier, prompting BlackRock to vote against the re-election of three directors in 2020.

The COVID-19 pandemic has also led to complaints that workers in industries such as food processing and transportation have been exposed to higher infection risks which employers have either ignored or dismissed. BlackRock made clear that it expected companies to take steps to mitigate risks to staff that could arise from their business practices. This was further evidenced in January 2021 when BlackRock voted against the re-election of the board of directors at Top Glove, the Malaysia-based rubber glove manufacturer. A quarter of the company's workforce became infected with coronavirus after some employees were forced to live and work in unsuitable premises.

The investment community is becoming increasing active in matters of board governance and will hold NEDs personally to account by voting against them when governance concerns arise.

Of course, it is important to point out that there is no "one-size-fits-all" approach to corporate governance. Companies should adopt a corporate governance code that implements policies and procedures they are readily able to maintain. Good corporate governance involves more than just providing an explanation against a chosen code, it involves embedding a positive culture, strong leadership, and robust systems and risk management.

Unlisted companies, which make up the vast majority of the private sector and range from multi-generation family-owned companies, through to SMEs and start-up companies, are not required to follow any governance code as such. It should be noted that many companies find that once they receive external investment or debt finance, compliance with either a code of governance or a governance framework or some sort becomes a requirement. Equally, companies both public listed and privately owned, may fall under to authority of one or more regulatory bodies, which may impose governance standards. All of this is additional to compliance with the Companies Act 2006.

With all the above being said, it should be noted that in 2021 proposals are underway to replace the FRC with the Audit, Reporting and Governance Authority (ARGA), a new regulator with the power to force accountants to split their audit and non-audit functions, force companies to correct errors in their accounts, and investigate directors themselves for financial reporting failures and claw back bonuses earned by board members where corporate failings are identified. It has been proposed that the new regulator will be able to apply the equivalent rules of the Senior Management Certification Regime (SMCR) as applies in financial services organisations, to all public listed and large privately owned companies – this means the ability to fine individual directors. Large privately owned companies are defined as; 2,000 or more employees globally or a global turnover of more than £200 million and a balance sheet of more than £2 billion globally.

Good governance is derived from a strong board with sound board members who understand and recognise that they are in post to serve the board on behalf of shareholders and other stakeholders. They understand that they have been entrusted with the fate and health of the company and are there to protect not only the company but also the community, country and indeed the ecosystem that the company is part of. A good board is active, responsive, and engaged at all times. For board members of a good board, corporate governance is the music in the background that makes everything run smoothly. They take challenges in their stride and are comfortable with difficult discussions and disagreements, viewing them as an opportunity to grow, both for themselves and for the company as a whole. NEDs should engage in and develop a number of unique problem-resolution and decision-making processes that are both highly complex in design and simple in execution. "Sophisticated simplicity" comes naturally to a good board. As a diverse board they are a strong collective of individuals, blending and harmonising seamlessly. Through this they display an expanded use of their minds, competencies, and tools. With this kind of board, challenge to the executive takes the form of constructive suggestions and input focussed on the best output for the organisation and the wider world. The executives feel supported and lifted when interacting with the board.

An organisation led by a Good board is likely to display some key characteristics showing the quality of the leadership and tone from the top. There will be a recognition that work must be meaningful to the overall health of the company, and all life. Not just the Executives but all staff and to the wider world. Sustainability across all areas is high on the agenda. Employee satisfaction will be high, stakeholders are satisfied that the company is run well and for the best interests of everyone and the communications are fully transparent. The board and executives take responsibility for the impact of their and the company's activities. The employees work together as teams and take responsibility within their teams. Ethical codes are taken seriously as is corporate governance. Regulation is viewed as something designed to maintain the health of the overall governance system and worked with accordingly.

It is useful to explore some of the similarities and differences, challenges, and benefits of different approaches to governance in the various organisations that make up the private sector as we consider type of legal entity below.

LEGAL STRUCTURES

As in the public and charity/voluntary sectors, in the private sector there is more than one type of legal entity available for the organisation of a business. A "legal entity" for business law purposes is any individual, company, business, or organisation that can legally enter into a binding contract with another legal entity. A legal entity can be composed of many people but has the capacity to operate in the same way as an individual, legally speaking. Incorporated businesses generally qualify as a legal entity.

Some examples of the most commonly used legal entities within the private sector are:

- Public limited company adds words to explain.
- Private company, limited by shares or guarantee.
- Mutual Organisations.
- Limited Partnerships.
- General Partnerships.

The majority of the legal entities listed above are governed by the Companies Act 2006 as well as other regulatory requirements that may apply to certain organisations. The legal entities governed by other legal provisions will be explored further in the sections below. Common to all organisations in the private sector is its management by private individuals without government involvement. The private sector receives necessary capital from its owners or shareholders/members and through borrowing. Different types of private sector undertakings have varied means of raising capital.

Looking at each type of private sector organisation in turn:

LISTED COMPANIES (PUBLIC COMPANIES)

The UK private sector comprises over 10,000 listed companies (also known as public companies), representing some 40 different sectors. Some of these companies are very large multi-nationals with global operational activities whereas others are much smaller and are only active in the UK market. The reasons for becoming a listed company are usually for raising capital and financing growth as well as enhancing the profile and prospects of a business. While we have touched on the governance requirements for public listed companies being some of the most onerous within the private sector, a variety of corporate scandals have resulted in further regulatory involvement. One of the most high-profile scandals in recent years was the financial crisis of 2007/2008. Regulatory bodies, involved in the financial sector introduced a senior management certification regime (SMCR), which covers the most senior executive and non-executive directors in certain financial services organisations.

The legislation, responsible for the SMCR was introduced to "reduce harm to consumers and strengthen market integrity by creating a system that enables firms and regulators to hold individuals to account". It is designed to ensure those in senior roles have the skills, knowledge and integrity to act in the customers' best interests, while setting a new standard of personal conduct for everyone working in financial services. Whereas governance codes are sometimes criticised for lacking "teeth", the SMCR includes provision for enforcement action to be taken against indiividual directors.

Niamh Corbett, director, Board Intelligence, commented, "The UK Senior Managers Certification Regime (SMCR) has become a global benchmark […] In the UK, companies have been fined, and individuals too". In recent years, the (FCA) has issued numerous fines against executive and non-executive directors in the UK (Channel Eye, 2021), for offences including failure to declare a conflict of interest, and lack of fitness or propriety, with fines ranging from the tens of thousands to over £70 million. Thinking about resigning now to avoid potential issues? It's probably too late. For NEDs thinking about resigning now to avoid potential issues, it's probably too late. In the UK, regulators have been clear they can go as far back as necessary when investigating failures by a Board. It is important to note that organisations regulated by the FCA, or its sister regulator the Prudential Regulation Authority (PRA), are not solely large listed companies. Regulated entities in the UK include a significant number of financial services organisations, which are mutuals – in other words owned by their members, rather than shareholders, these include Building Societies and Friendly Societies, which will be explored further in the sections below.

LEARNING POINT

In 2016, the financial regulator PRA introduced a requirement
for boards of regulated financial services firms to provide
evidence of effective challenge, by NEDs at board meetings
(www.bankofengland.co.uk, Mar.2016). The boards of a
number of organisations do this by sharing the minutes
of board meetings with the Regulator; however, it has
resulted in a positive culture and mindset change. NEDs are
reported as coming into the boardroom knowing that there
is an expectation of them, which will be externally shared,
to demonstrate constructively challenge – described by one
board member as like "someone marking one's homework". It
was carefully managed so that board minutes were presented
without specifying which NED raised a particular point, this
removed the pressure of NEDs "competing" to raise the same
key issue and by presenting a list of NED questions/areas
for further clarification together with the response given by
executive directors/management team, the board was able to
demonstrate appropriate NED challenge in a positive and non-
confrontational manner.

This approach not only satisfied the regulator but had a positive
effect on the culture and dynamics of the board, NEDs started to
see an expectation to provide constructive and effective challenge
at every board meeting and with this mindset, the levels of robust
debate increased.

UNLISTED PRIVATE COMPANIES

An unlisted private company is a company that is not listed on any
stock exchange. It is registered as a company which generally has a
minimum share capital and a minimum number of shareholders. In
the UK unlisted private companies are formed under the Companies
Act 2006.

The UK register of incorporated companies totalled 4.35 million by the end of March 2020, (GOV.UK, 2020), and most of these are not listed on a stock exchange. The unlisted enterprises lie at the heart of most countries' economies and account for a significant part of the UK's GDP and employment.

Most unlisted private companies are owned and controlled by small groups of individuals or groups of individuals. A large number of unlisted private companies are owned (either in part or in full) by private equity or venture capital firms and others are owned by members of a family. As highlighted above, mutual organisations are owned by their members and some would argue that mutuals belong in the "not-for-profit" sector, albeit the authors would argue they are, indeed, profit-making organisations who do not distribute those profits.

Following a few notable collapses in privately owned large companies (British Home Stores, Carillion, Thomas Cook, Patisserie Valerie, and LF Woodford Equity Income Fund) there has been an ongoing initiative by the UK government to develop a set of corporate governance principles for large private unlisted companies. The development of the Wates Corporate Governance Principles for Large Private Companies is part of this initiative.

The Wates Principles and Adherence Requirement

This reporting requirement applies to all companies that satisfy either or both of the following conditions:

- more than 2,000 employees;
- a turnover of more than £200 million, and a balance sheet of more than £2 billion.

The six Wates Principles are:

- Purpose and leadership.
- Board composition.
- Director responsibilities.

- Opportunity and risk.
- Remuneration.
- Stakeholder relationships and engagement.

Each company adopting and reporting against the Wates Principles has the freedom to operate their own corporate governance framework as decided by the owners and the board. Large companies do not tend to become large overnight; they tend to have been built and grown over many years. One of the issues this raises is that, in a number of cases, the CEO (possibly the founder) is a "larger than life" character with a strong will and dominance in the boardroom. If that individual is a majority shareholder, he/she has the power to hire and fire NEDs, this presents an undertesting dynamic a boardroom, how do NEDs fulfil their moral and legal duties to hold a dominant force to account?

It is interesting to note that the new Audit Reporting and Governance Authority (ARGA), which will replace the Financial Reporting Council (FRC), is expected to affect large privately owned organisations, as well as public listed companies. This body is expected to have greater powers to bring errant directors to account and clawback bonuses paid if firms subsequently collapse. In addition, it is proposed that ARGA will also impose similar requirements to those of the SMCR in financial services, to all directors of public listed and large privately owned firms, meaning that directors can be personally fined for misconduct in their role as directors.

MUTUALS

The term "mutual" is used as an umbrella term for several different ownership models. Mutuals are often described as being characterised by the extent to which members have democratic control of the business and share in its profits, and contrasted with "investor controlled" companies. However, could be seen as a misleading distinction, because all limited companies operate for the benefit of their members – the shareholders who invest in a company limited by shares, or the guarantors of a company limited by guarantee. The distinguishing characteristic of a mutual is that the organisation is owned by, and run for, the benefit of its members, who are actively and directly involved in the business; this includes employees, suppliers, or the community or consumers it serves, rather than being owned and controlled by external investors.

The legal structure of a mutual could vary depending on the type of organisations such as a co-operative or an employee-owned company. Some of the best-known mutual organisations in the UK are building societies as governed by the Building Societies Act 1987 (Legislation. gov.uk, 2011) and Friendly Insurance Societies as governed by the Friendly Societies Act 1992 (Legislation.gov.uk, 2011). Traditionally, many mutual organisations, selected non-executive board members from among their membership and it is important that a proportion of board members continue to be drawn from that pool; however, increasing regulation, especially in financial services organisations, has made it a necessity for many organisations to choose NEDs with specialist backgrounds (e.g. credit risk), from other organisations, such as shareholder-owned banks. With the exception of very large building societies like Nationwide, the levels of remuneration on offer have made it challenging to attract the right mix of skills and experience onto some mutual organisation boards. At the same time appointing NEDs who have a sympathetic approach to the values and culture of a mutual is vital to an engaged board that has a primary focus on providing benefit to its members rather than being primarily profits-driven.

EMPLOYEE-OWNED ORGANISATIONS

It is not unusual for employee-owned organisations to be created when a business founder(s), often also majority shareholder(s), wish to exit the business while allowing the organisation to continue on in almost its current form but with a new management team. This is an alternative to selling to a third party and a way of preserving the business name, heritage, and potentially high-quality jobs in the area.

While there are some large employee-owned organisations, which are well-known names such as John Lewis, many organisations that become employee-owned are SME businesses.

The employee ownership consultancy Baxendale (Baxendale, 2020) comments that from a governance view point, this is interesting as, when the organisation is privately owned and managed, perhaps by the founder who is both Managing Director and majority shareholder, there may be little need for any further accountability. Perhaps board meetings take place but many decisions would naturally be made by the founder, as both leader and majority shareholder of the organisation. The organisation may be very well run and employees may be comfortable in this arrangement and have a strong sense of loyalty to the founder's authority and decision-making. Once an organisation becomes employee-owned a different governance structure becomes a requirement. The employees/members are directly or indirectly the shareholders either through share option plans or an ownership trust.

Baxendale points out the in a sale to a third party, or a management buy-out, the shareholder rights pass to a new owner, and they are then able to appoint their own leaders, whether that is themselves or their appointees. In the eyes of the employees, the new leaders may or may not have the same authority to lead the company as the founder; but this is immaterial – the new owners have the majority shareholding and the control. The standard of governance is, and will continue to be, dependent on the individuals holding that majority control, and their attitude towards it.

In the case of the sale of a business to an employee ownership trust (EOT), the situation is quite different. The majority of shares are sold into the EOT; and ownership is controlled by a trustee or trustees who must take all decisions in the best interests of its beneficiaries, the employees. It is now the trust board that is holding those who are leading the business to account. Leadership is separated from ownership, although as the majority owner, the trust ultimately has the ability to control the composition of the board should it wish to. In reality it is unlikely to do so, unless things have gone badly wrong and cannot be resolved. This is the worst-case scenario power that it can use to hold the leaders of the business to account.

During the process of transition into employee ownership, and the setting up of the trust, there is an opportunity to stop and look thoroughly at both governance and control of the future employee-owned organisation;

- Who will control the trust?
- How will they be appointed?
- How will they hold the board to account?
- How often will they meet?
- How will they make decisions?
- What would they do if the board was underperforming?
- What other role might they have, in representing the voices of the employees, or as protectors of the culture or legacy of the business?

The board of trustees tend to consist of employees or members, independent directors, and potentially founders. All statutory duties apply to trustees as to directors of any company. Governance will be in accordance with articles of association, company, and trust law.

PRIVATE EQUITY (PE)/VENTURE CAPITAL (VC)-OWNED COMPANIES

Private companies (fully or partly) owned by Private Equity and Venture Capital investors will generally adopt a governance framework heavily influenced by the Private Equity firm that owns them. The PE/VC company will usually occupy a number of Board seats of their portfolio companies to ensure that their investee companies adhere to the strategic goals set by the PE/VC company. The companies owned by PE firms can vary from small family run businesses to large international corporations. PE/VC firms are keenly aware that the governance framework of their portfolio companies adds to (or detracts from), the overall return on their investment and therefore aim to get the governance practices in as good a state as possible prior to re-selling a portfolio company.

In addition to the directors some board meetings are also attended by observers. The right to appoint an observer may be a condition of an investment or sometimes a licence or other key contract. The rights of the observer may be laid down by contract but are usually enshrined in the company's articles. This will usually say who can appoint an observer, that the observer is entitled to notice of all board meetings and to receive all the board papers. The observer has no voting rights and in the past was generally barred from speaking at board meetings; however, now it is very common for their rights to extend to speaking at board meetings.

The usual purpose of appointing an observer is to give the appointer comfort as to the progress of the company. It is common practice for a university to appoint an observer to the board of its spin outs. This can be helpful for both parties. The university does not "interfere" in the running of the company but can see that the usually inexperienced directors have the business under control and provide information such as where additional help might be sought or what other facilities of the university might be available to the start up.

Of potentially more concern is the appointment of an observer by an investor. With an early-stage company bringing in its first investment the investor may have similar concerns to the university and want some comfort that its money is being spent wisely and that the company is making progress. You would expect this to be handled by the appointment of an investor director; however, where there are multiple investors a smaller investor may accept an observer in place of the right to appoint a director if other larger investors have a right to appoint a director. Where an investor has multiple investments, they may also be uncomfortable about taking on a board seat because of the difficulty of complying with their duties towards each of the investee companies without conflicts.

There are two potential major issues with the appointment of board observers, first, there is the question of accountability. A director has legal responsibilities towards the company and with that, potential liabilities. An observer has none and so his duty will be towards the organisation that appointed them. So, if they do speak at a board meeting, in whose interest are they making the point? Second, there is the question of influence and so transparency. The shareholders appoint the board and both they and third parties who interact with the company are entitled to believe that those are the decision makers. If there are observers in the room, are they influencing the decisions? If they speak, they could be influential but even if they stay silent their presence may be sufficient to swing the debate in particular directions. Even where an observer has no right to speak it is human nature that if they are in the room someone will speak to them and of course there is the question of how it looks to the outside world.

There are also issues for the observer. If he/she becomes involved in discussions and decision-making, could he be considered a shadow director and accidently find himself liable having failed to act in accordance with the duties laid on directors. If having carefully examined the request for an observer the company feels that such an appointment is acceptable to it then it becomes critical that the person so appointed and the board are all clear as to that person's position and the extent to which they can and cannot be involved in board discussions.

Private equity-owned organisations can also have a large individual majority shareholder, who may be the founder of the company. This can create cultural governance challenges as both the culture and approach to governance emanate from the top of an organisation and can be a reflection of the personality/style of the CEO, especially is that person is the majority shareholder.

LEARNING POINT

In 2016, a detailed report was released by the Business, Innovation and Skills Committee (ISC), which pointed to poor working conditions at the warehouses of Sports Direct. Its CEO and majority shareholder, Mike Ashley was heavily criticised in the report for not inspecting his warehouses regularly enough and for the concerning conditions employees were working in.

The company was accused of; paying its staff less than minimum wage, punishing employees for taking water breaks or time off for illness, employees on zero-hour contracts forced to work unpaid overtime or risk being denied more hours in the future and allegations of permanent contracts being offered in exchange for sexual favours. The report concluded that the Company should carry out a wide-reaching independent review of all corporate governance practices, its board oversight and effectiveness, acquisition strategy and associated due diligence.

In its blog on corporate governance failures, the NED Membership Group In Touch Networks (IN TOUCH NETWORK, May 2019) comments that there is a view that the top-down culture at Sports Direct was a major cause of these failings and had Mike Ashley not had a stake in the business, changes might have been implemented before reaching such a critical stage.

FAMILY-OWNED COMPANIES

Family-owned companies stand at the centre of the UK economy. They represent a significant amount of wealth, revenue, and jobs world-wide. Family-owned businesses have often first established family governance mechanisms outlining the mutual understandings between family members. The choice of family governance framework depends on the number of family members and their involvement within the business.

Generally, the family elder members will outline the vision and objectives of the business and possibly also serve on the board of directors.

Following on from this, the elder family members agree the relationship between family governance and the corporate governance of the business itself. A clear distinction between family governance and the governance of the business should be made. It is not uncommon for families to experience some difficulties in fully separating the interests of the family with the interests of the company. This is when an independent non-executive director can be invaluable in establishing degrees of separation and providing some independent oversight into the potentially conflicted decision-making.

The British Chamber of Commerce (The Chamber, 2011) published research by Family Business Place and the law firm Charles Russell Speechlys which suggested that:

- 55% cent of family businesses found succession to be a barrier to future success;
- 62% would consider selling up owing to difficulties handing on the business to children or relatives; and
- 90% of UK family businesses operated with no formal family governance structures in place, stunting their potential productivity and growth.

The research suggests that some of the governance issues are based on an "aversion to giving non family members senior leadership or strategy setting roles. The lack of formal governance leads to struggles with succession, complacency within the business, family disputes and even damage growth".

LEARNING POINT

The fifth generation of a family-owned organisation sought considerable debt funding for a large renewable energy

---

infrastructure project that would ensure the company's success and sustainability for many years (and generations to come). The bank noted the lack of an effective governance system within the company and even the MD noted decision-making was not easy and often involved lunch with his mother, followed by similar meetings with aunts, second cousins and so on. A condition of approval of funding was the establishment of an effective governance system, after advice from specialists, this took the form of the creation of a family council, to represent shareholders and a board of directors, including an independent (non-family member) chair and an independent non-executive director.

Decision-making became much more streamlined and transparent, while family interests were represented formally too. Importantly, the governance system was designed with the needs and aspirations of this particular family and organisation in mind and the independent chair and NED were selected for their business skills but also because they had themselves been members of a non-competing family-owned business, which allowed them to bring an added sensitivity and understanding to board discussions.

As with other types of organisations, governance arrangements in a family-owned company require a bespoke approach tailored to the operating environment, history, and aspirations of the family and other stakeholders.

PARTNERSHIPS

A partnership is a formal arrangement by two or more people to manage and operate a business and share in its profits or losses. There are several different types of partnership arrangements in existence; some have partners sharing liabilities and profits equally, while in others, partners have limited liability. There is also the "silent partner", in which one party is not involved in the day-to-day operations of the business. Professionals such as doctors, dentists, accountants, architects, investment professionals and lawyers may form a limited liability partnership where there are potential tax benefits to be derived when compared to a limited company.

Due to the hugely varied size and scope of partnerships it is difficult to promote an ideal structure or a typical partnership governance framework that covers the leadership, management, and decision-making structure of the firm, the responsibilities and accountabilities for decision-making, and so on. In larger practices, the governance system tends to be more flexible than other large private entities as external presence is limited to dedicated boards and there is less interaction, therefore, between the management or executive committee and the board for example. Invariably the more senior body is dedicated to setting and overseeing strategic matters of importance; however, duplication can exist in the management committee as they are also staffed primarily with partners of similar seniority and capabilities.

One of the governance challenges described, especially in larger partnerships, relates to agreeing strategic direction. One can imagine a large legal partnership where there are partners in a variety of disciplines such as corporate law, property, land and rural, private client, family law and litigation, agreeing one strategic direction for the partnership as a whole and gaining agreement from all Partners can take so long that by the time it is agreed, the operating environment has moved on and instead of implementing a strategy, a new one has to be agreed. The creation of a management or oversight board can provide a useful solution, albeit all full partners would have to vote to approve certain decisions.

SMALL, MEDIUM-SIZED ENTERPRISES AND MEDIUM-SIZED BUSINESSES (SMEs AND MSBs)

SMEs and MSBs are companies that employ 1 to 1,999 employees. They are often closely held companies with one or a handful of owners/

shareholders. As they grow from small to medium sized, they often look to adopt a governance framework which begins to more closely resemble that of the more structured governance processes used in listed companies.

The challenge for closely held companies is how to strengthen their governance without compromising the flexibility that many see as necessary to be agile enough in the marketplace. Most public companies have clear rules and procedures to ensure everything from regulatory compliance to risk assessment is taking place as it should as well as evidencing this. SMEs are often more wary of becoming too bureaucratic or process driven. Therefore, a phased development of their corporate governance framework is an effective way to ensure the company is governed appropriately.

LEARNING POINT

In 2021, it was reported that three men were disqualified from being directors of any UK company following a case brought by the Competition and Markets Authority (CMA). Following admission of a breach of competition law through the formation of cartel. (uk.finance.yahoo.com, 2021). The cartel saw two firms collude on rolled lead prices. The companies Associated Lead Mills (ALM) and HJ Enthoven (which trades as BLM British Lead) also arranged not to target certain customers in order to split the market between them, and agreed not to supply a new business because it risked disrupting existing relationships with customers.

Not only were the companies involved fined £1.5 million and £8 million, respectively, but the three directors faced further personal action against them. Board members should be aware that even in circumstances where the organisation does not apply a governance code where they might not be subject to an industry regulator, directors are subject to legal action if there is a breach of UK law, including the Companies Act, Health and Safety Legislation, and so on.

Private unlisted companies, not needing to adhere to the Wates Corporate Governance Principles, face choices in terms of their corporate governance framework. Some private unlisted companies choose to publicly state that they follow a specific Code of Corporate Governance. This will make sense in cases where they are considering attracting external investments or finance, working towards an IPO with a view to listing on a stock exchange or looking to sell the company. There is no doubt that having a robust corporate governance framework in place undertaking any of these substantial transactions will increase the value of the company and/or attract cheaper financing.

WHY BE A NON-EXECUTIVE DIRECTOR IN THE PRIVATE SECTOR

It is, of course, a highly responsible one that not only carries potential liabilities if not carried out well but also a great moral and fiduciary set of duties. While private sector board appointments include many benefits, such as on average, the best remuneration levels and the opportunity to influence and shape organisations that are responsible for wealth creation, and the vast majority of UK employment, the role brings challenges too. As in the public and charity/voluntary sectors, it is a very responsible role and one that needs to be taken very seriously. A diligent approach to questioning, analysing, scrutinising, constructively challenging, and decision-making.

Attractions of being a NED in the private sector include the following:

- Decision-making tends to be efficient and provide the business with the quickest and most cost-effective of solutions.
- Remuneration, on average, tends to be the highest for NEDs in this sector.

- Liaising with a range of shareholders from large institutions, private equity funds to private individuals, employees or families.
- Excitement – organisations in this sector can be fast-moving and involve corporate actions such as mergers and acquisitions.

There are a range of governance codes providing guidance on good practice in governance and the behaviour of board members, there is no *requirement* for training or qualifications, with perhaps the exception of the role of chair of the audit committee in public listed companies. However, training courses do exist from the *Financial Times* Non-Executive Director Diploma, the Institute of Directors Chartered Director Programme, The Good Governance Institute, and many others.

COVID-19 AND COMPANY GOVERNANCE

The COVID-19 pandemic has provided a stark reminder of the need for robust governance in all companies. During the pandemic many private companies, providing jobs for millions of people, struggled in adapting their activities fast enough in their response to the crisis. A sound corporate governance framework makes it possible to rapidly make decisions to implement necessary changes that will help guide progress through any crisis. As a highly varied sector, private sector organisations and their respective boards have been affected, and responded in different ways throughout the pandemic; however, the global management consultancy McKinsey & Company presented research on how boards in the sector had responded (www.mckinsey. com, Apr.2021). The report suggests that

> while overall corporate performance suffered during this time, boards were quick to rise to the challenge of navigating a global public-health and economic crisis. That is especially true with regard

to how boards operate; after many years of reports of only minimal improvements in how they work and their overall effectiveness, the latest results suggest that the pandemic has triggered new and improved ways of working that may outlast the pandemic.

Overall, the sector has seen greater collaboration between boards and management teams, board members have also adopted new ways of working and given more time to board-related work. McKinsey also point to greater flexibility in agenda setting, greater focus on strategy and company resilience. One area of change that boards in the sector appear to have embraced is investing in technology and tools to enable more digital collaboration and establishing ad hoc crisis committees.

KEY MESSAGES

- The private sector is the foundation of economic prosperity, tax revenues, and the majority of employment in the UK economy.
- Good governance is at the core of a successful private sector.
- Behaviours exhibited in the boardroom, in the senior leadership team and the organisation as a whole, will illuminate why the corporate governance is at the level it is.
- No amount of good governance processes and policies will help if board members do not embrace the principles of good governance.
- Achieving a purposeful, prosperous and well-run company where talented individuals want to work, and which has a positive impact on society and the wider world is enabled by a good board coupled with best practice corporate governance.

FURTHER READING

https://www.thecorporategovernanceinstitute.com/
courses/?utm_source=google&utm_medium=cpc&utm_

term=generic&utm_term=%2Bdirectorship%20
%2Bprogram&utm_campaign=Search+-+UK+-+Corporate+Govern
ance+Roles+Courses+-+Broad+MM&utm_source=adwords&utm_
medium=ppc&hsa_acc=5880302866&hsa_cam=11362773553&hsa_
grp=115000214287&hsa_ad=481949385975&hsa_src=g&hsa_
tgt=kwd-977218234936&hsa_kw=%2Bdirectorship%20
%2Bprogram&hsa_mt=b&hsa_net=adwords&hsa_
ver=3&gclid=EAIaIQobChMIzIT2v4H57wIVVofVCh
3CXwmMEAAYASAAEgIES_D_BwE

https://www.thecorporategovernanceinstitute.com/
courses/?utm_source=google&utm_medium=cpc&utm_
term=generic&utm_term=%2Bdirectorship%20
%2Bprogram&utm_campaign=Search+-+UK+-+Corporate+Govern
ance+Roles+Courses+-+Broad+MM&utm_source=adwords&utm_
medium=ppc&hsa_acc=5880302866&hsa_cam=11362773553&hsa_
grp=115000214287&hsa_ad=481949385975&hsa_src=g&hsa_
tgt=kwd-977218234936&hsa_kw=%2Bdirectorship%20
%2Bprogram&hsa_mt=b&hsa_net=adwords&hsa_
ver=3&gclid=EAIaIQobChMIzIT2v4H57wIVVofVCh3
CXwmMEAAYASAAEgIES_D_BwE

REFERENCES

Baxendale. (2020). Building trust: Employee ownership and governance.
[online] Available at: https://www.baxendale.co.uk/building-trust-
employee-ownership-and-governance/ [Accessed 4 May 2021].

Cambridge Dictionary. (2019). THE PRIVATE SECTOR | meaning in the
Cambridge English Dictionary. [online] Cambridge.org. Available at:
https://dictionary.cambridge.org/dictionary/english/private-sector.
[Accessed 13 Mar. 2021].

capital.com. (n.d.). Private sector definition. [online] Available at: https://
capital.com/private-sector-definition. [Accessed 11 Apr. 2021].

Channel Eye. (2021). Imminent risk of personal fines for NEDs warned by
Club NED. [online] Available at: https://channeleye.media/imminent-risk-
of-personal-fines-for-neds-warned-by-club-ned/ [Accessed
15 Mar. 2021].

Commonalities, Differences, and Future Trends Board Chairs' Practices across Countries Contents. (2015). [online] Available at: https://www.insead.edu/sites/default/files/assets/dept/centres/icgc/docs/board-chairs-practices-across-countries.pdf. [Accessed 9 Mar. 2021].

Flood, C. (Mar. 2021). [online] Available at: https://amp.ft.com/content/11285871-f0a7-4573-b638-5391e713eac8.

GOV.UK. (n.d.). Business population estimates for the UK and regions: 2019 statistical release (HTML). [online] Available at: https://www.gov.uk/government/statistics/business-population-estimates-2019/business-population-estimates-for-the-uk-and-regions-2019-statistical-release-html#:~:text=common%20legal%20form. [Accessed 15 Mar. 2021].

GOV.UK. (n.d.). Companies register activities: 2019 to 2020. [online] Available at: https://www.gov.uk/government/statistics/companies-register-activities-statistical-release-2019-to-2020/companies-register-activities-2019-to-2020. [Accessed 15 Mar. 2021].

IN TOUCH NETWORK. (n.d.). Businesses behaving badly: 3 Corporate Governance Failures. [online] Available at: https://intouchnetworks.com/en-gb/blog/corporate-governance-failures. [Accessed 5 May. 2021].

Legislation.gov.uk. (2010). Companies Act 2006. [online] Available at: https://www.legislation.gov.uk/ukpga/2006/46/section/172. [Accessed 14 Mar. 2021].

Legislation.gov.uk. (2011a). Building Societies Act 1997. [online] Available at: https://www.legislation.gov.uk/ukpga/1997/32/contents [Accessed 4 May 2021].

Legislation.gov.uk. (2011b). Friendly Societies Act 1992. [online] Available at: https://www.legislation.gov.uk/ukpga/1992/40/contents [Accessed 4 May 2021].

Ons.gov.uk. (2018). Public and private sector by size – Office for National Statistics. [online] Available at: https://www.ons.gov.uk/businessindustryandtrade/business/activitysizeandlocation/adhocs/008157publicandprivatesectorbysize.

Tcfdhub.org. (2019). TCFD Knowledge Hub – TCFD Knowledge Hub. [online] Available at: https://www.tcfdhub.org/ [Accessed 11 Jun. 2019].

The Chamber of Commerce. (2011). Applied Spectroscopy. [online] 65(1), pp. 5A6A. Available at: http://gtm.uk.com/wp-content/uploads/2015/01/Family-Businesses1.pdf [Accessed 4 May 2021].

uk.finance.yahoo.com. (n.d.). Three directors banned after companies formed lead cartel. [online] Available at: https://uk.finance.yahoo.com/news/

three-directors-banned-companies-formed-120239718.html?guccounter=1
[Accessed 11 Mar. 2021].

United Nations. (2015). The 17 Goals. [online] United Nations. Available at:
https://sdgs.un.org/goals. [Accessed 10 Mar. 2021].

www.bankofengland.co.uk. (n.d.). Corporate governance: Board
responsibilities. [online] Available at: https://www.bankofengland.co.uk/
prudential-regulation/publication/2016/corporate-governance-board-
responsibilities-ss [Accessed 4 May 2021].

www.mckinsey.com. (n.d.). What's next for boards of directors | McKinsey.
[online] Available at: https://www.mckinsey.com/business-functions/
strategy-and-corporate-finance/our-insights/how-boards-have-risen-to-
the-covid-19-challenge-and-whats-next [Accessed 4 May 2021].

CHAPTER TEN

Governance in the Public Sector

Rachel Gwyon and Arturo Langa

DOI: 10.4324/9781003142850-10

INTRODUCTION

The UK public sector is large, spending c. £928 billion representing around 35% of UK GDP in 2019/2020. It is a dynamic and changing sector, employing over 5.5 million people in the UK in September 2020, accounting for 16.6% of all those in paid work (www. ons.gov.uk, Dec. 2020). The National Health Service (NHS) alone is thought to be the 5th largest employer in the world.

The public sector is diverse and complex across the UK and devolved administrations, and commonly defined by government ownership, financial support or control, rather than the nature of the function carried out. Its ethos is one of service to others, accountability, and integrity. Within it, a wide range of bodies promote, fund, advise on, scrutinise, or deliver public services, often free or heavily subsidised at the point of delivery. They are sometimes called "arm's-length bodies" because they are politically impartial and operate at a distance from government, independent of their related minister.

Public bodies tend to have their own boards of non-executive directors, and sometimes include executive members too. Their longevity and focus help build capacity, expertise and the stakeholder relationships to underpin credible advice and quality services. These are often highly valued or perceived as critical by the public, and the resulting sense of purpose and impact provide for very satisfying board roles.

The key difference between governing public bodies and those in other sectors is the nature of Parliamentary accountability and scrutiny. Across the UK this accountability will be to the Westminster Parliament, Scottish Parliament, Welsh Parliament or Senedd Cymru (Welsh), or Northern Ireland Assembly. Scrutiny covers ministers and organisations themselves, their operation and stewardship of public funds. Such accountability has led to significant legislative requirements and guidance around how boards and their members should operate, from their functions to required individual board member behaviours, and organisational transparency.

While common founding principles and values underpin governance across the wider public sector, there is a diverse array of entities and structures, each with different degrees of delegated authority. This complexity is increased by the fact that arrangements within each part of the UK is governed by either Whitehall or the appropriate devolved administration, resulting in no single point of reference for a snapshot across all parts of the UK.

The public sector does not include organisations that deliver services under contract, or receive only a proportion of their income from public funding through grant-in-aid. While a sometimes fast-changing situation, it can surprise some to find that some organisations are not public bodies, such as Universities. However, a number of public bodies can also be limited companies or registered charities, even all three. One set of reporting requirements does not trump any other in such cases, showing the complexity facing board members and the degree of skill required.

DEFINING THE PUBLIC SECTOR ACROSS THE UK

Public bodies are those owned or controlled by government or local government.

The public sector is defined by the independent UK-wide Office of National Statistics (ONS), which has worked with reference to the European System of Accounts 2010. That means definition, or classification, is an issue for statisticians rather than ministers. EU requirements are for governments to produce accurate, consistent public sector finances, and national accounts and these, in turn, align with international accounting standards.

As the UK has now left the European Union, ONS will take over responsibilities that were previously delegated to the statistical office of the EU, called Eurostat. At the time of writing, ONS announced that it intends to continue to align with international standards and ensure international comparability of economic and social statistics as it develops its work under the Statistics and Registration Service Act 2007. For example, it has committed that labour market statistics will continue to be published in line with the UK Statistics Authority's Code of Practice for Statistics and in accordance with International Labour Organization (ILO) definitions and agreed international statistical guidance. Board members might expect a high degree of continuity post-Brexit, and application of familiar classification principles.

In considering if a body, or entity such as a joint venture, is public or private the level of government control is examined, whether exercised directly or indirectly. The control measures which ONS consider can vary over time, as best practice evolves. While not definitive, they include whether government:

- appoints those in control, can veto appointments, or be consulted on them;
- provides funding or rights to levy fees, including having control over how funding, income or profits are spent; and
- operates control over the day-to-day running of the body.

Once a body is deemed to be in the public sector, it is assigned to a sub-sector for inclusion in the relevant part of the national accounts. This point matters because certain limits, for example on the level of public borrowing, affect how financial tools and flexibilities are passed on to public bodies and boards. There are three sub-classifications, as shown in Table 10.1.

The devolved administrations (Scottish Government, Welsh Government, and Government of Northern Ireland) fall within the same central government classification as the UK itself (and England for which there is no comparable devolved assembly or devolution of powers). Powers to establish public bodies in Scotland, Wales, and Northern Ireland have been devolved to their respective administrations, so their ultimate form and function is determined by

Table 10.1 *The three sub-classifications of public bodies in the UK*

Central Government	Public Corporations	Local Government
Ministerial departments (England, Wales, Northern Ireland) or portfolios (Scotland)	Market bodies who finance their operations from the sale of goods or services, raising over 50% of their funding.	Body restricted to a specific locality.
Arm's-length bodies such as agencies or non-departmental public bodies. Non-market bodies controlled by Ministers	These can be controlled by UK Government, devolved administrations, or local government.	Non-market bodies controlled by local government

each government, within the same overall classification system. This can give rise to some interesting differences. For example, because of differences in the levels of government control operated across jurisdictions, further education colleges in England were classified to the private sector in 2012, but those in Scotland were re-classified back to the public sector in late 2015. Similarly, water services are in the private sector in England, but Scottish Water is a public corporation. Board members should not assume that familiarity with one regime reads across to another, and should always check the details of their own organisational context.

Arm's-length bodies are independent of the core of government in all four jurisdictions. This independence is achieved through government specifying what the organisation is to deliver and how it is expected to operate. There are a range of common misconceptions around such independence, for example that the board is free of government strategic or financial oversight and control, which is not the case.

Recognising a risk of diffusion of accountability, or that public sector activity might crowd out market enterprise, a range of controls operate around whether a public body can be created in the first place. It is not as simple as identifying a need, or a willingness to fund a service. Establishing any arm's-length body requires a clear specific and distinct purpose from its related part of the core government, and it cannot be given authority to make decisions or perform functions that only ministers or their core departments or portfolios should make.

For example, for bodies performing a UK-wide or England-only function, the lead minister will need to secure Cabinet Office and Treasury agreement to a clear perceived advantage in creating a new organisation. The UK Government policy direction has been to reduce the number of its bodies. A programme from 2010 to 2015 reduced the number of organisations by around one third and was estimated to have saved around £3 billion in administration costs.

Despite these controls, it is possible to become a public sector organisation through an ONS process called "reclassification".

LEARNING POINT

In 2014, Network Rail was reclassified to the public sector "at the stroke of a pen" by the Office of National Statistics. While some might consider this a rather dry topic, others saw it as nationalisation of the track operator. Issues had arisen over strategy, and the level of directors' pay and bonuses. Ministers sought tighter limits and oversight around such decisions, which brought implications for the assessment of whether government controlled the body.

The Network Rail Board had been accountable to "public members" and the classification shift produced certain changes. For example, it gave the Secretary of State greater power to appoint or remove the chair, greater say over the board and, by implication, the appointment of those public members. It also had consequences for how the organisation financed its operations, heralding a move away from Network Rail raising its own private debt against the value of its network, called the Regulated Asset Base.

In practice for the board this decision, not made by them, changed their operating context and delegated authorities almost overnight. Network Rail said of these changes at the time,

> For passengers and station users, this statistical change will mean little to their journeys. We recognise that, for Network Rail, it will mean greater accountability and transparency to parliament, taxpayers and fare payers, who rightly deserve to better understand the value of their significant investment in Britain's booming railway.

In early 2021, the UK Government announced the next chapter with the creation of Great British Railways to take over Network Rail infrastructure, alongside setting fares and timetables, collecting revenue, and running and planning the network. This shows how public board members should be ready for, and alive to the governance implications of, change.

HISTORY

A gencies, and other modern public body structures, came about as a consequence of major reform of the civil service initiated under Margaret Thatcher in the late 1980s.

Known as the "Next Steps" programme, the reforms aimed to separate the core of civil servants involved directly in policy-making and ministerial support functions, from the 75% to 95% of civil servants involved in the service delivery or executive functions of pre-devolution central government. The intention was to transfer this larger group into semi-autonomous agencies and, as the Institute for Government noted, this aimed to increase focus on external recruitment, financial and performance management, and customer relations. The intended result was greater efficiency and higher-quality services (www.instituteforgovernment.org.uk, 1987).

By the middle of 1993, just over 60% of the British civil service were working in so-called Next Steps agencies, or similar organisations (Butcher, 1995).

For board members, it is interesting that the Employment Rights Act 1996 (updated, and applying across all UK jurisdictions) requires employers to give time off to their staff to perform the duties of governing board members of certain public bodies particularly in, but not restricted to, the local government, education, or health sectors.

THE NATURE OF PUBLIC BODIES

There is now an almost dizzying array of labels for public bodies, such as executive agencies, non-departmental public bodies (NDPB), public corporations, tribunals, non-ministerial offices, health boards, commissioners, ombudsmen, and regulators. Some, but not all, will have a chair and board. Most Organisation for Economic Co-operation and Development (OECD) countries use public bodies for delivering types of government services.

Public bodies cover functions that affect everyday lives across diverse services. The services delivered vary widely in scale and nature, and include:

- services direct to the public, such as the National Health Service;
- services at a national level, for example protecting security or environment;
- services with a scrutiny or regulatory focus, working across services or markets such as energy or telecoms;
- advice to government; and
- services underpinning the function of government such as revenue collection.

Public bodies offer the benefits of focus on a particular service, community need, or locality; efficiencies in stakeholder engagement including the multi-agency working that is needed to make complex services work for the user; operational skill, effectiveness, and responsiveness.

Parliaments and assemblies, think tanks or critics, can point, from time to time, to accountability challenges. The greater the body's autonomy, the greater the specificity of performance and reporting expectations, to ensure clear purpose and accountability for effectiveness and efficiency.

The different administrations across the UK have established their own ways to guide ministerial teams, or public bodies themselves, through this complexity and can be a great source of board advice or assistance. Typically, they will:

- publish information about their public bodies;
- promote good governance and accountability, effectiveness, and efficiency;
- offer advice and guidance, including sharing best practice; and
- support new board members and an effective public appointments process.

COMMON LEGAL STRUCTURES OF PUBLIC BODIES

Arm's-length bodies (ALBs) are a specific category of public body that are administratively classified in each jurisdiction across the UK. They can also be called quangos, which stands for "quasi-autonomous, non-governmental organisations". When used by the press or critics of an organisation, this latter term is not usually complimentary, tending to be used to imply a lack of democratic legitimacy or accountability. ALBs include executive agencies, non-departmental public bodies (NDPBs), and non-ministerial departments, and there are over 300 of these types of body alone across the UK and devolved administrations at the time of writing, managing well over £200 billion of expenditure. Welsh Government-sponsored

Bodies are NDPBs and also known in Welsh as *Corff (plural: Cyrff) a Noddir gan Lywodraeth Cymru*, CNLC. Most public bodies across the UK are in one of the categories set out below.

EXECUTIVE AGENCIES

Executive agencies are clearly designated, financially viable, business units within ministerial departments or portfolios, and undertake executive functions rather than giving policy advice. They are closest to central government, with the shortest "arms". They have a clear focus on delivering specific outputs, for example, Prison Services. Their staff are usually civil servants. The CEO and any non-executive board chair are appointed through public appointment. Executives are likely to be board members alongside non-executives. Boards may have a combined CEO and chair, and in such cases it is the combined CEO/chair who appoints and can remove non-executive board members. The body will have its own published annual report and accounts, which are consolidated with the central government accounts.

A non-executive director's experience of an agency board was that, while the audit and risk committee was formed entirely of non-executives, the main strategic board contained a majority of executive director members. The key to effective working was striking the right balance between support to the chief executive officer and their team alongside insightful questioning and constructive challenge. How the non-executives worked together, to contribute the right mix of their combined skills and strengths to any particular issue, was also crucial to the overall strength and success of the board.

NON-DEPARTMENTAL PUBLIC BODIES (NDPBs)

NDPBs are not part of a government department or portfolio, and operate with independence, although a lead minister remains responsible to Parliament for their performance and effectiveness.

NDPBs show perhaps the greatest variety in form, structures and working methods, and can be used for trading activities. They exist in two principal types:

- Advisory NDPBs: mostly comprising external experts who operate in a personal capacity to form boards or committees which offer ministers independent and specialist advice. The Minister will appoint members, and the minister's team of civil servants will set the strategic framework. The Advisory NDPB itself is likely to be supported by a separate secretariat of civil servants to help support its work. Such bodies do not report their own accounts.
- Executive NDPBs: form the majority of public bodies, and are arguably at the end of the longest "arms". These have their own legal "personality", carrying out a service or function within a strategic framework determined by ministers. They are funded through grant-in-aid and may receive charitable donations or have levy or fee-raising powers. They produce their own annual reports and accounts, which are consolidated with central government. Ministers will appoint the non-executive chair and other board members. The board appoints the chief executive. Executives, including the CEO, are not board members. Executive staff are public, but not civil, servants. Such boards are likely to look and feel very recognisable to non-executives with a private or charitable sector background. It may help to think of them as a company with a single shareholder: the government. The level of activism shown by that shareholder will likely vary over time, depending on the context.

NON-MINISTERIAL DEPARTMENTS/OFFICES

Non-ministerial departments (UK, England, and Wales) or non-ministerial offices (Scotland) operate similarly to normal government departments but are more specialised. They generally cover matters for which direct political oversight is judged unnecessary or inappropriate, and account directly to Parliament. They can have their own subsidiaries, which may be executive agencies or non-departmental public bodies. They have their own budgets, and may have levy powers. They produce their own, non-consolidated accounts, and their staff are civil servants. Examples include the Charity Commission for England and Wales, the Competition and Markets Authority (UK), and The Scottish Courts and Tribunals Service.

HEALTH BODIES

While comparable to other bodies, in recognition of the degree of specialisation, health has its own sub-classification for public bodies. These include, for example, NHS Trusts (England); Health Boards (Scotland); Health and Social Care Trusts (Northern Ireland); Local Health Boards (Wales); Mental Welfare Commission for Scotland; NHS24.

PUBLIC CORPORATIONS

These are market bodies controlled by the UK Government, devolved administrations, or local government, as set out above. They are founded by legislation and include any type of public entity that is a market body, gaining over 50% of their income from purely commercial activities. Trading funds are often included in this category. The BBC is an example, founded by the 1922 Broadcasting Act, and is funded by the TV licence fee. Others include Scottish Water or the Crown Estate. Ministers retain an interest in the level of fees or charges that can be levied, although other bodies such as customer groups will also have a say.

Board members may find such organisational environments most similar to private or regulated industries, in that managing income as well as expenditure, in a scrutinised context, is likely to be a key element.

PARLIAMENTARY BODIES

These are set up by, and usually report directly to, parliament rather than a minister. They often deliver functions or services that require even greater distance from ministers and are even more focussed on political independence and accountability to Parliament, perhaps because they operate a more regulatory or oversight function. Usually staffed by public (not civil) servants, senior appointments may involve Parliament directly or parliamentary oversight. Examples include Independent Parliamentary Standards Authority (Westminster); National Audit Office (UK); Audit Scotland (Scottish Parliament); Audit Wales (Welsh Parliament), and Northern Ireland Audit Office (Northern Ireland Assembly).

Given the oversight role of parliamentary bodies, most board members will come across them when in receipt of an audit or scrutiny report relating to their own public body. Any such report is automatically published, and likely to attract Parliamentary Committee interest and follow-up, so it is worth paying very careful attention to the detail of findings and the nature of your board's response.

LEARNING POINT

Governance aspects of the "Next Steps" public body framework were quickly tested following their creation, and in a high-profile way.

In January 1995, the then English Prison Service was already an Executive Agency. Three prisoners escaped from Parkhurst top security prison. This unfortunate incident happened three months after another high-profile breakout, this time of five IRA inmates from another supposedly impregnable jail.

Public outrage followed with demands for accountability from the home secretary, Michael Howard. Parliamentary and public debate at the time was heated and focussed on where the responsibility lay for this security failure, and who should resign or be fired. Was it a failure of criminal justice policy, or a failure in operational delivery, putting the focus on the governance of the Prison Service?

Since it was the ministers who had determined there should be a difference between policy and delivery, focus was on the justification and strength of the new "wall" created between the two aspects.

An inquiry into events at Parkhurst prison and security at all jails found that there had been "a chapter of errors at every level and a naivete that defies belief". The Home Secretary summarily sacked the Prison Service CEO, Derek Lewis, saying that the "buck stopped with [the CEO] Mr Lewis and the prison management". Two non-executive directors of the board also resigned following Mr Lewis's removal.

These debates, and the outturn in terms of who left their roles, helped establish and indicate the strength of the framework of accountability that survives today.

In the modern context, board members might note that for an agency the government has a role in the appointment, and therefore removal, of the chief executive officer. For a NDPB, the equivalent influence is directly over the chair, with the board determining the fate of their chief executive.

Another question for public body board members, with their collective responsibility, is what type of accountability issue might constitute a resignation one for non-executives?

THE ROLE OF PUBLIC BODY BOARDS

Within their organisation boards provide strategic leadership, direction, support, and guidance. Board members have corporate responsibility for organisational performance and delivery of ministers' policies and priorities. They share collective responsibility for ensuring adherence to certain standards of financial propriety and regularity, as well as promoting the effective and efficient use of staff and other resources, including public funds. As with other sectors, a public sector board holds the chief executive to account.

Other than the role of ministers and parliamentary accountability, there is nothing immediately remarkable about such responsibilities in comparison with boards in either the charitable or private sectors. Indeed, experienced board members will recognise a high degree of similarity between the best practice principles applying to PLCs, and reflected in regimes such as the UK Corporate Governance Code (Financial Reporting Council, 2018), and those carrying into public sector accountability frameworks. Similarly, Companies' Acts principles and provisions are often also mirrored in public sector legislation or guidance.

As one example of how board responsibilities are viewed in the public sector, NHS Scotland produced a Blueprint for Good Governance (Mclaughlin, 2019). This sought to recognise the increasingly demanding environment that NHS boards across the UK operate in, and highlights how boards can ensure good governance to support the provision of high-quality, safe, sustainable health and social care services. Covering themes that will be familiar to board members in any sector, the blueprint helpfully points to three aspects of good governance: functions, enablers, and support, as outlined in Figure 10.1.

The nature of the differences with private boards relates to how the ministerial oversight and parliamentary accountability operates. For example, there is a very high degree of codification and specificity around a variety of aspects of public sector governance.

Each organisation should hold a clear, written document from government covering areas such as the body's legislative basis, its purpose, functions, duties, and powers. The key roles and responsibilities of ministers and their civil service officials are likely to be detailed, along with those of the chair, board, and chief executive. The precise nature of these can vary across jurisdictions and the policy

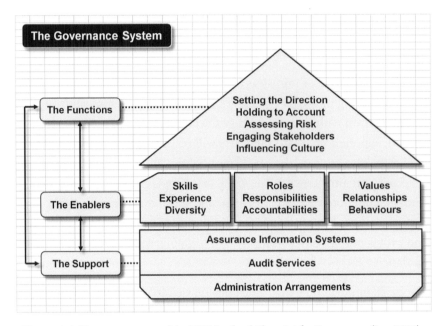

Figure 10.1 *The governance model – NHS Scotland Blueprint for Governance (Jan. 2019).*

area within which the body fits. Board members might check relevant extant guidance in the place at the time of their membership.

The framework should detail organisational aims, objectives, and targets. The level of delegation should also be clear: those decisions which the organisation is authorised or not authorised to make at its own hand. Examples include restrictions on establishing subsidiaries, around particular types of investment or related to projects above a certain financial value, or the level of fees charged for services.

Where an organisation is also a limited company it may also have articles of association. An obvious point might be for a board member to ensure these are coherent with the framework, as the two documents may have been updated at different times! In line with principles of transparency all these are usually published on the body's own website and shared with the related Parliament or Assembly.

A key difference between private and public sector bodies is the nature of decision-making – more often requiring co-decision or collaboration in the public sector. For example, legislation may specify that certain other organisations must be consulted, or agree, the strategic direction or particular decisions. This requires board members to become skilled in exercising "soft" power, supporting their organisations to build influence, rather than being able to direct the actions of others who perhaps have their own democratic legitimacy. While this can lead to stronger or enduring decisions overall, they may be reached more slowly, which some may find frustrating or misunderstand.

A number of individuals with private sector career backgrounds make the transition to non-executive roles in public bodies each year, usually very successfully. Some can be surprised at aspects of the different operating context, or express frustration at what they perceive as the short length of the "arms" they are at the other end of. In navigating the accountability and scrutiny required within a public body, one piece of advice offered by a former chair is to think how any decision or action could be perceived by your most trenchant critic if reported on the front page of a tabloid. If that test suggests the risk of potential difficulty, it is worth pausing and reflecting: transparency means such reporting is commonplace.

EXPECTATIONS OF INDIVIDUAL BOARD MEMBERS

Board members can expect to operate as a "critical friend" bringing a balance between supporting the executives and holding them to account for organisational performance.

The expectations placed on public body board members individually also explicitly extend to their personal behaviours, values, and ethics. Following 1994 concerns, when it emerged that some Members of Parliament had accepted cash in return for raising issues and asking questions in the Westminster Parliament, the prime minister established the UK-wide Committee on Standards in Public Life. This Committee itself continues to operate as an advisory Non-Departmental Public Body, and its initial remit was to "make recommendations as to any changes in present arrangements which might be required to ensure the highest standards of propriety in public life".

The Committee's first chair was The Right Hon Lord Nolan, a Lord of Appeal, leading to it becoming known as the Nolan Committee, and the scope of its work extended to members of Parliament, ministers and civil servants, executive quangos and NHS Bodies, and senior officers of local authorities. Reporting initially in 1995, the Nolan Committee identified the following principles of conduct expected in public office, which still apply today, including:

1. Selflessness.
2. Integrity.
3. Objectivity.
4. Accountability.
5. Openness.
6. Honesty.
7. Leadership.

For a full description of the Nolan Principles, please refer to page 70 in Chapter 2. These continue to apply to members of UK-wide and English boards, in Wales and Northern Ireland. The Nolan principles and practices also extended to the selection and appointment of non-executive directors (see below). As one example of how such principles can translate into practice, David Prince, former member of the Committee on Standards in Public Life, highlighted in 2016 (cspl. blog.gov.uk, Jul. 2016) that NHS board members in England were each required to sign a personal statement, which one might imagine would certainly focus the mind of any board member:

> To justify the trust placed in me by patients, service users and the public, I will abide by the (NHS Governing Body Standards) at all times when at the service of the NHS. I understand that I must act in the interests of patients, service users and the community I serve, and that I must uphold the law and be fair and honest in all my dealings.

In Scotland, the Nolan principles were also accepted at the time. They were later developed further and enshrined in statute through the Ethical Standards in Public Life (Scotland) Act 2000, which identified a further two principles: public service; and respect. Each Scottish public body is also expected to have a published Code of Conduct, based on the statutory requirements and covering the personal behaviour of board members. These are enforceable through reference to the (Scottish) Commissioner for Ethical Standards in Public Life.

Building on these ethical foundations, all boards should keep a register of interests. Best practice includes checking for updates before each board meeting and publishing the register. Board members should expect to detail any gifts and hospitality received above low monetary values; set out political affiliations or other non-financial interests relevant to the work of the body; and declare lobbying or access to ministers, political advisers, or top officials.

PUBLIC APPOINTMENTS

Chairs can usually expect to be appointed by ministers through a transparent public appointments process, and to have a say in the similar appointment of a suitably diverse group of non-executive directors. Applicants through a public appointments process should expect to need to demonstrate awareness of, and evidence of operating in compliance with, Nolan principles, and the broader list applying in Scotland. In each jurisdiction such processes are overseen by an independent public appointments commissioner, who sets the framework and expectations such as around diversity. Building on Nolan principles, interview panels will comprise an "independent member" whose role is to ensure these fair and transparent processes are followed. Legislative provision may set out the number of members of some boards, or the specific organisations or backgrounds to be represented on a board.

Individual and corporate reputation is critical to operating in the public sector. This scrutiny and focus starts at the public appointment stage.

Applicants might expect their past social media, and other forms of public comment, to be checked and probed. Previous spent convictions, ill-advised memberships of certain organisations, or past comments re-read in a modern context, could rule a candidate out from certain roles. Once on a board, members might take care of how their actions or comments, in any forum or context, could be perceived to impact their reputation or that of their organisation. As can be seen from the breadth of the Nolan principles, being a fit person for public office covers a range of tests and requirements.

Many non-executive directors have portfolio careers. It is worth thinking carefully about the past and current combination of roles and how they interact. Joining the board of one company might impact a potential future role with another. For example, early-stage companies often seek rounds of equity finance and operate in high-risk contexts, meaning they can face funding difficulties and even insolvency. While parts of the private sector may more readily understand such learning and experience, the potential reputational impact of having served on the board of an insolvent company could well preclude an individual from a future public board role in light of the requirement of public boards to be accountable for use of taxpayer funds.

LEARNING POINT

Scrutiny of board members can come from any source – even initiated by your organisation's own staff, as the chair of the Imperial College Healthcare NHS Foundation Trust found. Paula Vennells took up this role on 1 April 2019, after an executive career culminating as CEO of the public sector Post Office.

The issue was that sub-postmasters, who run post office branches, had been blamed over many years for unexplained accounting shortfalls. They were forced to pay back funds, bankrupting some. Others were prosecuted and even went to prison. Stress caused ill-health.

From 2009, Computer Weekly had been exploring and following the story that a new post office computer system called Horizon was behind accounting errors and that no money had, in fact, been lost. In December 2019, a multi-pound group litigation in the High Court ended with the Post Office conceding it had been wrong, apologising and paying damages.

The question then moved to one of governance and the personal character of leaders. Paula Vennells left the Post Office, one public body, before the conclusion of the High Court Case, to become Chair of one of the biggest Trusts in the NHS. After reading about the treatment of sub postmasters during her CEO tenure, a senior medic referred Vennells' chair appointment to the Care Quality Commission (CQC), which regulates health and social care in England. The referral came under powers for the CQC to regulate that board directors and members require to be "Fit and Proper Persons" (FPPR), and asked the CQC to review Imperial College Healthcare NHS Trust's arrangements for FPPR, calling for consultation with those affected at the Post Office (www.cqc. org.uk, Jun. 2018).

While originally defending its decisions and processes, and as the Criminal Cases Review Commission started to refer postmaster cases for consideration as miscarriages of justice, the NHS Trust commissioned an external legal review in 2020 of the tests it applied to the fitness of its Chair. That had not reported when Vennells stepped down in April 2021, also standing back from her private sector non-executive roles with Morrisons and Dunelm.

Stepping back does not conclude scrutiny: the Trust review has still to report; and the UK Government has announced a judicial inquiry into events at the post office. This will have statutory powers to call witnesses and secure evidence, which Vennells has welcomed, and had not reported at time of writing. There is potentially more governance learning to come.

WORKING EFFECTIVELY WITH MINISTERS AND THE CIVIL SERVICE

A government minister will have responsibility for oversight of the public body. As with any other part of their role, where ministers are advised and supported by the civil service, this is also true of how ministers work with their public bodies.

For NDPBs, a minister will likely be supported by a "sponsor team" of civil servants who perform specific roles, at a range of levels of seniority, relating to governance and building and maintaining effective relationships with the public body. This sponsorship role is the key interface through which the interests both of ministerial policy and the public body are developed.

The sponsor team will help promote good governance, ethical standards and share wider sectoral best practice. They are the ideal friend to help a board, especially the chair, navigate the complexity of wider government, or engage at the right time with the right people.

Civil servants hold specific responsibilities around ensuring the body's general compliance with relevant statutory and administrative duties, or relating to key processes such as around establishment, merger, or abolition; public appointments; facilitating ministerial agreement to strategy and vision; setting budgets and financial management arrangements; and reporting. While not usually attending board meetings, they are entitled to do so, although only as observers not participants. They hold very real responsibilities in their own right, as the example below shows, on which they can seek to engage with board members.

Sponsorship is two-way. Building a successful relationship with civil service interlocutors, as well as with ministers and their political advisers directly, will help board members ensure a shared understanding of priorities and resolve any tricky issues effectively. The ideal is an open, trusting, responsive, and mutually supportive relationship which provides a sound basis for constructive challenge both ways, and supports continuous improvement.

Sponsorship is principally a strategic role, and the level of ministerial oversight might flex to reflect the perceived strengths of each body, and the conditions and risks faced. For example, a closer degree of oversight might follow ombudsman referrals, or if external audit, or a Parliamentary Committee, has highlighted areas of concern. So, if the arm's length appears very short, it is worth board members checking relative perspectives on their organisation's performance, resilience, or governance with their sponsor team or minister. It may be that confidence and assurance is readily shared with ministers. In any event, a mutual understanding of challenges faced will have value in deciding the best way forward.

For agencies, the equivalent oversight role is taken forward by an individual "Fraser Figure", usually a very senior civil service role, that provides a link between agency chief executives and the parent government. This approach derives from the report "Making the most of Next Steps" (1991) by Sir Angus Fraser (Great Britain. Efficiency Unit and Great Britain. Prime Minister, 1991).

LEARNING POINT

The Northern Ireland Events Company (NIEC) was a public body formed in 1997 to boost Northern Ireland's image as a venue for high-profile sports and music events. It was sponsored by the Northern Ireland Government's Department of Culture, Arts and Leisure (DCAL). The appointment of a new Acting CEO in 2007 uncovered a potential deficit of £1.2 million, and the organisation collapsed later that year with debts totalling £1.6 million.

In 2008, the NI Department of Enterprise, Trade and Investment (DETI) launched an investigation which lasted six years and cost £1.2 million. Press interest on both sides of the border was high into what became the biggest scandal ever investigated by the

North's Public Accounts Committee according to the Irish Times (McDonnell, Feb. 2016).

The Northern Ireland Audit Office published its findings in September 2015 (Northern Ireland Audit Office, Sep. 2015). It found that the board had failed to provide adequate oversight, and weaknesses in DCAL's approach. Its most damning comments related to the CEO is as follows:

> In our opinion the standard of leadership provided by Janice McAleese fell well short of what is expected from an Accounting Officer. This included conflicts of interest which were poorly handled and covering up escalating financial losses with misleading and, on occasion, fabricated documentation which was provided to the Board and to DCAL. We are unaware of any other instance in the Northern Ireland public sector in which an Accounting Officer has failed so comprehensively to uphold the Nolan principles of conduct in public life and more specifically the requirements expected of an Accounting Officer as set out in DCAL's letter of appointment.

This was followed up by Stormont Public Accounts Committee scrutiny. In their February 2016 report the Committee agreed with DCAL that

> the NIEC saga represented.... a comprehensive failure on the part of DCAL to fully discharge its responsibilities in terms of sponsorship; it was a failure on the part of the NIEC Board to provide effective leadership, direction, support and guidance to the organisation; and it was a failure on the part of Janice McAleese, the Chief Executive of the company, to ensure that public funds were properly managed and safeguarded.
>
> (Public Accounts Committee Report on The Northern Ireland Events Company, Feb. 2016)

The committee went on to make recommendations about CEO appointment processes, the required board experience and skills mix, including financial skills, and called for all public body board members to learn the lessons about effectiveness of governance. While all board members had acted in a voluntary capacity, the committee noted their poor board attendance, concluding they had not made themselves aware of the time commitment and their responsibilities prior to accepting appointment. The committee further made recommendations about sponsorship, and the skills required for this role.

The implications did not end there. The BBC reported in early 2018 on the outcome of disqualification proceedings against board members and former senior executives (NI Events Company: Board Members Disqualified from Being Directors, 2018). These saw the board chair and nine other directors pledge not to act as a company director for nine and five years respectively. Janice McAleese, the CEO, was banned as a company director for 14 years and, in 2019, was also given a two-year sentence at Belfast Crown Court, suspended for three years, after admitting misconduct in public office.

IMPORTANT ASPECTS OF PUBLIC BODY GOVERNANCE

In addition to working effectively with ministers, there are other important aspects of public body governance that it is important for potential board members to know about. While in the private and charity/voluntary sector, board debates and decisions are highly confidential, public sector boards are expected to operate in a transparent manner. Matters such as setting the vision, strategy, and decision-making as well as finance are also approached in a different manner in public body boards, and these are explored below.

TRANSPARENCY

Public bodies are expected to have decision-making processes that are open, transparent, and informed by the needs of stakeholders, citizens, service users, and employees. The steps a body takes to ensure that it is operating in an open way will be influenced by its size and nature. Legislation or guidance across each part of the UK requires public bodies to publish certain types of information annually, for example relating to expenditure.

Public bodies might, for example, be expected to hold board meetings, or parts of board meetings, in public where it is practical and appropriate to do so. A body might also:

- publish summary reports and/or minutes of meetings;
- invite members of the public to a dedicated question and answer session at a board meeting;
- consult stakeholders and users on plans, priorities, and
- actions;
- use the internet to publish information, release video of board meetings, or make services available to the public.

Freedom of Information legislation has existed across all parts of the UK since the early 2000s. While precise provisions slightly differ between jurisdictions, all enshrine the principle of openness and afford rights of access to information held by public authorities. Public bodies can also expect to be required, through legislation or guidance, to release or publish environmental information or other types, such as around complaints handling, codes of conduct, or the names and salary details of senior staff. Public body websites should detail how to contact relevant Ombudsmen.

Transparency requirements include the accessibility of information, for example to someone with a visual impairment, or ensuring services are available in those languages required by users. Perhaps most notably, the Welsh Language (Wales) Measure 2011 relates to the use of Welsh in the delivery of public services. Its implementation is overseen by the Welsh Language Commissioner, who promotes and facilitates the use of Welsh; expands people's rights to use the language in their everyday lives; and ensures that public bodies comply with Welsh language standards.

VISION, STRATEGY, AND DECISION-MAKING

A public body will often set out its forward strategy in a multi-year corporate plan, perhaps also incorporating measures of success or key performance indicators. Unlike the private sector, an organisation's strategy is neither private nor the sole preserve of its board. The board should expect to be required to formulate their plan and strategy in collaboration with stakeholders, and to publish it once agreed. Ministers will also expect a role in agreeing the overall vision and strategy, priorities, broad resource requirements and that longer-term performance measures are appropriate and sufficiently stretching to reflect an effective and efficient use of public funds.

For perhaps obvious reasons, a board cannot decide on mergers, acquisitions, winding-up, or expansion of activities into a different jurisdiction.

Board members should expect interest in the longer-term impact of their strategic plans. Sustainable development, low carbon goals, wellbeing or the impact on future generations are examples of over-arching goals that may be of interest to ministers, parliaments, and assemblies across the UK. The Future Generations Commissioner for Wales, for example, encourages public bodies to take greater account of their long-term impact and has power to carry out reviews into the extent that they are meeting their related statutory duties.

DEALING WITH PUBLIC FUNDS

There are key differences between how finance operates in private/ charitable sectors and in public bodies, which are pertinent to the governance role of board members. For example:

- Recognising the requirements around stewardship of taxpayer funds, the public body CEO will be designated as accounting officer (UK, Wales, Northern Ireland) or Accountable Officer (Scotland), to whom funds are delegated by the appropriate civil service equivalent. Such roles bring certain personal financial responsibilities and accountabilities to Parliament, which the board cannot over-ride. It is incumbent on the chief executive to manage the combination of accountabilities to Parliament and the board well, and on board members to facilitate and support this.
- A public body will usually receive its budget annually. In some circumstances, such as if a multi-year government spending review has occurred, forecast budgets may be available over a medium-term multi-year period. Otherwise, the typical financial planning horizon is the April-March financial year. Budgets can be subject to change, up or down, at government behest during the financial year. Boards are responsible for ensuring sufficient financial resilience to handle such short-notice adjustments.
- Since all public bodies operate within the same financial system as their central or local government sponsor, board members should expect their organisation to face comparable controls such as inability to borrow at their own hand, hold reserves, or take significant investment decisions without prior, explicit agreement. Staff may be subject to ministerially determined pay policies, affecting the remuneration or severance levels which the Board can set.
- As part of the public sector, an organisation is required to operate within relevant rules applying to awarding grants to third parties, for example, limits on public support to private enterprises under the new UK Subsidy Control Regime, previously determined by EU State Aid rules.

The board is responsible for ensuring appropriate internal audit arrangements and for establishing an audit committee, which will often consider both financial and operational delivery risk and control systems.

The Parliament or Assembly in each part of the UK ensures an independent external audit function which reports publicly and is headed by a figure with statutory responsibilities, technically appointed by the Crown. The various lead officers and their audit organisations are as below:

- Westminster Parliament – Comptroller and Auditor General; National Audit Office
- Scottish Parliament – Auditor General; Audit Scotland.
- Welsh Parliament – Auditor General for Wales; Audit Wales
- Northern Ireland Assembly – Comptroller and Auditor General for Northern Ireland; Northern Ireland Audit Office

Board members of public bodies, health service organisations and government departments should usually expect external audit to be conducted independently and directly by one of the audit offices above, or by a private sector auditor appointed by that audit office, rather than the Board itself. The various national audit organisations share common aims to ensure transparency and scrutinise how public bodies manage and spend public money, including how they achieve value, efficiency, effectiveness, and improvement in the delivery of public services. They have powers to secure access to all required documents and records.

Consequently, board members should expect that their annual accounts require to be signed-off by the relevant public audit body, and that any issues arising will be the subject of a published, independent report. Alongside audit opinion, the audit organisations can typically undertake organisation-specific, or more general, value for money inquiries; governance reviews; audit of IT projects; project work or other ad hoc reviews.

Findings of any of these reports will be published to the relevant legislature, whose Public Audit Committee will often follow up with public hearings. Senior executives, especially the Accountable Officer, can expect to be called to give evidence to such Committees, particularly on reports raising concerns or issues around the longer-term sustainability of an organisation's financial model. The Board Chair may also be involved in such scrutiny.

For Councils and related local government bodies, arrangements are a little different. In Wales, external audit is also through Audit Wales. In the other jurisdictions, required audit standards are set out under statutory powers, in a Code of Audit Practice, by the relevant comptroller or auditor general. Audits and reviews are then carried out by the Accounts Commission (Scotland); local government auditor (Northern Ireland); or by an auditor appointed by Public Sector Audit Appointments Ltd (England).

LEARNING POINT

Natural Resources Wales (NRW), a Welsh Government–sponsored body, was created to ensure sustainable maintenance, use and enhancement of the Welsh environment and natural resources. It became operational in 2013, and from 2014 commenced sales of timber.

While noting that the financial statements in the 2017–2018 accounts gave a "true and fair view" the then auditor general for Wales, nevertheless, qualified his regulatory opinion (cdn. cyfoethnaturiol.cymru, n.d.). Any such move is rare, but for NRW it was for the third year running. The issue centred around whether 59 new contracts for timber sales awarded in 2017–2018 had been properly entered into; whether they were at or below market rates; and whether they complied with State Aid rules. The focus became on governance.

On the face of their published accounts, the auditor general for Wales noted that NRW had departed from its own policy of openly marketing timber; had not properly documented the decision-making process; had not followed its framework document requirement to refer novel or contentious decisions to its sponsor department in the Welsh Government; and had not followed its own internal scheme of delegation.

The auditor general wrote, "I therefore consider the transactions relating to these contracts to be unlawful and I have qualified my regularity opinion accordingly". This is strong stuff.

In comment to the Public Accounts Committee of the Welsh Parliament in their subsequent inquiry, he said,

> The fact that the issues raised in my report on NRW's 2017–18 financial statements are so similar to those included in my report on NRW's 2015–16 financial statements has confirmed that NRW did not treat the findings of 2015–16 report sufficiently seriously.
>
> (Natural Resources Wales Scrutiny of Annual Report and Accounts 2017–18, 2018)

While a new CEO of NRW had only recently come into post in February 2018, and remained to see through improvements, the Chair resigned in July. The board and new Chair took action, appointing Grant Thornton to carry out a full independent review of the issues, provided training in public law and state aid for those involved in contracts, and reviewed governance and financial schemes of delegation.

The Welsh Public Accounts Committee recommended publication of the independent report, sought a public action plan from the NRW board to implement its findings, and suggested a further public follow-up hearing to ensure progress.

WHY JOIN A PUBLIC SECTOR BOARD?

There are numerous reasons why you may wish to consider joining a public sector board, even if you have spent most of your career in the private or charity/voluntary sectors. You may have reached a point where you feel able to "give something back".

There can be a number of popular misconceptions about joining public sector boards, which this chapter may have helped dispel.

Just like organisations in other sectors, public sector bodies require board members who will bring commitment, strategic thinking, constructive challenge and solid governance skills. While potential board members may bring a specialism such as finance, HR or legal expertise, all board members should bring the ability and willingness to understand the whole organisation and the context within which it operates, as well as the inter-personal skills to work effectively with a very wide range of people and interests. While many public sector board roles are unremunerated, other than covering expenses, reasons to join a public sector body board include:

- the opportunity to "give back" and contribute to important public services;
- to gain valuable board experience of complex organisations and different stakeholder dynamics, potentially enhancing an ongoing executive career;
- exposure to a wide variety of fellow board members from diverse sectors, bringing a range of skill-sets.

A personal example was shared by an individual who, following a successful private sector executive career, and private sector and charity non-executive roles, found the prospects of "delivering for the nation" very attractive. She consequently joined a Scottish NDPB board to bring her commercial background and fresh perspective to bear, particularly around audit and risk management. She found her experience of a wide range of different business models was highly valued, and this breadth aided her transition to the public realm, noting its key difference of assurance being required to the accountable officer rather than the board as a whole. She found a purpose-led organisation very satisfying, and was impressed with the innovative, forward-looking approaches she found there.

Her advice to others would be to look to join Boards where you see a "fit" with your own motivations and perceive a high level of skill, understanding, and political acuity among fellow board members, particularly the chair. The challenges she reported lay in the lengthy and potentially off-putting public recruitment process, and in understanding how best to become knowledgeable and stay up-to-date around wider public sector issues.

COVID-19 AND PUBLIC BODY GOVERNANCE

The COVID-19 pandemic represented an unprecedented challenge to public services in all parts of the UK, and to the boards of public bodies. Responding effectively could be argued to be the largest single challenge that public services have faced in decades (www. instituteforgovernment.org.uk, 2020.) Every public body was affected as swift and large changes became evident in user demand, how and where citizens could or wanted to travel or work, and how they accessed or paid for services. Individuals, and organisations, changed how they considered and reacted to risk.

Much initial reporting focussed on the early changes made to keep organisations operational, and to provide vital public services. For example, a report by the House of Lords (A Critical Juncture for Public Services: Lessons from COVID-19, Nov. 2020) pointed to the

NHS rapidly upscaling its acute care capacity with the construction of Nightingale hospitals; and at the local level, 15,000 rough sleepers being safely re-housed. In addition, it highlighted how,

> many public service providers developed remarkable innovations to meet the challenge of COVID-19. Decisions which before the pandemic took months were made in minutes. Good personal and organisational relationships broke down longstanding barriers between the statutory and voluntary sectors. New ways to deliver services flourished. Digital technology was used more widely, and more successfully, than ever before.

Despite the rapid development and delivery of furlough support for workers, and in common with administrations across the UK, the House of Lords found risks of widening inequality, with those who were most disadvantaged to begin with worst affected. This can be expected to impact the focus of future public services, alongside learning from the resilience issues some services faced.

In a video blog, the Auditor General for Wales similarly noted how public bodies managed their immediate response with novel and innovative ways of working, tackling long-standing issues with real urgency. He highlighted how Audit Wales had changed its own methods, to help share best practice at speed including through a week-long virtual learning event covering a wide range of issues, from governance to engagement with communities through COVID-19.

Some COVID-19 impacts had immediate financial consequences. As services, such as education, moved online income fell, for example to Colleges. In another example, in December 2020 the Auditor General for Scotland reported that Business Stream (SWBS), a subsidiary of Scottish Water, might need between £47 million and £88 million in financial support due to the pandemic impact. Its retail, hospitality and small and medium business customers had experienced reduced water consumption. Taken together with a greater risk of water bills not being paid by some customers the risk to Business Stream, and its parent body, was found to have increased (Audit Scotland, Dec. 2020).

Other changes may be long-term. Lockdowns associated with COVID-19 meant most boards and many of their staff were newly working from home, using various new digital tools. Board meetings, Council meetings, even Parliamentary Committee scrutiny hearings all moved online. Some of this will doubtless generate learning and change for the future, including about the potential for broader attendance, and wider geographical representation, at public meetings.

Demand for public transport also fell dramatically, impacting sustainability of the business model of cost recovery from fares, and requiring taxpayer financial support. This may speed some more permanent changes: it was announced that Scotland's train services will be taken over by a new public sector body, transferring from the private rail operator Abellio. This makes permanent the temporary nationalisation which occurred due to COVID-19.

Over coming months and years it will become more apparent whether and how this level of innovation continues, and what long-term changes result. As governments in all jurisdictions consider their best priorities to recover the from the health, social and economic harm brought by the pandemic, there could be shifts in the nature or scale of future public investment, affecting public bodies and their boards. For example, between them the Auditor General for Wales, House of Lords and Scottish Government Infrastructure Investment Plan highlight the increased importance of digital infrastructure and connectivity; transformed digital public services; and digital inclusion, achieved through provision of devices to those in need and support for increased digital skills so no-one is left behind.

KEY MESSAGES

- Public bodies are set up by the government, but work separately and at arm's length. Being on a Board of one means regularly operating in complex and stimulating environments.
- Public bodies are often highly valued by users, offering rewarding Board roles.
- Key differences with other sectors arise from the nature of *public accountability*, which brings its own oversight and conduct requirements, covering the organisation and individual members.
- Public sector Boards do not have the ability to borrow, hold reserves, or take significant investment decisions without prior, explicit agreement. Employee remuneration and severance arrangements may also be subject to ministerially determined pay policies.
- Scrutiny levels are high, and cover every aspect of personal and corporate reputation.

FURTHER READING

https://www.gov.uk/government/organisations

https://www.gov.scot/publications/national-public-bodies-directory/

https://assets.publishing.service.gov.uk/government/uploads/system/uploads/attachment_data/file/942991/Code_of_Conduct_for_Board_Members_of_Public_Bodies_2019_V1.0_FINAL.pdf

https://www.gov.scot/binaries/content/documents/govscot/publications/advice-and-guidance/2015/04/board-guide-board-members-public-bodies-scotland-april-2015/documents/00475242-pdf/00475242-pdf/govscot%3Adocument/00475242.pdf

https://www.finance-ni.gov.uk/publications/public-bodies-guidance-including-board-guide-and-public-bodies-guides

https://www.cipfa.org/policy-and-guidance/publications/b/board-governance-essentials-a-guide-for-chairs-and-boards-of-public-bodies

REFERENCES

A Critical Juncture for Public Services: Lessons from COVID-19. (n.d.). [online]. Available at: https://publications.parliament.uk/pa/ld5801/ldselect/pubserv/167/167.pdf.

Audit Scotland. (n.d.). The 2019/20 audit of Scottish Water. [online]. Available at: https://www.audit-scotland.gov.uk/report/the-201920-audit-of-scottish-water [Accessed 24 May 2021].

Butcher, T. (1995). A New Civil Service? The Next Steps Agencies. *Governing the UK in the 1990s*, pp. 61–81.

cdn.cyfoethnaturiol.cymru. (n.d.). *Cyfoeth Naturiol Cymru – Dewis Iaith/Natural Resources Wales – Language Select*. [online] Available at: https://cdn.cyfoethnaturiol.cymru/media/686529/annual-report-and-accounts-201718 [Accessed 24 May 2021].

ComputerWeekly.com. (Oct. 2020). *NHS Trust Takes Another Look at Its Appointment of IT Scandal CEO*. [online]. Available at: https://www.computerweekly.com/news/252490996/NHS-trust-takes-another-look-at-its-appointment-of-IT-scandal-CEO [Accessed 17 May 2021].

cspl.blog.gov.uk. (n.d.). Why Standards Continue to Matter – Committee on Standards in Public Life. [online] Available at: https://cspl.blog.gov.uk/2016/07/08/why-standards-continue-to-matter/ [Accessed 3 May 2021].

Financial Reporting Council. (2018). THE UK CORPORATE GOVERNANCE CODE. [online]. Available at: https://www.frc.org.uk/getattachment/88bd8c45-50ea-4841-95b0-d2f4f48069a2/2018-UK-Corporate-Governance-Code-FINAL.PDF.

Gov. (1995). The 7 Principles of Public Life. [online]. GOV.UK. Available at: https://www.gov.uk/government/publications/the-7-principles-of-public-life.

Great Britain. Efficiency Unit and Great Britain. Prime Minister. (1991). *Making the Most of Next Steps: The Management of Ministers' Departments and Their Executive Agencies*. London: H.M.S.O.

McDonnell, F. (Feb. 2016). NIEC Failure "One of the Biggest Scandals" Since Devolution. [online]. *The Irish Times*. Available at: https://www.irishtimes.com/business/retail-and-services/niec-failure-one-of-the-biggest-scandals-since-devolution-1.2546479 [Accessed 10 May 2021].

Mclaughlin, C. (2019). [online]. Available at: https://www.sehd.scot.nhs.uk/dl/DL(2019)02.pdf.

Natural Resources Wales Scrutiny of Annual Report and Accounts 2017–18. (2018). [online]. Available at: https://senedd.wales/laid%20documents/cr-ld11883/cr-ld11883-e.pdf [Accessed 24 May 2021].

NI Events Company: Board Members Disqualified from Being Directors. (2018). *BBC News*. [online]. 15 Jan. Available at: https://www.bbc.co.uk/news/uk-northern-ireland-42664147 [Accessed 24 May 2021].

Northern Ireland Audit Office. (Sep. 2015). niec_full_report.pdf. [online]. Available at: https://www.niauditoffice.gov.uk/files/niecfullreportpdf [Accessed 24 May 2021].

Public Accounts Committee Report on The Northern Ireland Events Company. (Feb. 2016). [online]. Available at: http://www.niassembly.gov.uk/globalassets/documents/pac-2011-2016/reports/report-on-the-northern-ireland-events-company.pdf [Accessed 24 May 2021].

The Independent. (1995). *Prison Drama Ends in Political Farce*. [online]. Available at: https://www.independent.co.uk/news/prison-drama-ends-in-political-farce-1578591.html [Accessed 4 May 2021].

www.cqc.org.uk. (Jun.2018). Fit and Proper Persons: Directors | Care Quality Commission. [online] Available at: https://www.cqc.org.uk/guidance-providers/regulations-enforcement/fit-proper-persons-directors.

www.instituteforgovernment.org.uk. (1987). *StackPath*. [online] Available at: https://www.instituteforgovernment.org.uk/printpdf/our-work/more-effective-whitehall/civil-service-reform-past-lessons/next-steps-agencies-1988-97 [Accessed 15 May 2021].

www.instituteforgovernment.org.uk. (2020). *StackPath*. [online]. Available at: https://www.instituteforgovernment.org.uk/sites/default/files/publications/digital-government-coronavirus.pdf.

www.ons.gov.uk. (Dec. 2020). Public Sector Employment, UK – Office for National Statistics. [online]. Available at: https://www.ons.gov.uk/employmentandlabourmarket/peopleinwork/publicsectorpersonnel/bulletins/publicsectoremployment/latest [Accessed 3 May 2021].

CHAPTER ELEVEN

Governance in the Charity/Voluntary Sector

Patricia Armstrong and Margaret Wright

DOI: 10.4324/9781003142850-11

INTRODUCTION

The charity sector in the UK is both complex and dynamic, driven by passion, social ethos, and social value. Over the last few decades, the sector has expanded and grown considerably. The central tenet of the sector is the human desire to help others without personal gain. Charity is not a modern phenomenon. The term charity has Greek origins – *charis* originally meaning "grace" and *philanthropy* meaning "love of people". Charity was closely aligned to the development of religious organisations with early teachings ascribing to the view that the poor had rights and the wealthy had duties. Religious orders established the means to support the poor, sick, and hungry (Smith, 1995). Charities have been a vital part of life for millennia and they play a significant role in society today.

The organisation, leadership, and management of charities have a long history. Until the middle of the 19th century, charities served people without really understanding the root cause of their problems. The creation of the Charity Organisation Society in 1869 brought advancement in how charities were organised. A more strategic approach was adopted along with an emerging campaigning role.

However, the state started to intervene more in providing education and health. As this intervention grew, the charity sector became an "add-on" to state provision. The influence and service provision by the charity sector was further reduced with the development of the National Health Service and the welfare state.

The sector began to re-assert itself from the 1960s onwards as government departments provided funding and charities started to deliver a range of services that had previously been provided by the state. The 1980s saw the rolling back of the frontiers of the state and this presented opportunities for charities to bid for contracts to provide essential services.

The growth of the sector has continued at a pace and charities are now recognised as essential to providing support for disadvantaged groups.

The sector is evident is every walk of life from culture and sport to the environment and transport to health and welfare.

Charities touch all our lives one way or another. Whether it is from receiving a service or by volunteering, everyone in the UK benefits from the sector in one way or another. It may go unnoticed, for example, the Red Cross in attendance at events, the hospital services run by the WRVS, the volunteers repairing paths on our hills and mountains, the sector contributes enormously to the health, welfare, and economy of the UK.

Many public services are now provided by the charity sector through procurement and contracts. The growth in size, scope, and influence has led to some concerns about the independence of the sector with many organisations providing services on behalf of government (local and national and the NHS).

Adding to this complexity is that many charities have trading arms that operate as private organisations but the profit is fed into the charitable organisation. The economic and social impact of the sector cannot be underestimated.

The governance and accountability of the sector comes under increasing scrutiny and the importance of the charity trustees to guide and steer organisations is a vital role in the sector. The vast majority of charity sector board appointments are voluntary and unpaid. Trustees find the complexity of overseeing a charity is an excellent learning experience and can make a positive difference to their career prospects. The role is challenging, exciting, and ultimately very rewarding.

The authors of this chapter have a breadth of experience working in the voluntary sector, as chief officers, as board members and as chairs. We have brought this experience into the chapter through the learning points highlighted and through our view of the sector. We have tried to share our passion for the sector as well as our understanding and experience.

The sector is renowned for peer support and sharing of good practice and thus many of the examples and checklists we refer to are ones we have been using over the years. This means that they may have been drawn from others we have encountered and adapted to suit, probably so many times that we now call them our own and thus we may not have been able to trace back an original source document. We want to acknowledge the support and openness of colleagues in the sector for sharing their stories, knowledge, and experiences over the years.

DEFINING THE SECTOR

Defining the sector poses the first challenge due to its diverse nature. The terms voluntary sector, third sector, non-for-profit sector, community sector, charity, civil society, and non-governmental organisations (NGOs) are all used interchangeably. In much of Europe the term civil society is common. In the UK the terms voluntary or third sector are the most common terms used.

But what defines this sector? To be a registered charity in the UK, there must be public benefit, it must have volunteers and be not-for-profit, but not all voluntary sector organisations will become charities. Many will have charitable purposes but not *register* as a charity; others will be voluntary organisations or social enterprises. One thing they have in common is that any surplus funds at the end of a financial year are used to further the organisations aims.

Registered charities are regulated by the sector regulator. A charity regulator is a regulatory agency that regulates the charitable sectors in their respective jurisdictions. They can also be referred to as commissions, although that term can also refer specifically to the non-tax policy regulation of charities.

In the different jurisdictions, the relevant regulators are:

- The Charity Commission (England and Wales).
- Charity Commission Northern Ireland.
- The Office of the Scottish Charity Regulator (Scotland).

Key features of an organisation in the sector include:

- It is independent (separate from governments).
- It will be self-governing and control its own affairs through a voluntary board of management.
- It will not make a profit that is distributed to shareholders.
- It will have a degree of voluntary participation.

The sector is mostly made up of small "micro" organisations with very small turnovers – all the way up to some very large organisations with significant balance sheets, in the multi-millions.

Tables 11.1 and 11.2 are from UK Civil Society Almanac (ncvo, 2019):

Table 11.1 *Number of organisations by size and UK country, 2017/18*

UK Country	Micro	Small	Medium	Large	Major	Super-major	total
England	61,776	47,178	19,714	4,380	602	54	133,704
Wales	3,708	2,319	811	177	24	0	7,039
Scotland	10,040	6,345	2,714	557	64	2	19,722
Northern Ireland	2,077	2,114	1,581	350	5	0	6,127
UK	77,601	57,956	24,820	5,464	695	56	166,592

Source: NCVO, Charity Commission.

Table 11.2 *Income sources, 2017/18 (£m)*

Income Source	Micro and Small	Medium	Large	Major	Super-major	Total
The public	1,274.1	3,635.5	7,348.7	7,551.0	5,574.6	25,383.9
Government	291.3	1,691.1	4,341.8	6,088.1	3,278.9	15,691.2
National Lottery	30.4	157.8	217.7	147.7	21.9	575.6
Voluntary sector	167.6	698.0	1,164.5	1,124.9	1,988.6	5,143.6
Private sector	56.5	260.4	676.1	1,165.3	494.3	2,652.6
Investment	379.4	902.4	1,238.9	703.5	873.6	4,097.9
Total income	2,199.4	7,345.3	14,987.6	16,780.5	12,232.0	53,544.8

Source: NCVO, Charity Commission.

THE SCALE OF THE SECTOR

The number of organisations is just one aspect of the scale of the sector. There is also a significant paid workforce as well as a vast number of volunteers. Figures from 2019 (ncvo, 2019) indicate that across the UK:

- There is a paid workforce of 909,088 in 2019. This is a 5% growth on the previous year and a growth of 17% since 2010.
- There is a majority of the paid workforce working in organisations that have less than 50 paid members of staff.
- Over a third of the workforce is located in London and the South East of England.
- Over a third of the workforce is employed in social work activities.

Added to these numbers of paid staff, volunteers are a significant element of voluntary sector activity with:

- 19.4 million people having volunteered during 2018/2019 through a group, a club, or an organisation.
- More than half of the UK population getting involved in informal volunteering.
- Most people formally volunteering at some point in their life.
- Volunteers getting involved in different ways that reflect their lifestyle, values, and priorities.
- A small proportion of volunteering coming via employers, mainly from large organisations.

The sector also has a wide variety of "subsectors" or areas of work. For example:

- Social Services
- Culture and recreation
- Religion
- Grant making foundations

- Parent-teacher association
- Development
- Village halls
- Education
- International
- Health
- Youth clubs and uniformed organisations
- Environment
- Playgroups and nurseries
- Law and advocacy
- Housing

The largest of these subsectors is social services, which incorporates a wide variety of areas of work. Each of the subsectors can be further subdivided.

In defining the sector, we can see how diverse it is and understand the scale and value to the economy.

HOW IS THE SECTOR GOVERNED?

It is important to clarify what governance actually is. Governance is a *function* with the board being the *structure*. The laws in the UK are very clear that the board is accountable for governance and the functioning of the organisation. Governance is "the systems and processes concerned with ensuring the overall direction, control and accountability of an organisation" (Cornforth, 2014). The legal responsibility for a charitable organisation sits with the board that is made up of unpaid, part-time volunteers.

One definition of "good governance" is that the *board sets and oversees the achievement of its organisation's objectives* which helps to lead the organisation on "**a journey to success** – a journey led from the boardroom" (Governance Code for Community, Voluntary and Charitable Organisations in Ireland).

Another note on terminology. Different terms are used for example, board, management committee, council, executive committee. The difference between the terms usually reflects the legal structure of the organisation. In addition, the people who serve on the governing body may be called trustees or directors (trustees in the case of charity law and directors in the case of company law). For the purposes of this chapter, we will use the terms board members and trustees.

The trustees delegate responsibility for the running of the charity to paid employees. The employees report to the board but rarely are members of the board – more on that later.

Good governance is essential to ensure that a charity is successful, complies with legislation and regulations, and delivers on its purpose. It is especially important in the charity sector as the purpose of charities is for public good and to serve the beneficiaries. Good governance is the basis of effectiveness, risk management, and leadership.

Trustees who have the skills, drive, passion, and time will help ensure that the charity thrives and develops the building blocks to achieve the charity's vision. Having the right leadership and governance structures in place helps the charity achieve its outcomes and ambitions.

LEGAL STRUCTURES

Very many organisations in the sector are both a charity and a company, each bringing legal duties as both a company director and as a charity trustee.

| Companies Act | → | Companies House | → | Company Director |
| Charity Act in each nation | → | Charity Regulator | → | Charity Trustee |

As a company director there are legal duties within the Companies Act:

- Duty to act within powers.
- Duty to promote the success of the company.
- Duty to exercise independent judgement.

- Duty to exercise reasonable care, skill, and diligence.
- Duty to avoid conflicts of interest.
- Duty to not accept benefits from third parties.
- Duty to declare interest in proposed transactions or arrangements.

There is also a duty for directors to file returns, to prepare and deliver accounts to Companies House and to keep minutes of board meetings, and hold annual general meetings (AGM) where relevant. Directors may delegate the actual duties but they are still responsible in law for complying and making sure the information is sent to Companies House on time and accurately. Failure to comply can make the directors liable to a fine or even imprisonment.

As a charity trustee there are legal obligations. These may be slightly different depending on which UK regulator the charity is aligned to, but basically a trustee should:

- *Act in the interest of the charity*: trustees should put the interests of their charity before their own interest or those of any person or organisation.
- *Operate in a manner consistent with the charity's purpose*: trustees should carry out their duties in accordance with their governing document.
- *Act with due care and diligence*: trustees should take such care of the charity's affairs as is reasonable to expect of someone who is managing the affairs of another person
- *Ensure the charity complies with the provisions of the relevant legislation* such as filing returns, preparing and delivering accounts, and providing information to the public. Although in practice these functions may be undertaken by others, they are still the responsibility of the charity trustees.

As board members, the trustees are responsible for controlling the organisation's management and administration, and for ensuring that income and property are used for the purposes set out in the organisation's governing document and for no other purpose.

It is important in considering establishing a new charitable or not for profit organisation that sufficient thought is given to the most appropriate legal structure or legal entity to be used in the venture. There are a range of available structures and they generally have advantages and disadvantages which must be considered in the particular circumstances that you are dealing with.

It is important to remember that the legal structure of your organisation is quite separate from its charitable status. Only certain structures are appropriate for charities. Some structures can be adapted if, at a later date, there is a desire for the organisation to apply for charitable status.

In addition, certain structures provide protection for board members as a result of being incorporated and offering limited liability.

Types of legal structure are presented in Table 11.2.

MOST POPULAR LEGAL STRUCTURES IN THE SECTOR

Company Limited by Guarantee – a company limited by guarantee is incorporated under the legislation that governs companies (the Companies Acts). It is the most commonly used form for incorporated charitable institutions, but it is often used for a wide range of other non-charitable purposes usually characterised as "not for profit" – in other words, for purposes which are not aimed at private gain (or at least not directly). These include trade associations, clubs and societies, registered social landlords and scientific research associations. A company limited by guarantee has a two-tier governance structure (see below). It will have one or more "members" and one or more directors.

Company Limited by Shares – a company limited by shares is also incorporated under the Companies Acts and is the usual form adopted by those undertaking trading or other commercial activities in the UK. A company limited by shares has a share capital of one or more shares which it issues to its members. In a commercial context, the shares entitle the holder to a proportion of the company's profits and its assets in the event that it is wound up and are often issued in order to raise funds for the company from those subscribing for shares.

Charitable Incorporated Organisation (CIO)/Scottish Charitable Incorporated Organisation (SCIO) – the CIO and SCIO are relatively new forms of incorporated entity designed specifically for charitable activities. Before the introduction of the CIO or SCIO, anyone wishing to set up an incorporated charity would usually use a company limited by guarantee, adapted to ensure it could qualify as a charity. Adaption is required because limited companies were originally designed for commercial use rather than charitable activity. As a consequence, charitable companies are subject to regulation by both Companies House and the Charity Commission/Office of the Scottish Charity Regulator. The CIO/SCIO created a new legal entity bringing with it the advantages of incorporation without the burden of dual regulation and registration and the flexibility to create a constitution aimed specifically at charity activities and governance.

Trust – trusts were originally introduced as a way of protecting assets. The legal owners hold and control the assets for the benefit of other people, the beneficiaries. The trustees are under a duty to safeguard assets. Because a trust is unincorporated, it can only interact with the outside world via its trustees. This means that trustees must hold all the trust's assets in their own name or in the name of a nominee on their behalf. The trustees must enter all contracts relating to the trust personally. They will remain potentially liable even if they have retired as trustees unless there is provision for them to be released from their obligation.

Unincorporated Association – there are no statutory formalities which must be observed in order to set up an unincorporated or voluntary association. The terms of the agreement between members will usually be set out in a body of rules. The rules will vary from association to association but will usually contain provisions relating to the admission of new members, the retirement of existing members, the way in which assets are to be held and who will have day to day management and control of the association's activities. An association is not an incorporated body and so cannot hold assets or enter contracts on its own and does not confer any limited liability on its members or trustees.

Community Interest Company – Community interest companies (or CICs, as they are usually referred to) were introduced in 2004. They are intended to be a legal form earmarked specifically for those who wish to pursue some sort of enterprise in the interests of the public (or community) rather than their own personal economic interests. In other words, a CIC is an entity which can only function on a not-for-profit basis. The hope was that the CIC would develop as a brand for developing community interests in much the same way as the charity brand. The development of the brand has not materialised in the way that was perhaps anticipated. CICs can be incorporated under the Companies Act as a company limited by shares or guarantee. The provisions of the Companies Act apply to a CIC in the same way as they apply to any other company limited by shares or guarantee. However, there are certain modifications the most significant of which is the introduction of an "asset lock". Essentially a CIC's assets must be held for community interests' objects and any distribution to any of its members must be on an arm's length basis. In other words, a CIC must receive value in return for any payment it makes to a member for the goods or services supplied to it. There are also specific provisions that limit the amount of any dividend that can be paid to members.

A CIC cannot be registered as a charity. CICs are regulated by the CIC regulator. They do not qualify for the exemptions and release from tax which can be claimed by charities but are subject to a lighter touch regulatory regime. A CIC is likely to be more appropriate where tax is not a particular concern or where there is a desire to make limited distributions to members (which is not be possible with a charity). The potential disadvantage of the CIC is the lower degree of public recognition given to the CIC brand.

As part of the consideration of adopting the most appropriate legal structure early thought should be given to the most appropriate governance model that should be followed. In broad terms governance models can be split into two categories, single tier or multiple tiers.

The difference between them relates to the way in which decision-making is structured within the constitution.

YOUR CONSTITUTION

Once you have decided on your legal structure your constitution needs to be consistent with that structure. There will be some organisations which demand specialist provisions in their constitution and there are some circumstances where legal advice will be helpful in this regard. For each type of legal structure there are commonly found model constitutions, plus detailed clause by clause notes and optional additional clauses.

If charitable status is being sought reference should be made to meeting the charity tests guidance issued by The Charity Commission, Charity Commission NI, or OSCR.

Consideration should also be given to the type of organisation being taken forward as different models will apply where appropriate to each of these. The most common such arrangements are as follows:

Social enterprises – a trading business is required and a company limited by guarantee is the most commonly adopted structure;
Development trust – a key requirement for a development trust is to identify clearly what projects and initiatives the development trust will be delivering directly and those that will be carried through by other organisations; and
Social firms – a distinct type of social enterprise, working in a wide range of sectors with a specific social mission to create employment for people most disadvantaged in the labour market

including people who have a disability, as history of mental health problems or have a criminal record or a drug and alcohol dependency.

Alastair Keatinge, Lindsays, Solicitors states, "To enable an organisation to have the best chance of long-term success, thought and care should be given to selecting the most appropriate legal structure to operate the business of the organisation".

While there are several ways that governance can be organised and much depends on the size and type of organisation. One thing they all have in common is the requirement to have members. Members tend to be a community of interest and when they join the organisation, they have voting rights. Often members are "silent" and they are content with receiving information, newsletters and invitations to meetings or functions. Importantly though, the members have voting rights at the AGM or EGM and can influence the membership criteria, and who can serve on the board as Trustees and the direction of the charity.

In many charities though, some of the members may also serve on the board. The board is responsible for recruiting new Trustees and they should take previous experience, skills, and values into account. Once recruited, the membership votes at the AGM on whether the candidate can become a Trustee.

The simplest form of governance structure – *one tier* – the members are the board and the board are the members, they are one in the same people. Even with this one tier structure, many boards develop sub-committees with delegated authority to progress with specific areas of work. It should be noted, however, that the board as a whole is accountable for all decisions.

In a two-tier structure the members and the board are two separate entities. There will be a process for joining and becoming a legal member and this group of people effectively become the "top tier" of governance. The members are responsible for electing the board who will govern the charity in the best interest of the members. The members are the custodians of the charity and the board is accountable to them. A two-tier model involves two levels of decision-making:

- The members who take decisions in relation to amending the constitution, appointing board members, and so on;
- The board exercises overall control and supervision in relation to the organisation.

Two tier structures are common in intermediary charities who represent the interest of other organisations. For example, a sports association has many members who are independent organisations in their own right.

In larger organisations where there are a large number of members, a third tier of governance is often used. This is useful when the views of a wide and varied membership need to be considered. There is usually an election process in constituencies when members vote for a member of their constituency to represent them at council. The guides and scouts are good examples of this structure of organisation.

Councils have a role in electing the board and in some governance processes. In this governance model there needs to be a clear distinction between the roles and functions of the council and the board.

An example of a single-, two-, and three-tier structure is illustrated in Figure 11.1.

Whatever the structure, there needs to be clear processes in place for recruitment, induction, training and appraisal of trustees. A board is a team of people with the expertise and skill to work together to provide good governance and to support and guide the staff team to excel.

As discussed in detail in Chapter 1 (Governance and the Role of the Board), many charity/voluntary sector organisations have some form of committee structure. Board meetings need to be efficient and make best use of the time available. A committee structure can help the decision-making process. Committees can be formed by those members who

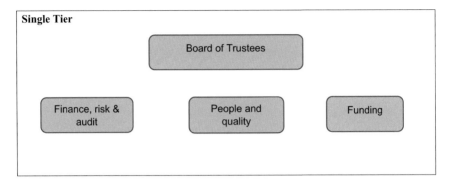

Figure 11.1 *Examples of a single-, two-, and three-tier structure with committees.*

have particular expertise and they review their area of work and provide advice to the board.

Whether a board has a committee structure or working groups, one thing is essential, that they have a clear remit, terms of reference and reporting mechanisms. Committees and working groups must add value to the board and be open to scrutiny.

LEARNING POINT

The founding board of a new charity were replaced by a new board (9 out of 11 were new). This was a planned process. The new board discovered that services were well established but the infrastructure of HR, H&S, Finance systems and IT needed improvement. The board quickly conducted a skills audit among themselves and determined, along with the CEO, the priorities. Sub-committees were established with Trustees putting their professional skills to good use. Each sub-committee developed clear terms of reference, authorities, and remit and appointed a chair of the committee. Each committee undertook to focus on a particular area of work and developed the infrastructure required. Once the systems were established the workload reduced. The sub-committees stayed in place but took a different focus, one of supporting the CEO to maintain, update, and comply with the systems.

The key learning from this is that sub-committees add to the efficiency of the board, shares the workload, helps new Trustees become familiar with the organisation in a specific area of expertise and is good for succession planning for the Board office bearers.

THE GOVERNING DOCUMENT

The board is responsible for the organisation's governing document. The terms used for the governing document varies depending on whether the organisation is a registered charity. Constitution tends to be used for non-registered charities and articles of association are used for those registered. Whatever the term the document is a written statement that clearly sets out the purpose, structure, and objectives of the charity. The document will have key information about:

- What the organisation does – its purpose.
- What powers it has to allow it to achieve the purpose.
- Trustee information – how many (maximum and minimum) how they are appointed and removed.
- Details of membership.
- Details of meetings, how often, in what format, decision-making powers and how they are recorded.
- How to change the governing document.
- What will happen if the organisation closes.

The governing document should be reviewed annually to ensure it remains relevant.

LEARNING POINT

A leading charity working with women decided to apply for funding to deliver a new service in partnership with another organisation. The service did fit with their overall strategy and the board approved the application, which incidentally was successful. The project involved working with men and in a neighbouring local authority area for a period of three years. While the board approved, no one thought to check the governing document, which stated that the charity worked exclusively with women and in a specified area.

On two counts the charity was working out-with their governing document which is in breach of charity regulations. The charity self-reported to the regulator and was assisted in making changes. The board now has a calendar of "checks" in place which includes an annual review of the governing document.

Understanding the delegated authority in the governing document is also vital for the Board to understand. For example, the CEO is an employee of the board and is supported and held to account. The board delegates authority to the CEO to employ, lead, manage, and develop the staff teams who deliver the organisational objectives. The Board will expect reports from the CEO/senior staff to help inform their decisions and keep them updated on the most current operational situations, stating where targets and objectives are met and where further action must be taken.

LEARNING POINT

A board of a medium sized charity (turnover circa £1m) did not realise that the CEO was an employee. All board members had joined within the tenure of the CEO. The board thought that the CEO was the employer of the staff and therefore developed employee terms and conditions, policies, and employee handbook. The CEO appointed an HR consultant to help with all HR issues and did not refer to the board for authorisation to make changes. When the CEO resigned and an Interim was appointed for six months, the board was surprised to learn that they were the employer and they had to approve terms and conditions, policy and handbooks for all employees.

A training programme was put in place for the board and they did learn and take on the full role as Trustees.

Trustees have general control of a charity and their duties are set out in law. They are subject to many duties and responsibilities both under common law and statute.

It is important to be clear about the differences between governance and managerial duties. The organisation will have an agreed delegation of authority which clarifies the lines between governance and management. Broadly speaking governance is concerned with strategy and direction while management is concerned with operational delivery.

It is often through the Chair / Chief Officer relationship that most boards have the clearest insight to the operational side of the organisation. It is often this relationship where cracks can begin to show if there are differing approaches or directions in vision and mission of the organisation. The chair needs to be supportive when the going gets tough, help give a clear steer on expectations and direction, but give constructive feedback when it's needed and sometimes be a sounding board and a listening ear. The chief executive needs to respect the chair's position, not bother them with the day to day running of the organisation but make sure they get it right about when to discuss things initially with just the chair and when to go straight to the board and finally, to work out how the "supervisory" element of the relationship should work, for example should the Chair carry our CEO appraisals?

In a global governance study by Cranfield University in 2009 and some follow-up work in Scotland it was shown that chairs and boards consistently scored the organisation as performing better than the Chief Executive and senior staff did. This was also identified in a further "Path to Impact" study carried out by ACOSVO and CO3 in 2018. Often the board reports show the more positive side of how well the organisation is doing, but the board members do not always see the challenges the staff have overcome to get to that point.

An important time is the transition stages when a new Chair comes in to post – it always takes a while to develop the relationship, work out how much or how little information they feel they need, how they like to prepare for meetings and how engaged they want to be in the work of the organisation. It can be difficult to get the balance right around the support element – on the one hand the board look to the staff to inform and support them in their understanding of the operations, but on the other, they are there to support the Chief Executive. There are dangers of both becoming too close and being too distant from each other and it is important to develop an open and trusted relationship where difficult conversations can be had if necessary. Although the chair is expected to lead the board and work most closely with the CEO and senior team, legally they have equal responsibility to all other board members (although depending on governing document, may have a casting vote in some instances).

LEARNING POINT

A new Chair took office and the Chief Officer realised that the style of working was not the same as the previous Chair. It took time to build the relationship and find what needed be discussed with the chair and what should be taken to the full board. Also, to redefine how much information needed to be shared and in what format. Finally, clarifying the definition of "operational" so both understood where the responsibilities lay, what had been delegated, and what sat at board level decision-making.

It was also a reminder on setting boundaries when working closely together. What could become a close friendship and a source of peer support, was also a clear governance relationship. If the boundaries are not clearly defined, there is a risk of conflict of interest if the relationship is too close.

Boards often appoint other Office Bearers in addition to the Chair, such as Vice Chair or Treasurer. The board will delegate responsibility to the office bearers and the roles should be clearly defined. A point to note though, office bearers do not have additional decision-making responsibility, they take an additional workload. For example, a treasurer will ensure that the financial reports are in order, understandable, and bring expertise to allow the board to make decisions. The Chair is usually the first point of contact for the CEO.

CONFLICTS OF INTEREST

Trustees must act, and be seen to act, in the best interest of the organisation and not for their own private interest or gain. There may be situations where trustee's own interests and the interest of the organisation arise simultaneously or appear to clash. Examples of this may be:

- A trustee may work for another organisation who will compete for the same contracts through a tendering process.

- A family member may be receiving services from the organisation.

Conflicts of interest are not actually a problem as long as there is a process for managing them. The organisations should have a register of interests, to be completed annually, which will record the following information for each trustee in relation to their board membership:

- Remuneration
- Related undertakings
- Unremunerated positions in public bodies and other organisations
- Interests in shares and securities
- Miscellaneous interests

An open approach to potential conflicts of interest helps to protect the reputation of the organisation and the individual trustee.

When considering a Trustee position, prospective Trustees should take account of their own interests – is a particular cause or a part of the sector that they have a passion for or are keen to be involved in? At the same time, before joining a Board, it is good practice to consider the question of possible conflicts of interest before there is commitment on either side. This is important where personal interests are deemed significant enough to make it difficult for the individual concerned to make a full contribution to the discussions and decision-making process.

If during the context of a discussion or decision-making process in a meeting, a potential conflict of interest emerges, the trustee should inform the board and if appropriate withdraw from the meeting for the duration of the relevant discussion. If this occurs, it should be clearly noted in the minute of the meeting.

WHY BE A CHARITY TRUSTEE?

People volunteer for all sorts of reasons; some may want to meet new people, while others may want to enhance their CV.

The Scottish Volunteer Forum in 2019 conducted a survey and respondents ranked the reason they volunteered. Gaining new skills was the most common reason given, followed by improving confidence and meeting new people. This suggests that for many people volunteer to improve their own personal situation. While "to support a cause they believe in" was 4th overall, it had the highest proportion of respondents. This suggests that a significant number of people, perhaps in certain types of organisation, are motivated for altruistic reasons.

LEARNING POINT

A senior manager from a private sector organisation joined the board of a local charity with a desire to "make a difference" and "give something back". They quickly realised that many myths they had heard about the sector being "amateur" were misjudged. They learned about the complexity of the sector and professionalism of the workforce and they saw it in a whole new light. They started to see it as a potential for a new direction in their working life. The following year they applied for a senior position in a national charity and were successful – partly through the knowledge and understanding they gained from their board position, along with the transferrable skills they now realise are possible between the sectors.

Whatever the reason, there are many benefits to volunteering as a charity trustee. For example:

- Physical and mental health
  - Gaining confidence and getting a sense of achievement
  - Meeting new people from all walks of life
  - Feeling useful
  - Having fun
  - Taking on a new challenge

- Career enhancement
  - Building new skills and confidence
  - Learning to work as part of a team
  - Enhances curriculum vita
  - Learning business skills and decision-making skills
  - Demonstrating your ability to take responsibility
- Skills development
  - Business skills
  - Communication and team working
  - Gain new experiences
- Contributing to your community
  - Doing something really special that benefits others
  - Being part of a community of interest
  - A sense of belonging

While there are many benefits, the role brings challenges too. It is a very responsible role and one that needs to be taken seriously. The idea of turning up at a meeting, having tea and biscuits while you hear about what has been happening and then going home is very far from reality. A diligent trustee must be able to question, analyse, scrutinise, constructively challenge and make decisions. You may also need to roll your sleeves up and get involved in ways you would not imagine for example, raising funds, taking part in charity challenges, attending events and being an advocate for the charity. Many a charity trustee can be heard to scream while abseiling down a tall public building, or enjoy planting trees in a community garden.

While there are guidelines for good practice and resources available, there is no *requirement* for training or qualifications. However, it is good practice for Trustees to keep up-to-date with the requirements for the role and any changes to legislation. There are annual Trustee weeks across the UK which gives Trustees the opportunity to learn and network. Many infrastructure organisations also offer training for Trustees.

COVID-19 AND CHARITY/ VOLUNTARY ORGANISATION GOVERNANCE

This chapter was written in the midst of the COVID-19 pandemic and the authors felt they had to acknowledge this as it has brought many challenges to the sector and its governance. Many organisations had their income severely reduced and some have had to increase support at the frontline to for those most in need. All have had to change the way they operate in some way, often by delivering services digitally. Decision-making has been rapid and against a backdrop of uncertainty. The pace of change and the level of risk have been unprecedented. Boards have had to realign strategic aims, objectives, and plans which were developed under different circumstances. COVID-19–specific risk registers were developed with mitigating actions to minimise risk. For some boards very difficult decisions have had to be taken such as redundancies, closure of organisations, and utilisation of reserves. For some, it has been an opportunity to progress a modernisation agenda which has been long awaited. The sector has been needed more than ever and the importance of robust governance has been at the forefront.

KEY MESSAGES

- Know the constitution and what the charitable purposes are. Make sure the governing document is reviewed annually.
- Ensure that the charity is compliant with all legislative requirements.
- Know what is expected, what the role and responsibilities of a trustee are, and understand that the board is the employer.
- Be prepared to offer time and expertise.
- Make time to develop good working relationships with other board members and with the CEO and senior staff.

FURTHER READING

https://www.gov.uk/government/organisations/charity-commission
https://www.oscr.org.uk/
https://www.charitycommission.org.uk/
https://www.charitycommissionni.org.uk/
http://www.acevo.org.uk/support/good-governance/
https://www.icsa.org.uk/knowledge/charity-resources
https://knowhow.ncvo.org.uk/governance
https://scvo.org/support/running-your-organisation/governance
https://youngtrusteesmovement.org/
https://www.acosvo.org.uk/chairs
https://www.associationofchairs.org.uk/resources/chairs-compass/
https://www.associationofchairs.org.uk/resources/download-qob/
https://www.associationofchairs.org.uk/working-as-a-team/
https://www.youtube.com/watch?v=CDPADIPElec

REFERENCES

Cornforth, C. (2014). Nonprofit Governance Research. In: *Nonprofit Governance*, Cornforth, C. & Brown, W. (eds.), London: Routledge, pp. 4–5.

https://www.acosvo.org.uk/sites/default/files/Boards_Governance_and_Leadership_of_the_ThirdSector.pdf.

Kakabadse, A., & Kakabadse, N. (eds.) (2009). *Global Boards: One Desire, Many Realities*. Basingstoke: Palgrave Macmillan.

Lee, Y. J. (2016). What Encourages Nonprofits' Adoption of Good Governance Policies? *Nonprofit Management and Leadership, 27*(1). doi.org/10.1002/nml.21226.

ncvo. (2019). UK Civil Society Almanac 2019. [online] Available at: https://data.ncvo.org.uk/.

Scottish Volunteer Forum. (2019). Available at: https://scottishvolunteeringforum.files.wordpress.com/2020/02/svf-volunteer-motivations-and-barriers-summary-report-1.pdf.

INDEX

appointments (to a board) 31, 33, 42, 66, 238, 242, 244, 249, 254, 262–5, 268, 287–8, 291, 308, 311–16, 318–19, 373–4
assessing risks 108–10
assurance 30, 60, 64, 74, 81–2, 98, 100–1, 110–13, 115, 118, 120, 122–3, 127–8, 130, 181, 243, 377, 387
audit 6, 11, 27, 30–1, 35, 42, 61, 111, 121–2, 143, 155, 167, 221, 224, 243, 272, 293, 295, 304, 331, 337, 349, 364, 367, 377, 383–4, 408, 409

board behaviours 238, 273, 275
board chemistry 238, 250, 265, 277, 282–3
board committees 30–1, 33, 167, 270
board composition 22, 61, 71, 155, 247–8, 268, 270, 278, 336
board diversity 252–3, 255
board induction 221
board matrix/board matrices 268, 270–2
board meetings 16–18, 22, 76, 155, 179–80, 184, 191, 195, 202–3, 209, 219–20, 223, 240, 243, 265, 269, 303, 335, 339, 342, 376, 380, 389, 401, 407
board recruitment 29–30, 76, 238, 241, 243–4, 248, 253, 256–8, 265, 298
board structure(s) 22, 26, 214, 239–40

challenges (faced by directors) 176, 186, 189–90, 251, 377

climate change 36, 125, 136, 138–9, 142–4, 147–8, 150, 153, 155, 161, 163–5, 169, 305, 326, 329
Companies Act (2006) 7, 10, 18, 20, 45, 95, 121, 174–5, 185, 211, 225–6, 233, 240, 323, 329, 331, 333, 335, 347, 402, 404
company secretary 7, 18, 88–9, 186, 208–9, 211–15, 217–25, 227–34, 240
competencies 40, 140, 266, 268–71, 332
conflicts of interest 9, 13, 76, 185, 197, 212, 234, 258, 378, 401, 413–14
constitution 7, 21, 264, 270, 403, 405, 407, 409, 417
COVID-19 103, 125–6, 136, 140, 143, 146–7, 151, 162, 166, 299, 330, 349, 388–9, 417
CV(s) 29, 269, 288–9, 292–3, 296, 304, 306, 312, 414
cyber security 36, 52

digital brand 288, 298, 300
director selection 268
directors' and officers' liability insurance 49, 51, 302, 305
director's duties 175, 209, 229
due diligence 27, 202, 259, 288, 291, 302, 304, 308, 319, 343

employee directors 184
Environmental Social Governance (ESG) 64, 99, 130, 136–43, 151–65, 167–9, 328–9
external advisors 42

future proofing 94, 125, 129

governance code(s) 20, 25–6, 38, 42,
    56–9, 61–5, 67, 69, 71, 74–6, 78–9,
    83, 85–6, 88–9, 95–6, 217, 230, 233,
    241, 245–6, 281–2, 327–8, 330–1,
    347, 369, 399
governance facilitator 217–18, 224–5
governance framework 27, 64, 83, 87, 98,
    111, 213–14, 216–17, 219, 221, 228,
    231, 331, 337, 340–1, 343, 346–9
governing documents 7, 18, 22, 32–3, 78,
    175, 211, 219, 240, 243–4, 246, 260,
    264, 284, 314, 316

identifying risks 106–8
independent board evaluations 280, 283
insolvency 10, 19, 43–6, 48, 52, 67

legal structures 196, 233, 338, 400, 402,
    405–6

networking 288–90, 297–8, 308, 316
newly appointed directors 199, 203, 278

qualifications 44, 186, 211–12, 251, 270,
    294, 349, 416

risk appetite 20, 96, 100–5, 109, 123–4,
    127–8, 241, 305
risk reporting 105, 154

securing a NED role 288–9, 306
skills matrix (matrices) 21, 238, 270–1
stewardship 13–14, 20, 66–7, 74,
    94–7, 152, 156, 163, 240, 328,
    356, 381
strategy 11–13, 15, 26, 33, 35, 38–41,
    46, 62, 82–3, 95–6, 100–1, 106–8,
    115, 119, 121, 124, 128–9, 138,
    141–4, 148, 150–2, 155, 160–1,
    168, 176, 179–81, 190, 196–7,
    200, 223, 241–2, 261, 270, 274,
    277, 292, 301, 303, 305, 327,
    343–4, 346, 350, 360, 376,
    380–1, 410–11
subsidiary boards 26–8, 293, 305, 388
succession planning 32, 83, 182–3,
    190, 220, 268, 270–1, 281, 312,
    329, 409
sustainability 16, 60, 64, 74, 76, 119, 122,
    128, 130, 136–8, 140, 142, 144–7,
    149, 152, 157, 159–60, 162, 164–5,
    167–9, 176, 194, 239, 303, 322, 326,
    332, 345, 384, 389

team dynamics 200, 203
transitioning from executive to
    non-executive 307

unhealthy cliques 48, 274

when to resign 47